Joan Joffe Hall

Joan Joffe Hall

THE FILMS OF THE

Jerry Vermilye

The Citadel Press

THIRTIES

Introduction By Judith Crist

Secaucus, New Jersey

ALSO BY JERRY VERMILYE

Burt Lancaster
Bette Davis
Cary Grant
Barbara Stanwyck
The Films of Elizabeth Taylor (with Mark Ricci)
Ida Lupino
The Great British Films
The Films of Charles Bronson

Acknowledgments

The author would like to express his gratitude to the following individuals and organizations who variously helped arrange screenings, supplied unusual still photographs, aided in informational research, or simply offered advice on film titles worthy of consideration:

Judy Caputo, John Cocchi, Kit Davies and the Learning Corporation of America, Constance Scrase-Dickins, Nancy Dennis, Frank Farel, Vic Ghidalia, Joe Judice, Bill Lloyd, John McAndrew, Ron Macht, Leonard Maltin, The Memory Shop, Ted Sennett, Allan Turner, and Douglas Whitney.

With special thanks to

Judith Crist

and

Al Kilgore

for considerations beyond the call of friendship.

And

a final salute to the movie companies themselves, which issued these films and hired the anonymous still photographers whose artistry illustrates this volume: Columbia, Metro-Goldwyn-Mayer, Paramount, RKO, Republic, 20th Century-Fox, United Artists, Universal, and Warner Bros.

Copyright © 1982 by Jerry Vermilye
All rights reserved
Published by Citadel Press
A division of Lyle Stuart Inc.
120 Enterprise Ave., Secaucus, N.J. 07094
In Canada: Musson Book Company
A division of General Publishing Co. Limited
Don Mills, Ontario
Manufactured in the United States of America by
Halliday Lithograph, West Hanover, Mass.

DESIGNED BY LESTER GLASSNER

Library of Congress Cataloging in Publication Data

Vermilye, Jerry.
   The films of the thirties.

   1. Moving-pictures—United States—Plots, themes, etc.   I. Title.
PN1997.8.V44   1982   791.43′75   82-12965
ISBN 0-8065-0971-6

CONTENTS

**For
Dolores and Al Kilgore**

''The old Hollywood that I knew is dead.
It only exists now in still photographs
and a few people's memories.''
—Olivia de Havilland (1980)

INTRODUCTION

by Judith Crist

It was the worst of times in the real world and the best of times in Shadowland for those of us who came into our independent moviegoing in the Thirties.

Those of us who entered the Thirties in our childhood were much like the middle-class children of the television era who started out with *Sesame Street* and then did their own dial-switching over a decade to find their favorite sit-coms and, in clandestine and unsupervised ways, their education in sex, violence, and pseudo-sophistication. We post-radio, pre-TV children came into the Thirties with only the taste of the great silent clowns (imagine a moviegoing life that started with *The Gold Rush*), and we grew into adolescence with the talkies. In our teens, we left the Thirties, as did the rest of the world, prepared for the total loss of innocence that came with the Forties.

The Thirties have been acclaimed as the golden decade in the fifty-year rise, decline, and fall of the Hollywood of studios and stars. In their course some 5,000 feature films were made, and at times some 80 million Americans a week were going to what was indeed, as television was to become, the opiate of the masses. Perhaps more important, it was a national medium, unifying us in a way that even network radio could not, providing the visuals of person and place to supplement the thesis. Unlike our elders—who were gorging in large part on six features a week, courtesy of a tri-weekly change of double-feature programs—we were once-a-week moviegoers (economics and parental discretion limited us), but any kid worth his or her piece of bubblegum and bag of penny candy (or even, for the foresighted, packed lunch) sat through the bill three times, entering the theater in the bright glare of a Saturday high noon and leaving in the dusk or darkness, frequently in the custody of an angry father who had roamed the aisles in search of his temporarily unloved one.

I've had to remind new born-yesterday generations that we had electricity, automobiles, and indoor plumbing in those days, and airplanes were no novelty. But when I consider what we learned from movies in the Thirties, I too get a sense of the prehistoric. Movie morality was, of course, as neanderthal as it was comforting. Virtue triumphed, evil and immorality were punished, and Jefferson Smith would survive. Mirror of our Thirties public morality, of course—summed up in the ultimate and triumphant *Gone With the Wind:* Scarlett, whom today we might consider a semi-liberated female of temperament, talent, and intelligence, was a Commandment-breaker and in the Thirties (if not in the Civil War era, for *GWTW* is strictly from the Thirties in concept and creation) that meant she got her come-uppance.

Despite the encroachment of Technicolor, the world was black and white, with morality indicated even by the color of cowboys' hats and women's hair. If you committed adultery (or what, with fadeout on an embrace, the sophisticates suspected was the big A), you were dying or dead by film's end; even married folks slept in twin beds (*vide* Judge Hardy and wife, and where Andy or his sister came from was anybody's guess), and no one could—or would—tell me that John Barrymore and Greta Garbo didn't spend that long night in the Grand Hotel simply gazing into each other's eyes—thereby giving the world its view of the two most exquisite profiles ever on screen. Twenty years later, when I first saw that movie in revival, I was a bit more sophisticated, and the simple eloquence of that love scene was overwhelming.

That's the word: eloquence. Movies found their technological voices in the Thirties, but it was still their silences that spoke—the silences and the faces. Swanson said it: they did have faces then, and my generation was rooted in movie-star individualities for our descriptions of people, beyond physical appearance, to temperament and persona. We were rooted in larger-than-life thirty-foot-high figures who gave us our reality and permitted us, time after time and for the duration thereof, to think of the world outside the theater as an illusion. We "grew up" with the stars: the Katharine Hepburn of *Little Women* grew up (in the many senses of character) to *Holiday;* Garbo went from Anna Christie to Ninotchka; only Judy Garland remained the eternal child for that decade—we didn't want to know her Dorothy wasn't really and truly twelve, any more than we wanted to know that the tornado was a black silk stocking. Some of us still don't. We want to retain those first illusions. And though the faces and the movie palaces have passed, the movies remain.

The movies of the Thirties were the best of movies and the worst of movies—and not until another fifty years go by will we be able to determine which were the great movies. Now, midway in the Thirties century, "greatness" is a purely personal accolade, and I honor Jerry Vermilye for not applying that overused adjective. His is a catholic selection of films, one that overflows with the juice of the variety that was the life of that decade's movies. Only a few of my favorites are missing; only a few of my nonfavorites are on hand.

And that's the joy of this book, which for me revives the joy of moviegoing in that faraway decade. In one of the great downtown theaters or one of the tackier nabes, there was always that fleeting moment of darkness, then the colophon, and then—a lighted screen, and we knew something wonderful was about to happen, before our very eyes. So turn the page.

REVISITING A GOLDEN AGE

In the Thirties, sobered by the Great Depression, Americans needed escape. And that's exactly what Hollywood provided, grinding out its dramas, melodramas, musicals, comedies and costume epics at a volume that now seems quite awesome, considering the current-day multi-million-dollar costs of just *one* motion picture. But in that decade between the stock-market crash and World War II, the big studios churned out movies sufficient to satisfy the considerable demands of constantly changing—often double-billed—film programs. And in that era, few of those assembly-line, audience-tailored films failed, for audiences' entertainment demands were then satiated by movie-going as they are now by television-watching.

Attempting to encompass the Thirties, that golden age of American moviemaking, by discussing a mere hundred films is, admittedly, sheer insanity. But, necessarily limited to that quota within the present volume, the author agonized long and hard over which titles to include and which to leave out. The decision was made not to limit the list to acknowledged classics (most of those have been covered elsewhere in this Citadel series), but to include a selection of relatively forgotten—and perhaps undeservedly neglected—films worthy of re-evaluation. A perusal of the contents pages will tell an informed reader that this book could hardly be entitled "The *Great* Thirties Films," because there are some undisputed losers scattered among the winners. Instead, an attempt has been made to represent a *cross-section* of Hollywood-produced motion pictures released in those largely escapist years. And it is hoped that the movies considered in these pages will stir up enough fond memories to compensate for the exclusion of so many well-remembered others.

Amazingly, Hollywood produced nearly five thousand motion pictures between the close of 1929 and the advent of the Forties. Corporations like Metro-Goldwyn-Mayer, Warner Bros., 20th Century-Fox, Universal, Columbia, RKO and United Artists accounted for most of the Thirties' film production, supplemented by an intermittent flow of minor-league product from such "poverty row" companies as Republic, Tiffany, Mascot, Chesterfield and Grand National. And although not every year in that decade was equally rich in noteworthy films, an effort has been made in this book to approximate ten titles from each. Some of the choices will likely elicit groans of *deja vu;* others will undoubtedly generate puzzled glances. Ultimately, the selection is a personal one, as are the assessments.

Inevitably, there will be those who deplore the exclusion of some favorite star or featured player herein, and for that the author begs the reader's indulgence. An early notion of centering only on those leading Thirties actors and actresses whose careers had not already been covered by a *Films of . . .* volume was discarded as being unfair to the reader not in possession of a Citadel bookshelf, as well as being unrepresentative of the decade in question. Limiting the selection to only one film each of such Thirties icons as James Cagney, Bette Davis, Clark Gable and Joan Crawford also resulted in too many important omissions. Nor was it possible to include *every* performer who ever starred in a Thirties film.

Talkies, unfortunately, marked the end of quite a few careers that had thrived during the silent era—Corinne Griffith, Milton Sills, Billie Dove, Vilma Banky, Laura La Plante, Thomas Meighan, Norma Talmadge, Rod La Rocque and Louise Brooks among them. But the ascending stars of that era are very much present and accounted for in these pages—if not necessarily in *all* of their best-remembered performances. Clark Gable, the Thirties' undisputed King of Hollywood, is observed at both the beginning of his fame in 1931 (*A Free Soul*) and at its 1939 apex (*Gone With the Wind*). But some will note the absence of such popular and award-laden Gable pictures as Frank Capra's wacky cross-country comedy with Claudette Colbert, *It Happened One Night* ('34), or *Mutiny on the Bounty* ('35), matching wits in the South Seas with scene-stealing Charles Laughton, or *The Call of the Wild* ('35), mixing romance and adventure in the Yukon with Loretta Young, Jack Oakie and a giant St. Bernard. Not to overlook Gable's combustible first teaming with his female counterpart, Jean Harlow, in the steamy, pre-Code melodramatics of *Red Dust* ('32).

Of the Thirties' ten Academy Award-winning Best Pictures, only three have been included, while *Cimarron* ('31), *Cavalcade* ('33), *It Happened One Night* ('34), *Mutiny on the Bounty* ('35), *The Great Ziegfeld* ('36), *The Life of Emile Zola* ('37) and *You Can't Take It With You* ('38) are, for various reasons, among the absent. And, although each of the Academy's Best Actor and Best Actress winners of the decade are included, it's not necessarily in the films for which they won.

On the other hand, there are so very many favorite motion pictures that vied for inclusion here and yet had to be rejected, regrettably, at the eleventh hour that it would seem churlish to end this preface without at least a quick survey of some noteworthy omissions.

British-born Charles Laughton made history by being the first performer to cop a Hollywood Oscar for a foreign-made picture (1933's *The Private Life of Henry VIII*, produced in England). But he also contributed a rich legacy of character performances to such Thirties hits as Cecil B. De Mille's lavish 1932 epic *The Sign of the Cross* (as the depraved

Clark Gable and Jean Harlow in Red Dust *(1932).*

emperor Nero), 1934's *The Barretts of Wimpole Street* (the stern and sinister father of an invalid Norma Shearer), and 1939's *The Hunchback of Notre Dame* (the deformed bell-ringer Quasimodo) in a most painstakingly detailed version of that Victor Hugo classic, which also introduced a glowing, young Maureen O'Hara to Hollywood.

Perhaps the decade's most prestigious leading lady, Norma Shearer made relatively few Thirties movies, and only *three* following the untimely 1936 death of her thirty-seven-year-old producer-husband Irving Thalberg. But one of her cleverest and most moving characterizations dominates the lavish and spectacular *Marie Antoinette* ('38), in which she ranges believably from tremulous youth to haggard middle age, as she bravely faces her inevitable execution.

The career of silent favorite Janet Gaynor—winner of the very first Best Actress Oscar for no fewer than *three* performances during the 1927/28 season—diminished to mostly trivial romantic comedies by the mid-Thirties. But, before retiring from the screen as the decade waned, she made two last, positive impressions as the rising young movie hopeful, opposite Fredric March's declining matinee idol, in the original *A Star Is Born* ('37) and in the delightfully serio-comic *The Young in Heart* ('38), as part of a family of charming con artists that included Douglas Fairbanks Jr., Billie Burke and Roland Young.

Stage-trained Paul Muni won his Academy Award for *The Story of Louis Pasteur* ('36). But he also gave striking delineations of a thinly veiled Al Capone in *Scarface* ('32), the Mexican lawyer who falls into the clutches of a lustful, conniving Bette Davis in *Bordertown* ('35) and that celebrated French novelist in *The Life of Emile Zola* ('37). And, while the actor was being accorded the pretentious billing of "Mr. Paul Muni," his Warners colleague Davis (already an Oscar winner herself for overacting in 1935's *Dangerous*) engaged in a long-running series of battles with her studio bosses before they came to realize the scope of her talents, and offered her such strong vehicles as the mob-targeted *Marked Woman* ('37), a spinster hiding a scandalous secret in *The Old Maid* ('39) and the flamboyant Virgin Queen of England in *The Private Lives of Elizabeth and Essex* ('39), pitting her against a somewhat less intense Errol Flynn. Davis's career would reach new heights in the Forties, as would that of Katharine Hepburn, an Academy Award winner for her ambitious fledgling actress in *Morning Glory* and heralded for her spunky Jo March in *Little Women*, both released in 1933. Once she had surprised Hollywood and her public with the deftness of her comic timing opposite the incomparable Cary Grant in *Bringing Up Baby* ('38), Hepburn found a welcome respite from such unpopular costume dramas as *A Woman Rebels* ('36) and *Quality Street* ('37).

A favorite leading man since 1932, Grant had begun his change from stiff-necked juvenile to jaunty young rogue opposite Hepburn in the eccentric failure *Sylvia Scarlett* ('36) before scoring in late-Thirties comedies with Irene Dunne and Constance Bennett, and capping the decade being fought over by vindictive wife Kay Francis and true-love Carole Lombard in *In Name Only* ('39). Lombard, a top comedienne since the mid-Thirties, displayed a keen dramatic flair in this soap opera, as well as in the same year's *Made for Each Other*, a funny-tender domestic drama with Jimmy Stewart.

Because of a tragic, fatal plane crash in 1942, Lombard's career barely survived the Thirties. Nor did Greta Garbo's. After the delightful East-West comedy *Ninotchka* ('39), there was only the sadly unsuitable *Two-Faced Woman* ('41) before her sudden and final retirement from the screen. Yet *Anna Karenina* ('35) and *Camille* ('37)—the latter widely acclaimed as her finest performance—offer continued proof of her dramatic artistry, while such diverse and exotic earlier vehicles as *Mata Hari* ('32), *As You Desire Me* ('32) and *The Painted Veil* ('34) remain celluloid monuments to the triumph of glamour and charisma over Hollywood hokum.

For the moviegoing public, that was an era of stars, not directors or producers. The big names were what counted, and no Thirties leading man enjoyed more gentlemanly popularity than the mid-fortyish Ronald Colman, whether kidnapped to Shangri-La in James Hilton's popular fantasy-drama *Lost Horizon* ('37), as look-alikes in love with the patrician Madeleine Carroll in Anthony Hope's Ruritanian romance *The Prisoner of Zenda* ('37), or as the blinded artist of Rudyard Kipling's *The Light That Failed* ('39), victimized by a Cockney slut, brilliantly embodied by young Ida Lupino.

But if Colman appeared to handle genteel, swashbuckling adventure well (for a middle-aged star), his sway over that area was challenged in the second half of the decade by a handsome newcomer from Australia named Errol Flynn. Flynn scored a sensation as *Captain Blood* ('35), followed by *The Charge of the Light Brigade* ('36) and a succession of mostly action stories and dramas—often cast opposite the beauteous Olivia de Havilland—that put him among the nation's top box-office stars by 1939.

Barbara Stanwyck, originally a Brooklyn chorus girl who first made it big on Broadway before hitting talkies in 1929, enjoyed her first Hollywood success under the dedicated direction of Frank Capra, in the sudsy dramas *Ladies of Leisure* ('30), *The Miracle Woman* ('31) and *Forbidden* ('32). In Capra's strange and exotic *The Bitter Tea of General Yen* ('33), she was an American in war-torn Shanghai who is both attracted to and repelled by a doomed, Oxford-

Douglas Fairbanks, Jr., Roland Young, Billie Burke, and Janet Gaynor in The Young In Heart (1938)

educated warlord (Nils Asther). In the Thirties, Stanwyck could not have been termed a "superstar," but her down-to-earth beauty, her directness, and her evident strength of character made her a favorite with the public, whether cast in drama, comedy or a period Western like Cecil B. De Mille's railroad epic *Union Pacific* ('39), in which she was a spirited Irish girl who finds adventure and romance with both a troubleshooter (Joel McCrea) and a gambler (Robert Preston).

Today it is all too easy to dismiss McCrea as a retired star of Fifties Westerns, for that is the genre in which he chose to phase out his long movie career. But in the Thirties, his tall, rugged good looks adapted as well to the drawing room as to the great outdoors, opposite such hard-working Thirties ladies as Ginger Rogers, Loretta Young and the Bennett sisters, Joan and Constance. In *The Silver Cord* ('33), he and Irene Dunne managed to escape the memorable grasp of his possessive mother (Laura Hope Crews). *Banjo on My Knee* ('36) was an entertaining comedy-drama of Mississippi riverboat folks, again opposite Stanwyck. In Edna Ferber's time-spanning *Come and Get It* ('36), about the rise of a lumber king (Edward Arnold), he romanced the beautiful, blonde Frances Farmer (as both a "bad" girl and her own innocent daughter). Farmer here displayed the talent and promise of an exciting screen future that was tragically thwarted by her own private demons.

In the realm of fantasy, cartoonist Walt Disney created a major movie milestone with the tuneful *Snow White and the Seven Dwarfs* ('37), his first full-length animated feature and a box-office bonanza that thrilled children of all ages with its delightful heroes and villains. Hollywood's other Thirties attempts at the fantastic sometimes proved heavy-handed and far less popular: *Alice in Wonderland* ('33) starred the unknown Charlotte Henry, surrounded by performers like Gary Cooper, Cary Grant and Edna May Oliver—all disguised under heavy makeup and masks; Shakespeare's *A Midsummer Night's Dream* ('35) also boasted a starry cast, topped by Jimmy Cagney, Dick Powell, Olivia de Havilland and Joe E. Brown, as well as extravagant sets and costumes. But the moviegoing public may have been frightened off by its "classic" label.

Fantasy of a far more saleable nature was popularized by a bandage-wrapped (but vocally powerful) Claude Rains in H.G. Wells' *The Invisible Man* ('33); Roland Young, Constance Bennett and Cary Grant in the delightfully wacky Thorne Smith ghost comedy *Topper* ('37); and the 1932 version of Edgar Rice Burroughs' jungle-adventure yarn *Tarzan the Ape Man*, which made an unexpected star of muscular Olympic swimmer Johnny Weissmuller and fostered a succession of sequels continuing through the Forties.

Along with sound came the large-scale song-and-dance picture shows, only a few of which have been touched upon in these pages. A giant milestone in this genre, of course, was *42nd Street* ('33) with its Busby Berkeley choreography, scores of pretty girls, and catchy songs by tunesmiths Harry Warren and Al Dubin. This film and its many successors quickly made popular musical stars of talents like Dick Powell, Joan Blondell and Ruby Keeler. The plots were often corny and predictable, but that didn't matter. Tune-flicks like *Footlight Parade* ('33), *Dames* ('34) and the *Gold Diggers* series dazzled Depression-era audiences with their kaleidoscopic dance numbers, camera effects, lavish sets, and a succession of wonderful melodies that one could go out humming. Al Jolson, who had played a major part in the advent of sound with 1927's *The Jazz Singer*, turned up in *Wonder Bar* ('34) and *Go Into Your Dance* ('35), but his movie days were already numbered. The matchless team of Astaire and Rogers, introduced in the supporting cast of *Flying Down to Rio* ('33), blazed through the Thirties like musical skyrockets in such well-remembered hits as *Top Hat* ('35), *Swing Time* ('36) and *The Story of Vernon and Irene Castle* ('39). And, while Fred and Ginger specialized in ballroom dancing, the equally unique Eleanor Powell could out-tap all of her Thirties Hollywood colleagues—which she demonstrated over and over again in the *Broadway Melody* editions of 1936 and 1938, and *Rosalie* ('37).

At the same time, there were the singers: Alice Faye, at first made up as a carbon-copy Jean Harlow for *George White's 1935 Scandals*, was better served later by the 20th Century-Fox beauticians in *Alexander's Ragtime Band* ('38), well teamed with Tyrone Power, Don Ameche and Ethel Merman. And if blonde Miss Faye was America's singing sweetheart of the late Thirties, she received some competition from a dark-haired, sultry-voiced ex-radio star named Dorothy Lamour, who introduced songs into exotic settings in *The Jungle Princess* ('36), *Swing High, Swing Low* ('37) and, especially, *The Hurricane* ('37), in which she sported a sarong, loved barrel-chested Jon Hall, and introduced the lovely ballad "Moon of Manakoora."

For a brief time in film history, "freak" musical performers like swimming star Esther Williams (of the Forties) and ice queen Sonja Henie enjoyed a tremendous vogue. Henie quickly rose to become a top box-office champion of the late Thirties through a combination of athletic skill and bubbly Norwegian personality in comedies-with-music like *One in a Million* ('36), *Thin Ice* ('37) and *Happy Landing* ('38). But producers would find it increasingly more difficult to supply stories appropriate to surround her skating acts, and in the late Forties, Sonja gave up the screen to tour with her ice show.

A phenomenon of another kind was that dimpled, pint-

Frances Farmer and Edward Arnold in
Come and Get It *(1936)*

*Roland Young, Cary Grant, and
Constance Bennett in* Topper *(1937)*

sized bundle of song-and-dance charm (and perennial moneymaker) Shirley Temple. Before she grew too big for the bright-little-girl image that Hollywood gave her, little Shirley was exploited to the hilt in such popular vehicles as *The Littlest Rebel* ('35), *The Little Colonel* ('35), *Captain January* ('36), *Heidi* ('37) and *Wee Willie Winkie* ('37), enjoying a fame and following that would transcend the years and pursue her well into middle age. As would that of another, somewhat older musical talent, Judy Garland, whose *Babes in Arms* ('39), opposite the equally dynamic young Mickey Rooney, and with its top-notch Rodgers-and-Hart score, deserves re-evaluation. Its success led to a hit series of Judy-Mickey musical comedies of the early Forties.

And then there were the opera queens who vied for movie fame equal to their Metropolitan Opera House celebrity: Lily Pons, introduced in *I Dream Too Much* ('35), oddly matched with Henry Fonda; Gladys Swarthout, debuting in *Rose of the Rancho* ('36) opposite John Boles; and Grace Moore, whose *One Night of Love* ('34) scored the only real hit of that lot. Otherwise, the cinema public seemed to prefer their arias from the girlish throat of Deanna Durbin or as served up by the lilting but mannered Jeanette Mac-Donald, whose first teaming with baritone Nelson Eddy in *Naughty Marietta* ('35) launched a major operetta-film revival.

Many of the silent screen's favorite icons found their lucrative careers severely curtailed by talking pictures, if not killed altogether. Yet some with perfectly fine speaking voices, like Lillian Gish, Mary Pickford and Gloria Swanson, were unable to match their former popularity. Gish's talkie debut in *One Romantic Night* ('30) failed to capture the public's fancy. Nor did the New York-made *His Double Life* ('33), a charming adaptation of Arnold Bennett's *The Great Adventure*, opposite droll Roland Young. Swanson entered the Thirties with style and an authoritative speaking voice that gave her no problems. But her vehicles were a random lot and, despite a professional, light-soprano voice that lent itself easily to Jerome Kern's *Music in the Air* ('34), she spent more time discussing movie projects than appearing in them—and eventually turned to the stage, as did Gish. Mary Pickford forsook acting completely after the failure of *Secrets* ('33), a time-spanning costume drama with Leslie Howard, and retreated behind the cameras to produce.

And, while many of these undeserved Hollywood has-beens were turning from films to the legitimate theatre, Broadway veterans like Henry Fonda, Margaret Sullavan and John Garfield brought their stage-honed techniques and methods to the silver screen. Already married and divorced in private life, Sullavan and Fonda were reunited briefly in 1936 for the delightful but today little-seen com-

edy *The Moon's Our Home*, in which they portrayed the love-hate battle between a best-selling writer and a tempestuous movie star. Garfield's sensational movie break-through came in *Four Daughters* ('38), in which he was an underprivileged youth mixed up with four motherless girls, portrayed by the three Lane Sisters (Priscilla, Rosemary and Lola) and Gale Page. When his rough-hewn appeal and street-blunted, New York-toned speaking voice caught on with moviegoers, Garfield was given a succession of under-dog roles like the fugitive boxer of *They Made Me a Criminal* and the social misfit of *Dust Be My Destiny*, both released in 1939.

And then there were the clowns. Many of the screen's best comedy players began their careers in silents and found that their pantomimic skills could carry them, albeit with varying degrees of success, into talkies. Charlie Chaplin, with only two movies produced in the Thirties, maintained complete silence throughout *City Lights* ('31). Harold Lloyd had had his best days in the Twenties, but enjoyed popular-ity with his strenuous antics in *Feet First* ('30) and *Movie Crazy* ('32). But Lloyd became too heavily enmeshed in plot in his later Thirties comedies, and suffered a decline in popularity, retiring when he thought that the public no longer "had any particular use for me as a comedian." Of far more durable popularity were the inimitable team of Laurel and Hardy, whose long, inspired partnership pro-duced a wealth of two-reel shorts, as well as such gag-laden feature-length classics as the incomparable *Sons of the Desert* ('33), the elaborate operetta *Babes in Toyland* ('34) and *Blockheads* ('38), which many consider to be the last of their vintage comedies.

And, while Stan and Ollie brought their public innocent laughter, escape from the troubles of a drab and depressing era, the wickedly naughty humor of stage veteran Mae West, introduced in picture-stealing support of George Raft, Constance Cummings and Wynne Gibson in *Night After Night* ('32), raised enough censorship hackles with her outrageously suggestive double-entendres, undulating walk and salacious glances in hits like *She Done Him Wrong* and *I'm No Angel* (both '33) to hasten the heavy Production Code crackdown that would severely hamper the American screen's freedom of expression for many years to come. Mae's post-Code Thirties features like *Belle of the Nineties* ('34), *Goin' To Town* ('35) and *Klondike Annie* ('36) became increasingly more tame. And while the lady tried to include as much borderline material as she could, it was a game that the unmatchable West often failed to win.

But these prefatory pages have barely touched upon the noteworthy Thirties films that have been excluded from this volume. In closing, one recalls *Min and Bill* ('30), with its inspired first teaming of those lovable cinema bulldogs, Marie Dressler and Wallace Beery; fast-rising radio star Bing Crosby crooning to Marion Davies in one of that waning silent actress's few good Thirties movies, *Going Hollywood* ('33); the chucklesome chills of those stormbound travellers trapped in *The Old Dark House* ('32); Joan Crawford's flashy Sadie Thompson, crossing moral swords with missionary Walter Huston's hypocritical disapproval in the unfairly maligned *Rain* ('32); the frightening side-show horrors of the bizarre *Freaks* ('32); Buster Crabbe's incredibly tireless derring-do as he tries to protect blonde Jean Rogers and battle dastardly Charles Middleton's Ming the Merciless in the comic-strip heroics of *Flash Gordon* ('36), the decade's most popular of all serials; a moody Phillips Holmes plotting Sylvia Sidney's demise in *An American Tragedy* ('31); the small town that gets set on its ear by a local author (Irene Dunne) who writes a sizzling best-seller in the hilarious *Theodora Goes Wild* ('36); the sheer melodramatic spectacle repeatedly offered an awed public by master showman Cecil B. De Mille in *The Sign of the Cross* ('32), *Cleopatra* ('34) and *The Crusades* ('35); Ethel, John and Lionel Barrymore teamed for their only movie, *Rasputin and the Empress* ('32); the slam-bang excitement of gangland thrillers like *Angels With Dirty Faces* ('38), in which likable hoodlum Jimmy Cagney plays hero to the Dead End Kids vs. Father Pat O'Brien; *G-Men* ('35), with Cagney on the *right* side of the law, for a change; and *Let 'Em Have It* ('35), pitting Richard Arlen's FBI agent against Bruce Cabot's scar-faced mad-dog mobster; the high-class tearjerking of Charles Boyer's star-crossed romance with Irene Dunne in *Love Affair* ('39); Frank Capra's charming fable about a small-town boy (Gary Cooper) upsetting the big-city slickers in *Mr. Deeds Goes to Town* ('36); and all those disaster-beset love stories successively altered by such spectacles as the earthquake of *San Francisco* ('36), the sandstorm of *Suez* ('38) and the deluge of *The Rains Came* ('39).

Adaptations of literary classics also struck box-office gold when filmed with the taste and care of director George Cukor's *David Copperfield* ('35), with Freddie Bartholomew as the boy David and Frank Lawton, as the man and surrounded by wonderful character actors like Roland Young, W.C. Fields and Edna May Oliver; George Stevens' *Alice Adams* ('35), in which Katharine Hepburn brilliantly walked a thin line between pathos and insufferable gaucherie as a small-town wallflower hopelessly in love with another girl's

fiance (Fred MacMurray); and William Wellman's *Beau Geste* ('39), with Gary Cooper, Ray Milland and Robert Preston as the three brothers who find adventure and death in the Foreign Legion because of a missing family sapphire. Stage adaptations also produced movies of note, including Adolphe Menjou and Pat O'Brien in a brilliant filming of that high-powered Twenties newspaper drama, *The Front Page* ('31); the touching Norma Shearer–Leslie Howard version of that much-filmed romantic drama *Smilin' Through* ('32); the social melodrama of *Dead End* ('37), focusing on the slumland problems of Sylvia Sidney, Joel McCrea and Humphrey Bogart; and Robert Montgomery's virtuoso change-of-pace depiction of a criminal psychopath, raising anxieties in Rosalind Russell and foolish, trusting old Dame May Whitty, in *Night Must Fall* ('37).

Social commentary was a risky box-office gamble in hard times like the Thirties, with results varying from the vivid realism of William Wellman's deliberately non-star *Wild Boys of the Road* ('33) to King Vidor's *Our Daily Bread* ('34), a well-intentioned Depression tale about a young couple involved in communal farming. But the public was more likely to seek admission when such movies offered the hard-hitting sensationalism promised by the Klan-oriented *Black Legion* ('36) or that harrowing pair of lynch melodramas, *Fury* ('36) and *They Won't Forget* ('37), which featured the brief distraction of a nubile, brown-haired young Lana Turner.

And while some filmmakers sought to illuminate important social issues, the majority continued to turn out escapist entertainments of an increasingly more ambitious nature, perhaps under the assumption that bigger was better. The 179-minute *The Great Ziegfeld* ('36) probably won its Best Picture Oscar as much for the size and scope of its musical production numbers as for its insights into the life of Broadway's master showman, Florenz Ziegfeld (as portrayed by William Powell). And the 141-minute *Anthony Adverse* offered rousing but episodic costume spectacle in its condensation of Hervey Allen's mammoth best-seller about an ambitious youth's progress (as embodied by Fredric March) in early nineteenth-century America.

But these introductory pages have only touched upon some of the memorable screen moments contributing to the Thirties' rich legacy of celluloid memories. Be that decade golden, silvered or frozen in platinum, Hollywood will not soon know its like again.

ANNA CHRISTIE

1930

Greta Garbo and Marie Dressler

CREDITS

A Metro-Goldwyn-Mayer Picture. Directed by Clarence Brown. *Screenplay and adaptation by* Frances Marion. *Based on the play by* Eugene O'Neill. *Photographed by* William Daniels. *Edited by* Hugh Wynn. *Costumes by* Adrian. *Running time: 74 minutes.*

CAST

Greta Garbo, *Anna Christie;* Charles Bickford, *Matt Burke;* George F. Marion, *Chris Christopherson;* Marie Dressler, *Marthy Owen;* James T. Mack, *Johnny the Harp;* Lee Phelps, *Larry.*

Garbo Talks! "Gimme a vhiskey. Ginger ale on the side. And don' be stingy, baby." With these words, spoken in a husky baritone, Greta Garbo, the silent screen's worldly goddess, made that perilous crossing to talking pictures that had kept a world of fans and colleagues in suspense. Along with Lon Chaney and Charlie Chaplin, she had continued to star in silent films while those around her either made the transition or saw their careers abruptly end. Garbo's vocal debut, cleverly selected to accomodate her Swedish accent, could not have been a better choice than Eugene O'Neill's 1921 stage play, *Anna Christie,* the story of a prostitute making the reacquaintance of her seaman-father, who had left her as a child in the care of predatory Minnesota-farm cousins.

O'Neill's play had already been well filmed in 1923, as a Blanche Sweet vehicle. And its 1930 remake reveals many of the problems of the early sound era, with its relatively static confinement to but a few basic sets—a barroom and the deck and cabin of a coal barge, plus one concession to "opening up" the story: a visit to a Coney Island amusement park.

But the restrictions imposed by the primitive sound equipment and its attendant restriction on camera movement made the "photographed play" look commonplace in 1930, and *Anna Christie's* director, Clarence Brown, was still new to the transition, having previously guided only one talkie *(Navy Blues)* and one part-talkie *(Wonder of Women).*

Although Garbo impressed both critics and audiences with her acting, there now seems too much head-and-breast-clutching anguish to her portrayal. But the basic honesty of her Anna—melded to the legendary charisma of that undeniable talent—still galvanizes us, even in the *Sturm und Drang* of O'Neill's turgid prose-poetry.

Greta Garbo and Charles Bickford

George F. Marion and Greta Garbo

Garbo's acting earned her a nomination for the Academy Award that went to Norma Shearer for *The Divorcee,* while Clarence Brown and William Daniels drew like approval for their respective direction and photography. But Garbo had talked now (she also *laughed*—long before *Ninotchka!*), and that low, deep accent blended well with her unique visual image. The star disliked her own performance in *Anna Christie,* heaping nothing but praise on sixty-year-old Marie Dressler (who, in a shameless display of uninhibited mugging, shares the film's pre-Garbo footage with George F. Marion, repeating his stage role as Anna's unsuspecting father). Immediately subsequent to Brown's *Anna Christie,* Garbo filmed a German-language version with a different cast under Jacques Feyder (director of her last silent film, *The Kiss*), and this she much prefers.

Fifty years after its initial release, *Anna Christie* seems a creaky remnant of another time and place, with its chief attraction the eternal fascination of Greta Garbo at the height of her luminous, world-weary appeal.

Ben Alexander and Lew Ayres

ALL QUIET ON THE WESTERN FRONT

1930

CREDITS

A Universal Picture. Produced by Carl Laemmle, Jr. *Directed by* Lewis Milestone. *Screenplay by* Del Andrews, Maxwell Anderson, George Abbott, *and (uncredited)* Lewis Milestone. *Based on the novel by* Erich Maria Remarque. *Photographed by* Arthur Edeson *and (uncredited)* Karl Freund. *Special effects photography by* Frank H. Booth. *Edited by* Edgar Adams *and* Milton Carruth. *Art direction by* Charles D. Hall *and* William R. Schmidt. *Synchronization and score by* David Broekman. *Dialogue director:* George Cukor. *Running time of roadshow version: 140 minutes (later cut to 103 minutes for reissue).*

CAST

Lew Ayres, *Paul Baumer;* Louis Wolheim, *Katczinsky;* John Wray, *Himmelstoss;* George "Slim" Summerville, *Tjaden;* Arnold Lucy, *Professor Kantorek;* Russell Gleason, *Muller;* Raymond Griffith, *Gerard Duval;* Ben Alexander, *Kemmerick;* Owen Davis, Jr., *Peter;* Beryl Mercer, *Mrs. Baumer;* William Bakewell, *Albert;* Joan Marsh, *Poster girl;* Scott Kolk, *Leer;* Yola D'Avril, *Suzanne;* Walter Browne Rogers, *Behm;* Renee Damonde and Poupee Andriot, *French girls;* Edwin Maxwell, *Mr. Baumer;* Harold Goodwin, *Detering;* Marion Clayton, *Miss Baumer;* Richard Alexander, *Westhus;* G. Pat Collins, *Berlenck;* Bill Irving, *Ginger;* Edmund Breese, *Herr Mayer;* Heinie Conklin, *Hammacher;* Vince Barnett, *Cook;* Fred Zinnemann, *Man.*

Beryl Mercer, Lew Ayres, and Marion Clayton

Erich Maria Remarque's grim pacifist novel about World War I, as viewed by the German footsoldier, was an expensive gamble for Universal Pictures. Its downbeat story of schoolboys facing up to both manhood and death on the battlefields of 1914–18 was filmed without "star names" and at what then represented a very high cost ($1,250,000)—the price of authenticity in its detailed sets, battle scenes, and realistic depiction of war's devastation.

Producer Carl Laemmle, Jr., chose as its director Lewis Milestone, then best known for the 1927 war comedy *Two*

Lew Ayres as Paul Baumer   *Louis Wolheim and Lew Ayres*

Arabian Nights, for which he had won the first, and only, Oscar for Comedy Directing. To help cast the film's leading roles, Milestone sought the aid of his stage-trained dialogue director, George Cukor, who selected twenty-year-old Lew Ayres. *All Quiet on the Western Front* made Ayres a star as Paul Baumer, who moves from patriotic schoolboy-enlistee to tragic battlefield casualty, when he's senselessly shot down by a sniper's bullet—in the film's celebrated climactic scene—as he reaches from his trench to catch a butterfly.

All Quiet on the Western Front was heaped with critical accolades, enjoyed a great popular success, and won Academy Awards for the 1929–30 season's Best Picture, as well as for Milestone's sensitive direction. Today its antiwar statement proves as powerful as it was over fifty years ago, standing proudly alongside such stunning antiwar motion pictures as Stanley Kubrick's *Paths of Glory* (1957) and Joseph Losey's *King and Country* (1964).

In 1979, a three-hour, $6-million TV adaptation of *All Quiet on the Western Front,* starring Richard Thomas in the Ayres role, failed to erase memories of an antique that, for all its awkward sincerity, still exemplifies early-sound Hollywood at its skillful best.

THE DIVORCEE

1930

CREDITS

A Metro-Goldwyn-Mayer Picture. Directed by Robert Z. Leonard. *Screenplay by* John Meehan, Nick Grinde, *and* Zelda Sears. *Based on the novel* Ex-Wife *by* Ursula Parrott. *Photographed by* Norbert Brodine. *Edited by* Hugh Wynn *and* Truman K. Wood. *Art direction by* Cedric Gibbons. *Gowns by* Adrian. *Running time: 83 minutes.*

CAST

Norma Shearer, *Jerry;* Chester Morris, *Ted;* Conrad Nagel, *Paul;* Robert Montgomery, *Don;* Florence Eldridge, *Helen;* Helene Millard, *Mary;* Robert Elliott, *Bill;* Mary Doran, *Janice;* Tyler Brooke, *Hank;* Zelda Sears, *Hannah;* George Irving, *Dr. Bernard;* Helen Johnson, *Dorothy.*

Having married MGM's production chief Irving Thalberg in 1927, Canadian-born Norma Shearer was a ripe target for criticism of her exalted status as queen of the Metro lot. But if the plum roles came her way, she undoubtedly deserved them. Working her way up from an extra in 1920, Shearer had ambition, and what she lacked in traditional movie-star beauty, she more than made up for in determination. By the time talking pictures arrived, she had learned all that she needed to know about good grooming and smart clothing, as well as the best camera angles and lighting for her imperfect face and figure.

She also had class and, most important, the one attribute that no amount of work and ambition could achieve: genuine star quality, that uncanny ability to draw and maintain audience attention, no matter how inferior her vehicle.

Her performance in *The Divorcee* won Norma Shearer her only Academy Award, despite nominations for various other roles. It was a film that she had fought to make, enlisting the aid of noted Hollywood glamour photographer George Hurrell to shoot her in sophisticated poses suggesting her capable of portraying the liberated woman-of-affairs described in its source novel, Ursula Parrott's popular paean to sexual freedom, *Ex-Wife.* The Hurrell gamble paid off for Shearer, who now altered her on-screen image to portray a series of free-living young women whose restive, straightforward approach to free love and chic, contemporary sophistication blended well with her cool, classic good looks. The actress's popularity now increased considerably, and from 1930 to 1934 she was among the top audience movie favorites, in Britain as well as the U.S.

The Divorcee represents soap opera of the glossiest variety, and a recital of its complex plot merely stupifies the listener as Shearer's sexually enterprising Jerry whirls in and out of liaisons with the opposite sex, represented by Robert Montgomery, Conrad Nagel, et al. All of which occurs before, during, and after her marriage to a newspaperman portrayed by Chester Morris, a philandering fellow with no tolerance for a wife who trades adultery for adultery. At the close of a plot that seems to allow its entire cast to bed one another, the sadder-but-wiser Shearer and Morris are finally reunited in Paris on New Year's Eve.

It was generally agreed that *The Divorcee* represented a great improvement on Parrott's best-seller, garnering both acclaim from the press and attendance records from its audiences, culminating in the Oscar Shearer won over the intense competition of Nancy Carroll, Ruth Chatterton, Greta Garbo, and Gloria Swanson.

Norma Shearer and Chester Morris

James Kirkwood, Nancy Carroll, and Phillips Holmes

THE DEVIL'S HOLIDAY

1930

CREDITS

A Paramount Picture. Directed, written, and scored by Edmund Goulding. *Photographed by* Harry Fischbeck. *Edited by* George Nichols, Jr. *Song: "You Are a Song" by* Goulding *and* Leo Robin. *Running time: 78 minutes.*

CAST

Nancy Carroll, *Hallie Hobart;* Phillips Holmes, *David Stone;* James Kirkwood, *Mark Stone;* Hobart Bosworth, *Ezra Stone;* Ned Sparks, *Charlie Thorne;* Morgan Farley, *Monkey McConnell;* Jed Prouty, *Kent Carr;* Paul Lukas, *Dr. Reynolds;* ZaSu Pitts, *Ethel;* Morton Downey, *Freddie the Tenor;* Guy Oliver, *Hammond;* Jessie Pringle, *Aunt Betty;* Wade Boteler, *House detective;* Laura La Varnie, *Mme. Bernstein.*

By 1930, Paramount contract player Nancy Carroll had won great popularity with her vivacious Irish beauty and charm, portraying the ingenue heroines of light musical fare like *Close Harmony* and *Honey,* with an occasional foray into melodramas like *Dangerous Paradise.* But the opportunities given her for serious dramatic acting were rare, and it was another actress's tragic death that brought Carroll one of her best roles. Jeanne Eagels had appeared in only five films, most notably 1929's *The Letter,* when she died at thirty-five of a heroin overdose. Eagels was to have starred in *The Devil's Holiday* and, after her demise, Paramount first considered retailoring the film for Ruth Chatterton. But, fortunately for Carroll, there were those who well recalled her flinty chorus girl opposite Gary Cooper in 1928's *The Shopworn Angel* and realized her rightness for

Norma Shearer, Helen Johnson, and Conrad Nagel

Phillips Holmes and Nancy Carroll

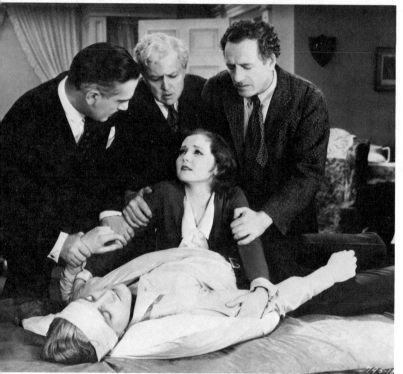

Paul Lukas, Hobart Bosworth, James Kirkwood, Nancy Carroll, and Phillips Holmes

The Devil's Holiday. The role of Hallie Hobart offered the Manhattan-born redhead an actress's dream: the opportunity to portray a young woman forced by circumstance to reform from hardboiled, man-hating fortune-hunter and party girl to face the responsibilities she owes the now seriously ailing husband she had once deserted. Manicurist Hallie's character is far from admirable, but Nancy Carroll's natural charm immediately wins us over, even though we know Hallie takes advantage of men to increase her bank account and improve her wardrobe. To this end, she meets and, not unexpectedly, enchants naive young David Stone (Phillips Holmes), a millionaire wheat-farmer's son in town to purchase machinery from the salesmen with whom Hallie is in league.

When his family opposes their marriage plans and his brother (James Kirkwood) rudely insults her, Hallie determines to get even by going through with the wedding, then demanding $50,000 of David's father (Hobart Bosworth) for a divorce. That accomplished, she leaves to resume her former way of life. But her conscience torments her, and she seeks solace in parties and drink. Meanwhile, David lies seriously ill as the result of a fall suffered in a fight with his brother over Hallie, and, when realization of her love for David brings her back to the Stone home and a return of the $50,000, she offers David something to live for.

The Devil's Holiday was written and directed by Edmund Goulding, who had just guided Gloria Swanson successfully through her first talkie, *The Trespasser.* Carroll's convincing portrayal of Hallie Hobart's reformation owes more to Goulding the director than Goulding the author, for his stereotyped screenplay is often far from convincing. But despite an annoying vocal tendency toward gushing falsetto, Carroll's emotionally taut acting provides the movie's chief pleasure.

Film critics were surprised at the depth of her performance, and *The Devil's Holiday* nearly won Carroll the Best Actress Oscar that went to Norma Shearer for *The Divorcee.*

THE UNHOLY THREE

1930

CREDITS

A Metro-Goldwyn-Mayer Picture. Directed by Jack Conway.
Screenplay by J. C. Nugent *and* Elliott Nugent. *Based on
the story "The Terrible Three" by* Clarence Aaron Robbins
*(later published as "The Unholy Three" and "The Three
Freaks"). Photographed by* Percy Hilburn. *Edited by* Frank
Sullivan. *Art direction by* Cedric Gibbons. *Costumes by*
David Cox. *Running time: 72 minutes.*

CAST

Lon Chaney, *Echo;* Lila Lee, *Rosie;* Elliott Nugent, *Hector;*
Harry Earles, *Tweedledee the Midget;* John Miljan, *Pros-
ecuting attorney;* Ivan Linow, *Hercules;* Clarence Burton,
Regan; Crauford Kent, *Defense attorney.*

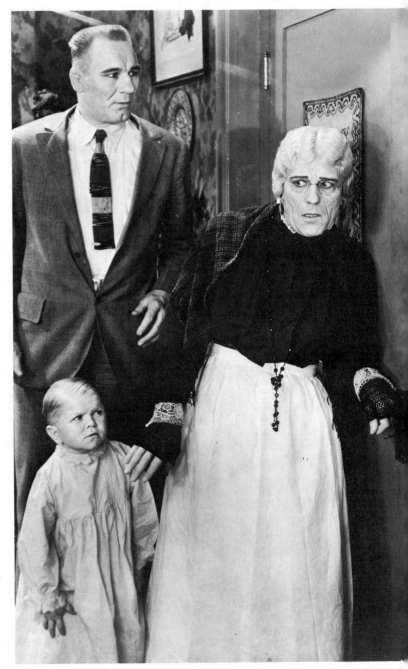

Ivan Linow, Harry Earles, and Lon Chaney

In 1929, when all of Hollywood was nervously facing the
transition to sound, Lon Chaney, the screen's uncontested
master of makeup and pantomime, maintained that he
would never switch to talking pictures. Despite an acting
background that included the theater, this sixteen-year
movie veteran had little faith in a vocal ability to match his
established screen image: "I have a thousand faces," he
confirmed, "but only one voice."

Chaney soon changed his tune, partly as the result of a
new $5,000-a-week contract he'd negotiated with MGM, and
partly to disprove the rumors that, because both of his
parents had been mute, he couldn't speak. But talk he did,
and in the 1930 remake of his 1925 hit, *The Unholy Three,*
Chaney employed five different voices in the role of a ventriloquist who impersonates not only his dummy but also a
sweet little old lady, a parrot, and a little girl! As proof of
the actor's vocal versatility, MGM publicity chief Pete
Smith even got Chaney to sign affidavits affirming that all
of these voices were his own.

The Unholy Three's sound version, directed by Jack Conway, adheres closely to the story line of Tod Browning's
popular silent predecessor. Circus ventriloquist Professor
Echo (Chaney) works in league with a pair of sideshow
freaks, strongman Hercules (Ivan Linow) and the depraved
dwarf Tweedledee (Harry Earles, repeating his role from the

Lon Chaney, Elliott Nugent, and Lila Lee

Ivan Linow, Lila Lee, Lon Chaney, and Harry Earles

1925 original). With Rosie (Lila Lee) they operate a pickpocketing sideline. Echo opens a pet shop, which he runs disguised as "Mrs. O'Grady," with the aid of his three colleagues and an unsuspecting young man named Hector (Elliott Nugent, who also collaborated on the film's screenplay with his father, J. C. Nugent). Their purpose: clever burglaries, the victims of which are the shop's unsuspecting clients. The movie's complex plot involves love and jealousy, murder and vengeance before a climax in which both Hercules and the evil Tweedledee are killed off, and Echo unintentionally suffers a vocal lapse that gives his "little old lady" away. At the picture's end, he's sent off to jail, leaving Rosie in the arms of Hector.

The Unholy Three was nearly as popular as a talkie as it had been when filmed without words, although it is generally agreed that the story's prior incarnation was atmospherically superior, thanks to Tod Browning's flair for the bizarre and unusual. For Lon Chaney, the remake presaged as successful a vocal screen career as the one he had enjoyed in some one hundred and fifty-nine silents, the most famed of which remain *The Hunchback of Notre Dame* (1923) and *The Phantom of the Opera* (1925).

But 1930's *The Unholy Three* was to be Chaney's farewell. On August 26, 1930—just seven weeks after the opening of his first talking picture—the film world's irreplaceable "man of a thousand faces" died. The ironic cause: throat cancer. He was only forty-seven.

Lon Chaney and Lila Lee

HELL'S ANGELS

1930

CREDITS

A Caddo Company Production for United Artists. Produced and directed by Howard Hughes *and (uncredited)* Marshall Neilan, Luther Reed *and* James Whale. *Screenplay by* Harry Behn, Howard Estabrook, *and* Joseph Moncure March. *Original story by* Marshall Neilan *and* Joseph Moncure March. *Photographed by* Gaetano (Tony) Gaudio *and* Harry Perry. *Color scenes in Technicolor. Edited by* Douglas Biggs, Perry Hollingsworth *and* Frank Lawrence. *Art direction by* Julian Boone Fleming *and* Carroll Clark. *Music by* Hugo Riesenfeld. *Running time: 125 minutes.*

CAST

Ben Lyon, *Monte Rutledge;* James Hall, *Roy Rutledge;* Jean Harlow, *Helen;* John Darrow, *Karl Armstedt;* Lucien Prival, *Baron von Krantz;* Frank Clark, *Lieut. von Bruen;* Douglas Gilmore, *Capt. Redfield;* Roy Wilson, *Buddy;* Jane Winton, *Baroness von Krantz;* Evelyn Hall, *Lady Randolph;* William B. Davidson, *Staff Major;* Wyndham Standing, *RFC Squadron Commander;* Lena Malena, *Gretchen;* Carl von Haartmann, *Zeppelin commander;* Stephen Carr, *Elliott;* Hans Joby, *von Schlieben;* Pat Somerset, *Marryat;* Marilyn Morgan/Marian Marsh, *Girl Selling Kisses;* F. Schumann-Heink, *First officer of zeppelin;* William von Brinken, *von Richter.*

Howard Hughes was a twenty-one-year-old Texan heir to the Hughes Tool fortune when he first became involved in Hollywood silent-film production, a subject which had long fascinated him. But his first venture, *Swell Hogan* (1926), was considered too poor for release and was permanently shelved. That same year Hughes had better luck as producer of *Everybody's Acting,* a Betty Bronson comedy which was favorably received. In 1927, he launched his own independent Caddo Production Company, with the very successful *Two Arabian Nights,* starring William Boyd and

Louis Wolheim. It won Lewis Milestone the first Academy Award for Best Direction—and encouraged Hughes to produce his spectacular aviation film, *Hell's Angels,* based on a Marshall Neilan–Joseph Moncure March story that involved two English brothers who become World War I fliers and rivals for the same fickle girl's affections.

Neilan was set to direct the movie, but when production began in 1927, disagreements between them caused Hughes to replace him with Luther Reed, who apparently shot most of *Hell's Angels'* original silent version—at a then-staggering cost of some $2 million. But, with the coming of sound, Hughes first decided to add audible effects to the movie's spectacular footage of aerial dogfighting—and then determined that *Hell's Angels* would have to be a full-fledged "talkie." The wonderful flying sequences were adjudged still usable, but all of the dialogue scenes involving stars Ben Lyon, James Hall, and Greta Nissen—would require extensive reshooting. In the case of Nissen, a thick Norwegian accent made it necessary to replace her altogether, and Hughes chose a teen-aged bit player named Jean Harlow.

Thanks to Howard Hughes' canny "Platinum Blonde" publicity campaign and what was then considered extreme sexual frankness in pre-Code dialogue and costuming, *Hell's Angels* made a star of Harlow. Her flat, nasal voice and crude acting skills notwithstanding, it was mainly Harlow who caught the attention of this film's audiences—and *then* the exciting aerial action scenes of battling biplanes and an awesome zeppelin. For the rest, *Hell's Angels* is a sometimes laughable, incredible melodrama of sibling rivalry and wartime sacrifice.

Fifty years later, the $4-million *Hell's Angels* is a creaky antique whose reputation as a "legendary classic" may confound younger audiences. But despite its risible dialogue, it remains a cinema landmark for the rough-diamond early Jean Harlow—and, of course, those still-thrilling flying sequences, a tribute to both the movie's stunt pilots and its special-effects artists.

Douglas Gilmore, Jean Harlow, James Hall, and Ben Lyon

Douglas Gilmore and Jean Harlow

ABRAHAM LINCOLN

1930

CREDITS

An Art Cinema Corp. Production for United Artists. Produced by M. Schenck. *Directed by* D. W. Griffith. *Production supervised by* John W. Considine, Jr. *Screenplay by* Stephen Vincent Benet *and (uncredited)* Gerrit Lloyd. *Photographed by* Karl Struss. *Edited by* James Smith *and* Hal Kern. *Art direction by* William Cameron Menzies *and* Park French. *Music arranged by* Hugo Riesenfeld. *Costumes by* Walter J. Israel. *Running time: 91 minutes.*

CAST

Walter Huston, *Abraham Lincoln;* Una Merkel, *Ann Rutledge;* Kay Hammond, *Mary Todd Lincoln;* E. Alyn Warren, *Stephen Douglas;* Hobart Bosworth, *Gen. Lee;* Fred Warren, *Gen. Grant;* Henry B. Walthall, *Col. Marshall;* Frank Campeau, *Gen. Sheridan;* Francis Ford, *Sheridan's aide;* Lucille La Verne, *Midwife;* W. L. Thorne, *Tom Lincoln;* Helen Freeman, *Nancy Hanks Lincoln;* Ian Keith, *John Wilkes Booth;* Oscar Apfel, *Stanton;* Otto Hoffman, *Offut;* Edgar Deering, *Armstrong;* Russell Simpson, *Lincoln's employer;* Charles Crockett, *Sheriff;* Helen Ware, *Mrs. Edwards;* Jason Robards, Sr., *Herndon;* Gordon Thorpe, *Tad Lincoln;* Cameron Prudhomme, *John Jay;* James Bradbury, Sr., *Gen. Scott;* Jimmie Eagle, *Young soldier.*

By 1930, the directorial prestige of film pioneer David Wark Griffith had diminished to an extent that he found it difficult to finance his projects. *Abraham Lincoln,* his first all-talkie, was filmed during a period of ill health that forced Griffith to abandon the production (he termed it "a nightmare of the mind and nerves") once the cameras had stopped shooting. As a result, the movie was edited by others—with somewhat uneven results. Many scenes have power and demonstrate the Master's touch. But the finished product is plodding and necessarily episodic, skimming as it does through Lincoln's entire life, from his log-cabin birth in 1809 to the 1865 Ford Theater assassination. And so we have the major highlights: young Abe's romance with the doomed Ann Rutledge, the rail-splitting early years as a young lawyer, the Lincoln-Douglas debates, the Presidency,

Kay Hammond and Walter Huston

the Civil War, and his violent dispatch by the flamboyant John Wilkes Booth. Behind it all is portrayed his rocky marital relationship with Mary Todd Lincoln, that controversial and somewhat historically muddy First Lady.

Griffith had hoped to get Lincoln biographer Carl Sandburg to write this screenplay, but was put off by Sandburg's asking price. So he engaged another distinguished writer, Stephen Vincent Benet, who received solo credit for this screenplay, although both Gerrit Lloyd and Griffith himself made unsung additions to it.

Griffith's name affords the 1930 *Abraham Lincoln* some prestige, but it is forty-six-year-old Walter Huston's masterful, age-spanning portrayal that holds the movie together. Of necessity, historical facts are telescoped in this chronicle, while famous speeches and quotations are juxtaposed with whatever visual images best suited Griffith. Historical accuracy is dealt with rather cavalierly. Much of this works, with scenes of lyric beauty and dramatic power set off by a succession of historical sequences notable only for their hollow pageantry. How much of this is due to Griffith's absence during the film's editing is subject to conjecture.

But *Abraham Lincoln* represents the once-great director's last work of any cinematic distinction. After that, there was only 1931's *The Struggle,* a low-budget New York-filmed treatise on alcoholism that audiences laughed at and United Artists quickly withdrew from distribution.

Walter Huston and Una Merkel

Ian Keith, Kay Hammond, and Walter Huston

THE SEA GOD

1930

Richard Arlen and Fay Wray

Richard Arlen (in diving suit)

On location off Catalina Island: Richard Arlen, director George Abbott, and Fay Wray

CREDITS

A Paramount Picture. Written and directed by George Abbott. *Based on the story "The Lost God" in* Where the Pavement Ends *by* John Russell. *Photographed by* Archie J. Stout. *Running time: 75 minutes.*

CAST

Richard Arlen, *Phillip "Pink" Barker;* Fay Wray, *Daisy;* Eugene Pallette, *"Square Deal" McCarthy;* Robert Gleckler, *Big Schultz;* Ivan Simpson, *Pearly Nick;* Maurice Black, *Rudy;* Robert Perry, *Abe;* Fred Wallace, *Bill;* Willie Fung, *Sin Lee;* Sol K. Gregory, *Duke;* Mary De Bow, *Mary;* James Spencer, *Sanaka Joe.*

The legendary George Abbott, producer, writer, and director—famed for his direction of Broadway musical comedies like *Where's Charley?, The Pajama Game,* and *Damn Yankees*—is less well known as a film director. But in the Fifties, he was responsible for the screen versions of that last-named pair of musicals, and from 1929 to 1931 he directed some eight motion pictures for Paramount, including a number of sudsy vehicles for Claudette Colbert *(Manslaughter, Secrets of a Secretary)* and Tallulah Bankhead *(My Sin, The Cheat).* Understandably, he then returned to the theater. Mainly, these were modest program pictures of the type ground out by Hollywood studios to fulfill quota commitments to their cinemas, whose change of fare was often on a weekly and/or double-feature basis. To this end, a movie like *The Sea God,* which had its New York opening at Broadway's Paramount Theater, where it shared the stage with a lavish revue called *Hello Paree,* had no pretensions other than modest escapist entertainment.

In what *The New York Times* called a "hectic muddle," Richard Arlen and Fay Wray impersonated the young romantic leads in this utterly fantastic tale of South Seas adventurers, pearl diving, and cannibals. It was best suited for children's matinees. With heavyset Eugene Pallette humorously on hand as Arlen's sidekick and hammy Robert Gleckler carrying on in the old techniques of hiss-boo silent-era villainy, director Abbott undoubtedly had his hands full. Arlen is handsome and stalwart, and pre–*King Kong* Fay Wray is as pretty as she is game for the rugged land-and-sea location work, but what is perhaps most interesting about *The Sea God* is its blend of studio-built "jungle" sets and its extensive use of very real outdoor scenery, shot on and around Southern California's famed Catalina Island, without any resort to process photography. When Abbott takes his company out on the water for an island-to-island sailboat race, his audience is out there, as well, with camera movements completely in accord with the natural environment. It is a pleasure to watch.

The movie's plot (Abbott's own adaptation of a John Russell story called "The Lost God") strains credulity at every coincidental turn, culminating with a diving-suited Arlen, his air hose severed underwater, surfacing to wade ashore amid superstitious cannibals, who are conveniently frightened off by this "sea god."

Hollywood no longer turns out crude comic strips like *The Sea God*—which may be just as well. But as a relic from a bygone era, it can still provide the undemanding with a brief seventy-five minutes of innocent fun.

OUTWARD BOUND

Leslie Howard, Douglas Fairbanks, Jr., Helen Chandler, Alison Skipworth, Beryl Mercer, and Montagu Love

1930

CREDITS

A Warner Bros. Picture. Directed by Robert Milton. *Screenplay by* J. Grubb Alexander. *Based on the play by* Sutton Vane. *Photographed by* Hal Mohr. *Edited by* Ralph Dawson. *Costumes by* Earl Luick. *Running time: 82 minutes.*

CAST

Leslie Howard, *Tom Prior;* Douglas Fairbanks, Jr., *Henry;* Helen Chandler, *Ann;* Beryl Mercer, *Mrs. Midget;* Alec B. Francis, *Scrubby;* Alison Skipworth, *Mrs. Cliveden-Banks;* Lyonel Watts, *Rev. William Duke;* Montagu Love, *Mr. Lingley;* Dudley Digges, *Thompson the Examiner;* Walter Kingsford, *The policeman.*

Sutton Vane's allegorical stage melodrama about the post-mortem destination of the human soul was the most provocative Broadway play of 1924, eliciting either fascination or passionate dislike. Transcribed to the Hollywood

Alison Skipworth, Dudley Digges, and Lyonel Watts

41

*Douglas Fairbanks, Jr., Helen Chandler, Lyonel Watts, and
Dudley Digges*

Lyonel Watts, Beryl Mercer, and Leslie Howard

screen in 1930, *Outward Bound* retained original cast
members Beryl Mercer, Dudley Digges, Lyonel Watts, and,
in his movie debut, Leslie Howard, under the direction of
stage-oriented Robert Milton. It was not a great success,
and even less so in its updated 1944 remake, *Between Two
Worlds.*

Most of *Outward Bound*'s action occurs aboard a
mysterious, fog-shrouded ocean liner whose passengers include: Henry (Douglas Fairbanks, Jr.), and Ann (Helen
Chandler), ill-starred lovers who discover they can't live
without one another; Tom Prior (Leslie Howard), a high-
strung, alcoholic wastrel; his mother, Mrs. Midget (Beryl
Mercer), whose identity is at first concealed from him; Mrs.
Cliveden-Banks (Alison Skipworth), a snobbish dowager; the
Rev. William Duke (Lyonel Watts), a dedicated missionary
of the London slums; Mr. Lingley (Montagu Love), an obnoxious, middle-aged businessman; and Scrubby (Alec B.
Francis), apparently the mystery ship's only steward. Eventually, they are joined aboard by the Examiner (Dudley Digges), who determines the passengers' respective fates. All, as
it turns out, are dead, except for young Ann and Henry,
whose suicide attempt ultimately fails when their dog
breaks a window pane and saves them from asphyxiation.

Outward Bound impressed and moved many who saw it in
1930, its verbosity and slow-moving narrative apparently
not detracting from the spiritual mystery of its unusual
character study. But, reevaluated from the distance of fifty
intervening years, the movie creaks badly. The acting of
Howard, Digges, Skipworth, and Love still holds up, but
Beryl Mercer's whining performance becomes irritating,
and the insipid sentimentality of the dialogue allotted to
Ann and Henry isn't alleviated by the cloying histrionics of
Chandler and young Fairbanks.

The movie is at its best technically, with sets and
photography adding much to the film's other-worldly atmosphere. According to cinematographer Hal Mohr, he devised
realism for the first part, and the addition of an umber fog
for the middle portion. Finally, when the ship and its
passengers are "out beyond," he recalls, "I had everything
sprayed a light gray, so all the detail of the set was lost completely. And on top of that, I photographed through heavy
gauze and used the fog machines."

The New York Times listed *Outward Bound* sixth among
its choice of 1930's ten best films. But, despite its thought-
provoking subject matter, this rather static excursion into
the supernatural now simply looks dated.

THE SILVER HORDE

1930

CREDITS

An RKO Radio Picture. Directed by George Archainbaud. *Produced by* William Le Baron. *Screenplay by* Wallace Smith. *Based on the novel by* Rex Beach. *Photographed by* Leo Tover. *Edited by* Otto Ludwig. *Art direction by* Max Ree. *Running time: 75 minutes.*

CAST

Evelyn Brent, *Cherry Malotte;* Louis Wolheim, *George Balt;* Joel McCrea, *Boyd Emerson;* Raymond Hatton, *Fraser;* Jean Arthur, *Mildred Wayland;* Gavin Gordon, *Fred Marsh;* Blanche Sweet, *Queenie;* Purnell Pratt, *Wayne Wayland;* William Davidson, *Thomas Hilliard;* Ivan Linow, *Svenson.*

Joel McCrea and Jean Arthur

Michigan-born Rex Beach (1877–1949) earned his considerable reputation as a writer of red-blooded fiction with his 1906 novel *The Spoilers,* about gold-rush Alaska and its rugged inhabitants. *The Silver Horde,* published in 1909, derived its title from the gleaming salmon whose presence in Alaskan waters motivated a rich fishing-breeding-canning industry. With this as his background, Beach wove yet another popular tale of greed, intrigue, and romance involving the single-minded men and women who plundered Alaska's natural resources. One character common to both novels is Cherry Malotte, a dance-hall entertainer of, not surprisingly, "questionable" repute. In *The Spoilers,* Cherry contends with "respectable" Helen Chester for the hero's affections, and emerges either the winner or the loser, depending on which of its five movie versions one is most familiar with.

In 1920, Goldwyn Pictures Corp. produced a film version of *The Silver Horde* with Myrtle Stedman as Cherry Malotte and costarring Curtis Cooksey, Betty Blythe, and Frederick Stanton. In it, reformed bad girl Stedman joins forces with Stanton, winning out over their villainous competitors in the fishing industry and stealing him away from the snobbish heiress he had intended to marry. Downgrading this romantic drama, the critics were more impressed with the film's Seattle location footage, with its salmon-fishing scenes.

The story's 1930 reincarnation at RKO resulted in an entertaining little melodrama, enhanced by a fine cast and Ketchikan, Alaska, locations, strikingly captured in near

Louis Wolheim, Joel McCrea, Evelyn Brent, and Raymond Hatton

Evelyn Brent and Joel McCrea

documentary fashion by cinematographer Leo Tover. Again critical comment was especially favorable for those scenes of fishing and the process of canning. At a tight seventy-five-minute length, director George Archainbaud keeps *The Silver Horde* from flagging with brawling action and romantic intrigue.

Evelyn Brent had starred in a raft of underworld yarns during the Twenties, and her brooding countenance and determined manner made her ideal for this movie's female lead, a woman as direct and sure in handling business as she is with men. Hers was a style that would soon become the domain of Barbara Stanwyck. Brent's vocal ability and her excellence in this film make it difficult to fathom why her career progressively declined with the Thirties. For handsome young Joel McCrea, as her partner in business and, eventually, romance, *The Silver Horde* was his biggest break to date. Jean Arthur has the movie's ingenue role, but in 1930 she possessed little of the charm later to be associated with her Frank Capra pictures; her holier-than-thou society deb deservedly loses McCrea to Brent. Louis Wolheim scores solidly as an unscrupulous cannery owner, and silent star Blanche Sweet does well in a small role that would mark her untimely farewell to the screen.

The Silver Horde typifies the very essence of the motion picture—an action yarn that includes something for everyone, as enlightening as it is entertaining.

LITTLE CAESAR

1931

CREDITS

A Warner Bros./First National Picture. Directed by Mervyn LeRoy. *Executive producer:* Hal B. Wallis. *Produced by* Darryl F. Zanuck. *Screenplay by* Francis Faragoh *and* Robert N. Lee. *Based on the novel by* W. R. Burnett. *Photographed by* Tony Gaudio. *Edited by* Ray Curtiss. *Art direction by* Anton Grot. *Costumes by* Earl Luick. *Running time: 80 minutes.*

CAST

Edward G. Robinson, *Cesare Enrico "Rico" Bandello;* Douglas Fairbanks, Jr., *Joe Massara;* Glenda Farrell, *Olga Strassoff;* William Collier, Jr., *Tony Passa;* Ralph Ince, *Diamond Pete Montana;* George E. Stone, *Otero;* Thomas Jackson, *Lt. Tom Flaherty;* Stanley Fields, *Sam Vettori;* Armand Kaliz, *DeVoss;* Sidney Blackmer, *The Big Boy;* Landers Stevens, *Comr. McClure;* Maurice Black, *Little Arnie Lorch;* Noel Madison, *Peppi;* Nick Bela, *Ritz Colonna;* Lucille La Verne, *Ma Magdalena;* Ben Hendricks, Jr., *Kid Bean;* George Daily, *Machine gunner;* Ernie Adams, *Cashier;* Larry Steers, *Cafe patron;* Louis Natheaux, *A hood.*

Edward G. Robinson and Douglas Fairbanks, Jr.

Early in 1931, with the release of *Little Caesar*, the Hollywood gangster film found popularity on U.S. screens with an impact that resounded throughout the Thirties. Most of the best, excepting Howard Hughes's independently produced *Scarface* (1932), emanated from Warner Bros., as exemplified by *The Public Enemy* (1931), *The Petrified Forest* (1936), and *Angels With Dirty Faces* (1938). These films made motion picture stars of Broadway-trained "tough guys" like James Cagney and Humphrey Bogart—much as *Little Caesar* did for a short, stocky, bulldog-faced stage actor named Edward G. Robinson.

Little Caesar might not have reached the screen at all had not its young director, Mervyn LeRoy, had the faith that a movie public saturated with escapism was ripe for the gritty realism of this hard-hitting Chicago mobster yarn. LeRoy had read W. R. Burnett's novel prior to its publication, and he convinced studio boss Jack Warner that audiences were ready for just such a change in film fare.

Bit players, Douglas Fairbanks, Jr., Glenda Farrell, and Thomas Jackson

The final shoot-out: Edward G. Robinson

Yet, despite its rise-and-fall story of a single-minded small-time hoodlum who becomes a notorious gangland big shot, *Little Caesar* wasn't a violent movie. It didn't portray graphic bloodshed, nor did it approximate the street language of today's screen. But the film's impact is strong and its violence implicit. And Edward G. Robinson, off-screen a gentle and refined actor, enacts the title role with a naturalism that more or less typed him in sinister parts throughout much of his long career. Because of the actor's intense believability as the swaggering, power-mad Rico Bandello, his pathetic demise, as he's gunned down behind a roadside billboard, remains a classic moment of Thirties cinema. And his dying last line—"Mother of Mercy, is this the end of Rico?"—lingers as an unforgettable epitaph to the decade's first great gangster movie.

For thirty-seven-year-old Robinson, *Little Caesar* did what seventeen years of stage and screen experience had not: it made him famous, establishing those familiar vocal and physical mannerisms that would make him an impressionists' favorite. *Little Caesar* remains a movie milestone, although it now creaks badly and shows its age—especially when compared with William Wellman's still-powerful *The Public Enemy*, released later that same year.

DRACULA

1931

CREDITS

A Universal Picture. Directed by Tod Browning. *Screenplay by* Garrett Fort. *Based on the novel by* Bram Stoker *and the play by* Hamilton Deane *and* John Balderston. *Photographed by* Karl Freund. *Art direction by* Charles D. Hall. *Edited by* Milton Carruth *and* Maurice Pivar. *Music by* Tchaikovsky *and* Wagner. *Running time: 84 minutes.*

CAST

Bela Lugosi, *Count Dracula;* Helen Chandler, *Mina Seward;* David Manners, *John Harker;* Dwight Frye, *Renfield;* Edward Van Sloan, *Prof. Van Helsing;* Herbert Bunston, *Dr. Seward;* Frances Dade, *Lucy Weston;* Charles Gerrard, *Martin, sanatorium guard;* Joan Standing, *Maid;* Moon Carroll, *Briggs;* Josephine Velez, *Grace, English nurse;* Michael Visaroff, *Innkeeper;* Daisy Belmore, *Coach passenger.*

Some twenty-five years after his death, and fifty years after filming the Universal screen version of his 1927 Broadway stage *Dracula*, this horror melodrama remains the movie for which Bela Lugosi is best remembered. Who could forget that lugubrious Hungarian accent pronouncing such deathless dialogue as "I never drink—*wine*," or, in response to the offscreen howling of wolves, "Listen to them . . . chil-dren of the night. What mu-sic they make!"

After the 1931 release of *Dracula* (a role for which the late Lon Chaney had been announced), Lugosi enjoyed a lengthy career in a succession of thrillers of varying merit until his death in 1955. But to many the name Lugosi means Dracula and Dracula means Lugosi, despite such subsequently successful Draculas as Christopher Lee, Louis Jourdan, and Frank Langella.

Bram Stoker's 1898 novel had originally been filmed in the German director F. W. Murnau's imaginative *Nosferatu* (1922), with Max Schreck as a monstrously grotesque, claw-fingered vampire count. In contrast, Bela Lugosi resembles nothing so much as some intense, tuxedoed magician, whose voluminous cape seems as likely to disclose rabbits as bats. Yet that requisite air of quiet, pervading evil is inherent in his masterful performance, sustained by Tod

Helen Chandler, Bela Lugosi, and Dwight Frye

Frances Dade and Bela Lugosi

Browning's overly cautious direction. Especially helpful is the camera-work of Karl Freund, who suffuses *Dracula's* introductory Transylvanian sequences with an uncanny mood and atmosphere quite lacking when the story subsequently moves to London and the film takes on the stilted appearance of a photographed play. Audiences became so accustomed to cinematic blood-letting in the Sixties and Seventies that today the 1931 *Dracula* assumes a positively Victorian quaintness when, as the count prepares to sink his fangs into a victim's throat, Browning pans discreetly away or cuts to a subsequent scene.

In many ways, Browning's *Dracula*, with its notable lack of background music, harks back to the silent era, a sensation reinforced by the slow, deliberate pace of Lugosi's acting, as well as to the melodramatic excesses which Browning permitted of character actor Dwight Frye's mad, vampirized Renfield and David Manners's effetely ineffectual young hero. As the film's Dracula-coveted blonde heroine, Helen Chandler simply looks mesmerized and haunted throughout.

Despite countless sequels and remakes, Lugosi's decidedly dated black-and-white *Dracula* remains the classic vampire thriller.

Helen Chandler and David Manners

Marlene Dietrich and Gustav von Seyffertitz

Marlene Dietrich and Victor McLaglen

Marlene Dietrich as X-27

DISHONORED

1931

CREDITS

A Paramount Picture. Directed by Josef von Sternberg. *Screenplay by* Daniel H. Rubin. *Based on the story* "X-27" *by* Josef von Sternberg. *Photographed by* Lee Garmes. *Art direction by* Hans Dreier. *Costumes by* Travis Banton. *Running time: 94 minutes.*

CAST

Marlene Dietrich, *Mary/X-27;* Victor McLaglen, *Lt. Kranau;* Lew Cody, *Col. Kovrin;* Gustav von Seyffertitz, *Austrian Secret Service chief;* Warner Oland, *Gen. von Hindau;* Barry Norton, *Young lieutenant;* Davison Clark, *Court martial officer;* Wilfred Lucas, *Gen. Dymov;* Bill Powell, *Major;* George Irving, *Contact at cafe;* Joseph Girard, *Russian officer;* Ethan Laidlaw, *Russian corporal;* William B. Davidson, *Firing squad officer;* Buddy Roosevelt, *Russian officer.*

Marlene Dietrich, now over eighty and still one of the screen's legendary greats, rose to early-Thirties prominence as the Trilby of that egocentric Svengali, writer-director Josef von Sternberg. Starting with the German-made *The Blue Angel,* von Sternberg starred her, between 1929 and 1935, in seven of his exotic, strikingly photographed motion pictures, in the process of which his wife sued the already married Dietrich for alienation of her husband's affections. Their cinematic alliance ended with *The Devil Is a Woman,* a movie the actress has always termed her favorite.

Dishonored, the third of this septet, casts Dietrich as a World War I streetwalker–turned–Mata Hari, a calculating and fatalistic beauty who disclaims fear of either life or death. With her omnipresent black cat, she's involved in a series of perilous spy missions, during which she causes the downfall of a traitorous colonel (Warner Oland), falls against her will for a Russian spy (Victor McLaglen), and dies before a firing squad for treason. Granted one last request, Agent X-27 insists that she be allowed to wear a streetwalker's garb "from when I served my countrymen instead of my country." And, in a final scene that can now only be considered "camp," she flings away her blindfold, faces the firing squad with hands on hips, and, when the officer in charge falters at his duty, uses the delay to apply a last touch of lipstick before she's shot down.

Dishonored (a meaningless title to which both Dietrich and von Sternberg strenuously objected) still entertains half a century later, primarily because of Dietrich and what film critic Richard Watts has aptly termed her "almost lyrically ironic air of detachment." With Lee Garmes's stunningly beautiful photography and the painstaking care of camera-conscious director von Sternberg, despite the film's trivial plot, its visual imagery remains indelible.

Many have charged brawny character actor Victor McLaglen's "miscasting" with destroying the love story's effectiveness. But the sheer glamour and personality of Marlene Dietrich (in her prime, at thirty) makes *Dishonored* a movie to remember, whether she's swaggering and posturing with the brazen confidence of a high-priced harlot or delivering her dialogue with the turtle-paced insinuations and pauses attributable to von Sternberg's heavy German hand.

Barry Norton, Marlene Dietrich, and bit players

Constance Bennett and Joel McCrea

BORN TO LOVE

1931

CREDITS

An RKO-Pathe Picture. Directed by Paul L. Stein. *Story and screenplay by* Ernest Pascal. *Photographed by* John Mescall. *Edited by* Claude Berkeley. *Running time: 84 minutes.*

CAST

Constance Bennett, *Doris Kendall;* Joel McCrea, *Barry Craig;* Paul Cavanagh, *Sir Wilfred Drake;* Frederick Kerr, *Lord Ponsonby;* Anthony Bushell, *Leslie Darrow;* Louise Closser Hale, *Lady Agatha Ponsonby;* Mary Forbes, *Duchess;* Elizabeth Forrester, *Evelyn Kent;* Edmund Breon, *Tom Kent;* Reginald Sharland, *Foppish gentleman;* Daisy Belmore, *Tibbetts;* Martha Mattox, *Head nurse;* Fred Esmelton, *Butler;* Eddy Chandler, *Capt. Peters;* Robert Greig, *Hansom cabby;* Billy Bevan, *Departing British soldier;* Bill Elliott, *Extra at hotel desk.*

Constance Bennett, the eldest of stage star Richard Bennett's three beautiful daughters (Joan and Barbara were the other two), had entered movies in 1922 at eighteen. By 1931, she was married to a marquis (her third husband) and was the highest paid of Hollywood actresses, displaying an equal capacity for both comedy and romantic drama. In motion picture soap operas of the Depression era, she often loved not wisely but too well, and frequently found herself an unwed mother.

In *Born to Love,* the first of four melodramas in which she was romantically supported by handsome, stalwart Joel McCrea, Bennett played an American hospital nurse, serving in World War I London, who meets and quickly falls for U.S. aviator McCrea during an air raid. They're soon living ''in sin,'' a situation advocated by Bennett, since Army rules prevent an officer's *wife* from remaining near the front lines. Later, he's reported missing in action, and she

Joel McCrea and Constance Bennett

Louise Closser Hale, Constance Bennett, and Paul Cavanagh

gives birth to his child. Time passes and she accepts the marriage proposal of a disabled British officer (Paul Cavanagh), becoming his bride. But then McCrea reappears and upsets the proverbial apple cart. Bennett meets with him; Cavanagh believes the worst and divorces her, winning custody of the child, who later dies. But McCrea is understandably on hand to comfort Bennett (who has now paid for her "sins") in the film's bittersweet fadeout.

Born to Love, with its audience-wise blend of carnal love, mother love, and sacrifice, typifies the so-called women's pictures of the early sound era, with Constance Bennett's role interchangeable among such stars as Helen Twelvetrees, Barbara Stanwyck, Kay Francis, and a host of others. But in 1931, Bennett was on top of the heap, and her cool blonde sophistication was only ruffled by the occasionally overwrought demands of sudsy melodramatics. In *Born to Love,* director Paul L. Stein tends to encourage her in some of the head-clutching, scenery-chewing excesses of the silent screen. But he's also capable of such subtleties as depicting his stars in a double-bed rendezvous by focusing his camera on one bedpost and their abandoned clothing while the lovers' voices are heard off-camera. One is spared the now-obligatory (even on TV) shot of bare-shouldered, sheet-covered actors—and it's almost a relief.

TARNISHED LADY

1931

Tallulah Bankhead as Nancy Courtney

Tallulah Bankhead, Edward Gargan, and Osgood Perkins

Phoebe Foster, Alexander Kirkland, and Tallulah Bankhead

CREDITS

A Paramount Picture. Directed by George Cukor. *Screenplay by* Donald Ogden Stewart, *based on his story "New York Lady." Photographed by* Larry Williams. *Edited by* Barney Rogan. *Running time: 83 minutes.*

CAST

Tallulah Bankhead, *Nancy Courtney;* Clive Brook, *Norman Cravath;* Phoebe Foster, *Germaine Prentiss;* Alexander Kirkland, *DeWitt Taylor;* Osgood Perkins, *Ben Sterner;* Elizabeth Patterson, *Mrs. Courtney;* Eric Blore, *Jewelry counter clerk;* Ed Gargan, *Man in the bar.*

Tallulah Bankhead had appeared in four silent pictures as a teen-ager before going to England, where she passed the Twenties as the American toast of the London stage. But, with the close of that decade and a slackening of British theatrical activity, Tallulah grew restless and chose to accept an offer to return to the States and sign a Paramount contract for five films at $50,000 apiece. What she didn't learn until later was that studio publicity flacks were promoting her as a follow-up to their most glamorous foreign import, Marlene Dietrich.

In rapid succession, she made three 1931 films whose titles alone underscore Paramount's one-track thinking: *Tarnished Lady, My Sin,* and *The Cheat.* Bankhead herself was appalled at a coming attractions trailer for *My Sin* that touted her as "Tallulah the glamorous. Tallulah the mysterious. Tallulah the woman," concluding "We gave you Marlene Dietrich. Now we give you Tallulah Bankhead!"

Tarnished Lady was her first feature since the 1928 British-made *His House in Order*—and her very first talkie, although the stage-trained intonations of that whiskey baritone gave the microphones no problem. But this movie, a soap opera about a New York socialite, takes her from penthouse to second-rate cabaret as she flits between an initially loveless marriage (to Clive Brook), much to the dismay of her bitchy and tenacious society rival (Phoebe Foster), and despite the young man (Alexander Kirkland) Bankhead still appears to prefer. But the Wall Street crash decimates Brook's wealth, and a baby helps "tarnished" Tallulah rearrange her priorities and effect a reunion with Brook.

Tarnished Lady drew some critical approval for Bankhead but proved a flop with the public, whose disinterest continued through her four subsequent vehicles for Paramount. Director George Cukor, who made his solo bow with this movie (after several codirecting assignments), admits that Donald Ogden Stewart's screenplay was "silly," but he credits its ultimate failure on his star's lack of natural empathy with the medium: "Tallulah was a most exciting, brilliant actress on the stage . . . but I don't think her quality of excitement ever quite worked on the screen."

Tarnished Lady remains an interesting failure, *because* of Tallulah Bankhead and our familiarity with her larger-than-life legend of later years. Hitchcock's *Lifeboat* (1944) and Preminger's *A Royal Scandal* (1945) have proven her potential as a screen actress. Yet film was not to make her famous—especially not as an imitation Dietrich!

Miriam Hopkins and Maurice Chevalier

THE SMILING LIEUTENANT

1931

CREDITS

A Paramount Picture. Produced and directed by Ernst Lubitsch. *Screenplay by* Ernest Vajda *and* Samson Raphaelson. *Based on the operetta* The Waltz Dream *by* Leopold Jacobson *and* Felix Doermann (Biedermann) *and* Hans Muller's *novel* Nex der Prinzgemahl. *Photographed by* George Folsey. *Edited by* Merrill White. *Music and lyrics by* Oscar Straus *and* Clifford Grey. *Music direction by* Adolf Deutsch. *Songs:* "One More Hour of Love," "That's the Army," "Breakfast Table Love," "Jazz Up Your Lingerie," *and* "Live for Today." *Runnning time: 102 minutes.*

CAST

Maurice Chevalier, *Niki;* Claudette Colbert, *Franzi;* Miriam Hopkins, *Princess Anna;* Charles Ruggles, *Max;* George Barbier, *King Adolf;* Hugh O'Connell, *An orderly;* Robert Strange, *Adjutant von Rockoff;* Con MacSunday, *The emperor;* Janet Reade, *Lily;* Elizabeth Patterson, *Baroness von Halden;* Harry Bradley, *Count von Halden;* Werner Saxtorph, *Joseph;* Karl Stall, *Master of ceremonies;* Granville Bates, *Bill collector.*

Miriam Hopkins and Claudette Colbert

Comedy spliced with a sly, sophisticated approach to sexual matters, was the Hollywood domain of German-born director Ernst Lubitsch (1892–1947). His sardonic sense of humor, often masking darker aspects of the human condition, helped create that special quality in his films known as the "Lubitsch touch."

In the Twenties, Lubitsch established a reputation for stylish, sparkling silent comedies long before the merely suggestive became blatantly explicit. With *The Love Parade* in 1929, he conquered the talking screen with a hit musical that made an American star out of French singer Maurice Chevalier.

The Smiling Lieutenant was a remake of the 1925 *Ein Walzertraum (A Waltz Dream)*, which featured Willy Fritsch and Mady Christians. In the story's Lubitsch incarnation, Chevalier portrays Niki, a guards officer whose live-in lover Franzi (Claudette Colbert) is a vivacious violinist. When Niki is assigned to assist the visiting Princess Anna (Miriam Hopkins) and her father, the King (George Barbier), his charming manner captures her heart. And, afraid that his dowdy daughter might otherwise remain a spinster, the King promptly arranges their marriage—which fails to disrupt Niki's liaison with Franzi. The Princess confronts her rival, who takes pity on this plain Jane and helps turn her into Cinderella, before nobly leaving Vienna so that Niki can better appreciate the newly revealed charms of his wealthy bride.

The "Lubitsch touch" works wonders with this slice of Ruritanian soufflé, and a happy blend of cast, direction, and subject matter helped win *The Smiling Lieutenant* an Oscar nomination for Best Picture. But *Grand Hotel* took that award. Chevalier, singing solo and dueting with Colbert, is in his element. She, in turn, is superb in a particular highlight of the film, the delicious scene in which she instructs Hopkins (an unexpectedly subdued performance) in how to improve her appearance in the number "Jazz Up Your Lingerie."

The Smiling Lieutenant was filmed at Paramount's East Coast Astoria studio, as was its French-language version, simultaneously shot as *Le Lieutenant Souriant*, in which all three stars repeated their roles.

Claudette Colbert and Maurice Chevalier

George Barbier, Miriam Hopkins, and Maurice Chevalier

Clark Gable and Norma Shearer

Lionel Barrymore and Norma Shearer

A FREE SOUL

1931

CREDITS

A Metro-Goldwyn-Mayer Picture. Directed by Clarence Brown. *Screenplay by* John Meehan. *Based on the play by* Willard Mack *and a novel by* Adela Rogers St. Johns. *Photographed by* William Daniels. *Edited by* Hugh Wynn. *Art direction by* Cedric Gibbons. *Gowns by* Adrian. *Music by* William Axt. *Running time: 91 minutes.*

CAST

Norma Shearer, *Jan Ashe;* Leslie Howard, *Dwight Winthrop;* Lionel Barrymore, *Stephen Ashe;* Clark Gable, *Ace Wilfong;* James Gleason, *Eddie;* Lucy Beaumont, *Grandma Ashe;* Claire Whitney, *Aunt Helen;* Frank Sheridan, *Prosecuting attorney;* E. Alyn Warren, *Bottomley, Ace's Chinese boy;* George Irving, *Defense Attorney Johnson;* Edward Brophy, *Slouch;* William Stacy, *Dick;* James Conlin, *Reporter;* Sam McDaniel, *Valet;* Lee Phelps, *Court clerk;* Roscoe Ates, *Men's room patron who is shot at;* Larry Steers, *Casino proprietor;* Francis Ford, *Skid-row drunk;* Henry Hall, *Detective;* Bess Flowers, *Birthday party guest.*

Norma Shearer, Clark Gable, and Leslie Howard

James Gleason, Norma Shearer, and Lionel Barrymore

In today's films, actors no longer support a star. Instead, *everyone*'s a star or costar or guest star or *special* guest star. And a few are "superstars." In *A Free Soul,* Norma Shearer is starred. The Metro queen's name appeared in giant letters over the movie's title, with all others billed routinely (in much smaller type) below it. Leslie Howard, Lionel Barrymore, Clark Gable, and James Gleason all supported her equally—in billing. But Barrymore stole the picture as Shearer's alcoholic lawyer-father, and Gable drew an electrifying portrait of charming villainy as an aggressive, sexually attractive gangster whose manhandling of his mistress (Shearer) excites her as much as it did the film's distaff audiences.

Based on the magazine serial by Adela Rogers St. Johns, *A Free Soul* was published in book form in 1924. Four years later it was dramatized by Willard Mack and enjoyed a Broadway run of one hundred performances under the direction of a young, pre-Hollywood George Cukor. In its cast, Kay Johnson, Lester Lonergan, Melvyn Douglas, and George Baxter played the roles enacted on screen in 1931 by, respectively, Shearer, Barrymore, Gable, and Howard. Mrs. St. Johns had based her original fiction on elements in the real-life relationship between herself and her father, Earl Rogers, a brillant criminal lawyer.

A Free Soul recounts an unlikely tale, but Clarence Brown's inspired direction drew such intense performances from the talented cast that both he and Shearer won Academy Award nominations. Largely as a result of his shatteringly realistic drunk scenes, Barrymore took home a Best Actor Oscar and landed a lifetime MGM contract. Shearer's liberated society girl is self-consciously overmannered, but this was among her greatest early talkie hits. For the macho-charismatic Clark Gable, *A Free Soul* was his springboard to Metro stardom.

In 1953, MGM released a grade-B remake of this story under the title *The Girl Who Had Everything* with Elizabeth Taylor, William Powell, and Fernando Lamas in the respective Shearer, Barrymore, and Gable roles. It made little impact.

David Manners, Helen Chandler,
Richard Barthelmess, John Mack
Brown, Elliott Nugent, and bit players

David Manners, Helen Chandler, and
Richard Barthelmess

THE LAST FLIGHT

1931

CREDITS

A Warner Bros./First National Picture. Directed by William Dieterle. *Screenplay by* John Monk Saunders, *based on his novel, Single Lady. Photographed by* Sid Hickox. *Edited by* Al Hall. *Art direction by* Jack Okey. *Costumes by* Earl Luick. *Running time: 80 minutes.*

CAST

Richard Barthelmess, Cary Lockwood; Helen Chandler, *Nikki;* David Manners, *Shep Lambert;* John Mack Brown, *Bill Talbot;* Elliott Nugent, *Francis;* Walter Byron, *Frink;* Luis Alberni, *Spectator at bullfight.*

Helen Chandler and David Manners

In recent years, critics and film scholars have "rediscovered" this unusual (for 1931) blend of dark humor, flip dialogue, and psychological insights anchored to a Lost Generation story of wounded air veterans trying to forget World War I with the aid of wild times and drink in 1919 Paris. Its derivative debts to F. Scott Fitzgerald and Ernest Hemingway are inescapable, yet it easily surpasses the Fifties adaptations of *The Last Time I Saw Paris* and *The Sun Also Rises*. Here, credit is due to the well-paced and economic guidance of German director William Dieterle (in his U.S. movie debut) and, especially, the script developed from his own novel, *Single Lady*, by John Monk Saunders, then best known for such male-dominated air service movies as *Wings* and *The Dawn Patrol*.

The Last Flight commences with scenes of aerial combat, but quickly shifts to terra firma, centering on four survivors who choose a life of cosmopolitan expatriation rather than face a return to their families and conventional American values. Caught up in an alcoholic haze born of happy desperation, they form a nonsexual alliance with a wacky flapper, Nikki (Helen Chandler), who shares their inclination to drink, as well as a liking for turtles in her bathtub and nonsequiturs in her thinking. Nikki's whimsical reply to any question of choice: "I'll take vanilla!"

Nikki becomes the group's mascot and falls for their leader Cary (Richard Barthelmess), who doubts her sincerity and flees to Lisbon, with his friends in pursuit. There, the

Helen Chandler, Walter Byron, Richard Barthelmess, Elliott Nugent, John Mack Brown, and David Manners

comedy-drama reaches its apocalyptic climax when, during a bullfight, the reckless Bill (John Mack Brown) jumps into the ring and is gored to death, followed closely by the murder of Nikki's unwanted suitor (Walter Byron) by drug-addicted Francis (Elliott Nugent) and the demise of alcoholic Shep (David Manners) after he's hit by a stray bullet. Mourning the death of comradeship, Cary and Nikki leave Lisbon together.

The Last Flight, a movie ahead of its time, failed to impress either critics or audiences in 1931. But its fine ensemble performances, rich textures, and unexpectedly matter-of-fact approach to love and friendship, life and death make it compellingly offbeat entertainment for those film buffs fortunate enough to have rediscovered it.

A month after this film's release, a short-lived musical adaptation—entitled *Nikki*—opened on Broadway with Douglass Montgomery, Fay Wray, and Archie Leach (a year before he changed his name to Cary Grant) in the Manners, Chandler, and Barthelmess roles.

THE GUARDSMAN

1931

Alfred Lunt and Lynn Fontanne

Lynn Fontanne and Alfred Lunt

Alfred Lunt, Lynn Fontanne, Maude Eburne, and ZaSu Pitts

CREDITS

A Metro-Goldwyn-Mayer Picture. Directed by Sidney Franklin. *Produced by* Irving Thalberg *and* Albert Lewin. *Screenplay by* Ernest Vajda *and* Claudine West. *Based on the play by* Ferenc Molnar. *Photographed by* Norbert Brodine. *Edited by* Conrad A. Nervig. *Running time: 83 minutes.*

Alfred Lunt, The actor; Lynn Fontanne, *The actress;* Roland Young, *The critic;* ZaSu Pitts, *Liesl the maid;* Maude Eburne, *Mama;* Herman Bing, *A creditor;* Ann Dvorak, *A fan.*

Ferenc Molnar's stage play is a champagne-light comedy of marital infidelity and its considerations. In the hands of mediocre players, this material could be stultifying; but as played by Alfred Lunt and Lynn Fontanne, it's devastatingly amusing, delightfully sophisticated entertainment.

Both actors had appeared separately in silent films, but the living theater was *their* medium and *The Guardsman,* a 1931 screen version of their 1924 Broadway hit, marked the Lunts' one and only costarring vehicle for the screen. This was unfortunate, for their unique brand of brittle high comedy was seldom glimpsed in standard Hollywood product, and the movie colony boasted no stars who could even approximate their blend of class, style, technique, and theatrical rapport.

The Guardsman is a frothy sex farce which owes much to the relative freedom of that pre-Code era. A jealous, temperamental team of stage actors have reason to doubt their long-standing professional and personal relationship. When the wife starts playing Chopin on her piano and drifting off into private reveries, the husband reasons that she is being unfaithful, and he impersonates a would-be rival—a Russian-accented, mustachioed, and amorous guardsman—for whom his wife seems a veritable pushover. But does she believe he's really an exciting *stranger*? Or does she know all along that it's her own husband in disguise? The narrative leaves one in doubt, a factor abetted by the sly acting of Miss Fontanne. Where, indeed, does artifice end and truth begin?

With their incomparable talent for expert ensemble acting and subtle nuance, the Lunts made *The Guardsman* one of 1931's best films, a factor recognized by America's National Board of Review and *The Film Daily,* both of which named the movie one of its year's ten best. Directing Lunt and Fontanne in their teaming film debut must have exhilarated veteran director Sidney Franklin, who later admitted: "I went to school on *The Guardsman.* What I learned from this experience—by being with the Lunts for several weeks—I couldn't have picked up in a lifetime."

The Guardsman's success as a star vehicle is abetted by superb character acting from the incomparable Roland Young, as their bemused critic-friend; Maude Eburne, as Fontanne's irrepressible mother; and ZaSu Pitts, as their maladroit servant.

Molnar's play was musicalized as *The Chocolate Soldier* and filmed in the Forties with Nelson Eddy and Risë Stevens. But 1931's *The Guardsman* is the version to remember.

SAFE IN HELL
(The Lost Lady)

1931

CREDITS

A Warner Bros./First National Picture. Directed by William A. Wellman. *Screenplay by* Maude Fulton *and* Joseph Jackson. *Based on a play by* Houston Branch. *Photographed by* Sid Hickox. *Edited by* Owen Marks. *Art direction by* Jack Okey. *Running time: 68 minutes.*

CAST

Dorothy Mackaill, *Gilda Carlson;* Donald Cook, *Carl Bergen;* Ralf Harolde, *Piet Van Saal;* Morgan Wallace, *Bruno;* Victor Varconi, *Gomez;* Ivan Simpson, *Crunch;* John Wray, *Egan;* Nina Mae McKinney, *Leonie;* Gustav von Seyffertitz, *Larson;* Cecil Cunningham, *Angie;* Charles Middleton, *Jones;* Noble Johnson, *Bobo;* George Marion, Sr., *Jack;* Clarence Muse, *Newcastle.*

Dorothy Mackaill as Gilda Carlson

British-born Dorothy Mackaill was a former showgirl with both West End and Broadway (Ziegfeld) experience when she broke into American movies in 1921. Her career as a Hollywood leading lady lasted little more than a decade, although she was a good actress whose voice enabled her successfully to cross from the silent era into talkies. But few of her films have survived.

In 1931's *Safe in Hell,* Mackaill portrayed a born loser. Her Gilda Carlson in this odd but interesting little melodrama is assuredly a tough cookie, but with a soft side. In New Orleans, Piet Van Saal (Ralf Harolde), a slick customer from her past, precipitates her downfall when, in an effort to resist his advances, she appears to have killed him during a struggle that results in the incineration of a New Orleans hotel. Since her presence in his room was noted by a bellhop, Gilda flees that city, just one step ahead of the law, with the aid of Carl Bergen (Donald Cook), her seaman-boyfriend, who stows her aboard his ship and sets her up in what's apparently the only hotel on Tortuga, a West Indian island that offers legal refuge for any and all fugitive lawbreakers.

Now saved from extradition, Gilda encounters the "hell" of the film's title when she's temporarily left there by Carl when his ship sails off and she finds she's the island's only white woman, thus stimulating the lustful thoughts and actions of Tortuga's seedy (if not downright sinister) male population, who variously attempt to have their way with her. But Gilda repels them all—until one evening when the

Charles Middleton, Morgan Wallace, Dorothy Mackaill, Victor Varconi, and John Wray

Dorothy Mackaill and Donald Cook

Maude Fulton–Joseph Jackson screenplay has her character undergo a sudden about-face with the facile explanation that she would have gone mad had she not donned her evening dress, left the sanctuary of her room, and joined their dinner table for some needed food, drink, and relaxation.

The plot now thickens with the machinations of sinister Bruno (Morgan Wallace), the sadistic island executioner, who frames her, and the unexpected appearance of Piet, who had incredibly survived that incident in New Orleans. Before sailor Carl's inevitable return, Gilda kills Piet in self-defense with the gun Bruno had given her for protection—and the full intent of later prosecuting her for illegal possession! As the film ends, Gilda walks off with Bruno, escorted to her execution by his goons.

Out of this sordid material, director William A. Wellman (*Wings, The Public Enemy*) develops a tightly coiled little film that offers more in sixty-eight minutes than many a two-part TV movie of today. *Safe in Hell* is occasionally overwrought and exaggerated. But audience interest seldom flags, and above all there is always the intriguing Dorothy Mackaill, whose appeal lies somewhere between that of a gutsier Marion Davies and a more feminine Talullah Bankhead, with both warmth and intensity to spare.

DR. JEKYLL AND MR. HYDE

1932

CREDITS

A Paramount Picture. Produced and directed by Rouben Mamoulian. *Screenplay by* Samuel Hoffenstein *and* Percy Heath. *Based on* The Strange Case of Dr. Jekyll and Mr. Hyde *by* Robert Louis Stevenson. *Photographed by* Karl Struss. *Edited by* William Shea. *Art direction by* Hans Dreier. *Costumes by* Travis Banton. *Running time: 90 minutes.*

CAST

Fredric March, *Dr. Henry Jekyll/Mr. Hyde;* Miriam Hopkins, *Ivy Pearson;* Rose Hobart, *Muriel Carew;* Holmes Herbert, *Dr. Lanyon;* Edgar Morton, *Poole;* Halliwell Hobbes, *Brig. Gen. Carew;* Arnold Lucy, *Utterson;* Tempe Pigott, *Mrs. Hawkins;* Colonel McDonnell, *Hobson;* Eric Wilton, *Briggs;* Douglas Walton, *Student;* John Rogers, *Waiter;* Murdock McQuarrie, *Doctor.*

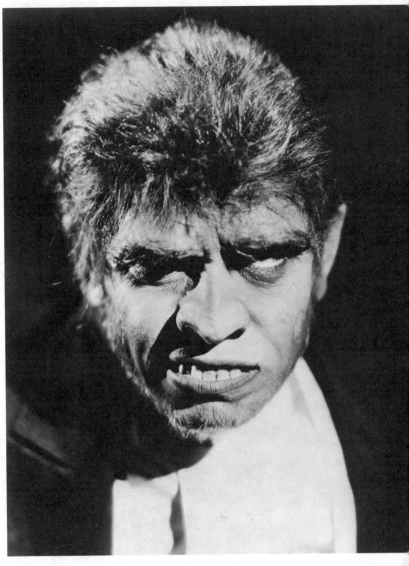

Fredric March as Mr. Hyde

Halliwell Hobbes, Rose Hobart, and Fredric March

Robert Louis Stevenson's short 1886 novel has since been filmed many times and under many titles, with variations as bizarre as a sex-change orientation in 1971's *Dr. Jekyll and Sister Hyde* and a 1973 *musical* adaptation for TV. But this classic terror tale of literature's most celebrated split personality has seldom been better served than in Paramount's 1932 version, produced and directed by that master cinema stylist, Rouben Mamoulian. It was only Mamoulian's third motion picture—and his *only* excursion into the uncanny. He had come from a solid stage background in comedy, drama, and opera and had already won acclaim for the taste and innovational touches of his *Applause* (1929) and *City Streets* (1931).

Working from an intelligent screenplay by Percy Heath and Samuel Hoffenstein, Mamoulian fought to cast Paramount contract actor Fredric March, who replaced that studio's original selection, Irving Pichel. Mamoulian's instincts were justified; March's bravura performance won widespread approval, brought him the first of his two Academy Awards, and pushed him into the vanguard of important Hollywood stars. A clever use of lighting and

Fredric March and Miriam Hopkins

makeup considerably aided his exciting transformation from handsome young Jekyll to the animalistic Hyde. But the actor's skills with voice, body language, and characterization served to remove all but the vaguest of similarities between these distinct alter egos. A half-century after its creation, March's *Dr. Jekyll and Mr. Hyde* remains a strong and frightening impersonation.

But this isn't the movie's only fine performance. Miriam Hopkins is at her best as Ivy Pearson, the sluttish cabaret entertainer, and her sexually insinuating scenes with both Hyde and Jekyll fairly crackle with pre-Production Code electricity. This screenplay itself makes no bones about fleshly desires and frustration. And, though the camera does not explicitly depict the Hyde-Ivy relationship, there is little doubt as to its carnal side—or his sadistic treatment of her. By contrast, Rose Hobart is attractive and warmly supportive as the "good" girl, but the scripts allows her little beyond that. Ironically, this was the role that Miriam Hopkins *wanted* to play, and it took much persuasion by Mamoulian to convince her otherwise.

With brilliantly conceived photography by Karl Struss and an inventive deployment of sound, this *Dr. Jekyll and Mr. Hyde* stands as a monument to the creative genius of Rouben Mamoulian and his production team.

James Cagney and Ann Dvorak

THE CROWD ROARS

1932

CREDITS

A Warner Bros. Picture. Directed by Howard Hawks. *Screenplay by* Kubec Glasmon, John Bright, *and* Niven Busch. *Story by* Howard Hawks *and* Seton I. Miller. *Photographed by* Sid Hickox *and* John Stumar. *Edited by* Thomas Pratt. *Art direction by* Jack Okey. *Music by* Leo F. Forbstein. *Running time: 85 minutes.*

CAST

James Cagney, *Joe Greer;* Joan Blondell, *Anne;* Ann Dvorak, *Lee;* Eric Linden, *Eddie Greer;* Guy Kibbee, *Dad Greer;* Frank McHugh, *Spud Conners;* William Arnold, *Bill Arnold;* Leo Nomis, *Jim;* Charlotte Merriam, *Mrs. Spud Connors;* Regis Toomey, *Dick Wilbur;* Harry Hartz, Fred Guisso, Fred Frame, Jack Brisko, Ralph Hepburn, Phil Pardee, Spider Matlock, Lou Schneider, Bryan Salspaugh, Stubby Stubblefield, Shorty Cantlon, Wilbur Shaw, and Mel Keneally, *Drivers;* James Burtis, *Mechanic;* Ralph Dunn, *Official;* Sam Hayes, *Ascot announcer;* John Conte, *Announcer;* John Harron, *Red, Eddie's pitman;* Robert McWade, *Tom the counterman.*

Eric Linden and James Cagney

That cocky, street-smart bravado and innate Irish belligerence that made a natural actor of New York City–born James Cagney helped develop him into one of Warners' most popular stars of the Thirties. After several inconsequential roles, he first hit it big in director William Wellman's 1931 gangster classic *The Public Enemy,* in which he romanced a novice Jean Harlow, pushed a grapefruit in poor, whining Mae Clarke's face, and wound up a stiff on his mother's doorstep. Cagney's impact in that one landmark film was sufficient to catapult him into the top echelon of screen popularity. Having signed with Warners for a miserable $400 per week in 1930, the actor rose, by the decade's end, to a then impressive $368,333.

James Cagney, Guy Kibbee, Frank McHugh, and Eric Linden

Ann Dvorak and Joan Blondell

The Crowd Roars typifies the sort of fast-moving melodrama that Warner Bros. churned out so prodigiously in the early Thirties. Screenwriters Kubec Glasmon, John Bright, and Niven Busch had done better. But with the male-action–oriented Howard Hawks directing, and a solid supporting cast that featured Joan Blondell, Ann Dvorak, Guy Kibbee, and Frank McHugh, the results pleased 1932 moviegoers, if not the reviewers. And the slam-bang racetrack footage, with its spectacular smash-ups, was sufficient for recycling in a 1939 remake, *Indianapolis Speedway.*

This is the one about the devil-may-care, hard-living racing driver (Cagney) who tries to keep his nice younger brother (Eric Linden) from following in his footsteps—including the company of "dubious" women like his own girlfriend (Ann Dvorak). When junior takes up with a "dame" (Joan Blondell) of whom big brother disapproves, the boy marries her and goes on to driving fame, while our sour-grapes nonhero hits the downward trail, after causing a fatal track accident that results in the death of a pal (Frank McHugh). But, by the picture's close, necessity has patched up the brothers' differences and reunited them in the winner's circle.

Within the restrictions of the race-car genre, the cast delivers as well as could be expected, with he-man Cagney even carrying off a difficult crying scene in Ann Dvorak's arms without causing embarrassment. *The Crowd Roars* is nothing Cagney and company need feel ashamed of, and it happens to be one of that actor's few early films (along with *The Public Enemy*) to maintain any kind of regular TV visibility today.

GRAND HOTEL

1932

John Barrymore and Greta Garbo

Ferdinand Gottschalk, Greta Garbo, and Rafaela Ottiano

John Barrymore, Lionel Barrymore, and Lewis Stone

In 1931, MGM production chief Irving Thalberg came up with a clever solution for Depression-era box-office doldrums: the multistar motion picture. While glittering personalities like Greta Garbo, John Barrymore, Joan Crawford, Wallace Beery, and Lionel Barrymore could easily carry a film on his or her own, Thalberg cunningly reasoned that filmgoers would be unable to resist a movie that combined all of these powerhouse talents in one entertainment package.

Grand Hotel originated as a German play by Vicki Baum that had achieved a 1930 Broadway run of 257 performances featuring Eugenie Leontovich, Henry Hull, Hortense Alden, Siegfried Rumann, and Sam Jaffe. Produced and distributed at a reported cost of $700,000, the filmed *Grand Hotel* brought MGM rentals of some $2,594,000 and walked away with the 1931–32 Academy Award for Best Picture.

Under Edmund Goulding's imaginative direction, this actors' showcase presents a veritable microcosm of humanity as it focuses on life, love, and death in a luxury Berlin hotel during the course of forty-eight consecutive hours. As the hostelry's guests whose lives fatefully intermingle, Garbo embodies a fading ballet star facing her moment of truth; John Barrymore is the suave jewel thief whose love rejuvenates her; Crawford plays an ambitious "little stenographer" with flexible morals; Beery's the tough industrialist who elicits Crawford's services; and Lionel portrays a lowly bookkeeper determined to spend his dying days in the lap of luxury.

Together, and with the fine support of players like Lewis Stone, Jean Hersholt, and Rafaela Ottiano, this MGM constellation weaves magic. Garbo's performance (here's where she declares that wish to be "alone") was much praised in 1932, although it now looks somewhat phony and exaggerated—a larger-than-life departure from her usual understated acting. And one might question why, despite the Teutonic setting, Wallace Beery alone employs a German accent, while Crawford and the Barrymore brothers speak in their usual American tones. But *Grand Hotel's* flaws are minor, and its entertainment value is strong.

In 1945, MGM remade the film as *Weekend at the Waldorf* with Ginger Rogers, Walter Pidgeon, Lana Turner, Van Johnson, and Edward Arnold. Fifteen years later, Vicki Baum's play was restored to its original form in a contemporary German version, *Menschen im Hotel*, starring Michele Morgan, O. W. Fischer, Sonja Ziemann, Heinz Ruhmann, and Gert Frobe. And, as this book is being written, there is Hollywood talk of still another version to come. Yet no amount of remakes seems to dim the memory of 1932's classic *Grand Hotel*.

CREDITS

A Metro-Goldwyn-Mayer Picture. Directed by Edmund Goulding. *Screenplay by* William A. Drake. *Based on* Vicki Baum's *play Menschen im Hotel. Photographed by* William Daniels. *Edited by* Blanche Sewell. *Art direction by* Cedric Gibbons. *Gowns by* Adrian. *Running time: 115 minutes.*

CAST

Greto Garbo, *Grusinskaya;* John Barrymore, *Baron Felix von Geigern;* Joan Crawford, *Flaemmchen;* Wallace Beery, *Preysing;* Lionel Barrymore, *Otto Kringelein;* Lewis Stone, *Dr. Otternschlag;* Jean Hersholt, *Senf;* Robert McWade, *Meierheim;* Purnell B. Pratt, *Zinnowitz;* Ferdinand Gottschalk, *Pimenov;* Rafaela Ottiano, *Suzette;* Morgan Wallace, *Chauffeur;* Tully Marshall, *Gerstenkorn;* Frank Conroy, *Rohna;* Murray Kinnell, *Schweimann;* Edwin Maxwell, *Dr. Waitz;* Mary Carlisle, *Honeymooner;* John Davidson, *Hotel manager;* Sam McDaniel, *Bartender.*

Dolores Del Rio

BIRD OF PARADISE

1932

CREDITS

An RKO Picture. Produced by David O. Selznick. *Directed by* King Vidor. *Screenplay by* Wells Root, Leonard Praskins, *and* Wanda Tuchok. *Based on the play by* Richard Walton Tully. *Photographed by* Clyde De Vinna, Edward Cronjager, *and* Lucien Andriot. *Choreography by* Busby Berkeley. *Art direction by* Carroll Clark. *Music by* Max Steiner. *Running time: 80 minutes.*

CAST

Dolores Del Rio, *Luana;* Joel McCrea, *Johnny Baker;* John Halliday, *Mac;* Richard "Skeets" Gallagher, *Chester;* Creighton Chaney/Lon Chaney, Jr., *Thornton;* Bert Roach, *Hector;* Napoleon Pukui, *The King;* Sofia Ortega, *Mahumahu;* Agostino Borgato, *Medicine man.*

The stunningly exotic beauty of Dolores Del Rio—the first Mexican actress ever to become an international film star—had weathered the transition from silent films to talkies. But roles had to be carefully chosen to accommodate her accent and somewhat rudimentary acting talents. *Bird of Paradise*, loosely based on an old stage play, fit the bill. The actress had relatively little dialogue, the plot was pure escapist romance, and few thespian subtleties were demanded, either of her or her leading man, Joel McCrea.

The movie's plusses lie in its appeal to the senses, namely in the striking black-and-white Hawaiian location photography of Clyde De Vinna, who had won a 1928 Oscar for *White Shadows in the South Seas*, and Max Steiner's richly evocative background score, designed to illustrate everything from Polynesian native dancing and choral chants to idyllic, star-crossed romance. In an era when original music was considered an unnecessary distraction to filmgoers, Steiner's first comprehensive start-to-finish score was a somewhat bold idea of the movie's producer, David O. Selznick. Selznick was then head of production at RKO, and it was his notion to turn out a motion picture teaming Del Rio and McCrea in a South Seas romance, to be directed by King Vidor, whose most recent films had ranged from pseudobiographic Western (*Billy the Kid*) to sentimental drama (*The Champ*). But Vidor found Richard Walton Tul-

Dolores Del Rio and Joel McCrea

ly's play *Bird of Paradise* hopelessly dated and uninteresting; Selznick countered, "I don't care what story you use as long as we call it *Bird of Paradise* and Del Rio jumps into a flaming volcano at the finish."

Bird of Paradise cost RKO more than a million dollars, a high expense at the time. And it is to Selznick's credit that the finished produce looks as good as it does, for its script was literally slapped together during a necessarily brief production period, mostly on the location voyage to Hawaii, where the weather did not always cooperate. But Del Rio and McCrea had other commitments, and *Bird of Paradise* had to be shot quickly, with final scenes completed in Hollywood.

Unfortunately, this lush 1932 romantic drama is little seen today, largely because of the 1951 Technicolor remake starring Debra Paget, Louis Jourdan, and Jeff Chandler. As so often has happened, an inferior newer version prevents the television exposure of an earlier, and often classic, *original* movie.

TROUBLE IN
PARADISE

1932

Herbert Marshall and Miriam Hopkins

CREDITS

A Paramount Picture. Produced and directed by Ernst Lubitsch. *Screenplay by* Grover Jones *and* Samson Raphaelson. *Based on the play The Honest Finder by* Laszlo Aladar. *Photographed by* Victor Milner. *Art direction by* Hans Dreier. *Music by* W. Franke Harling. *Gowns by* Travis Banton. *Running time: 86 minutes.*

CAST

Miriam Hopkins, *Lily Vautier;* Kay Francis, *Mariette Colet;* Herbert Marshall, *Gaston Monescu/La Valle;* Charlie Ruggles, *The Major;* Edward Everett Horton, *Francois Filiba;* C. Aubrey Smith, *Adolph Giron;* Robert Greig, *Jacques the butler;* George Humbert, *Waiter;* Rolfe Sedan, *Purse salesman;* Luis Alberni, *Annoyed opera fan;* Leonid Kinskey, *Radical;* Hooper Atchley, *Insurance agent;* Nella Walker, *Mme. Bouchet.*

Cynical, sophisticated wit was the very essence of producer-director Ernst Lubitsch's Hollywood career, and his sly sense of visual humo; is nowhere more evident than in this 1932 comedy classic. Years later Lubitsch told his biographer, Herman G. Weinberg, "As for pure style, I think I have done nothing better or as good as *Trouble in Paradise*."

The film's Samson Raphaelson–Grover Jones screenplay derives, as did so many Hollywood films of the Thirties, from Continental source material—in this case, a Hungarian play by Laszlo Aladar. Its substance is slight, but good acting and the deft hand of Lubitsch and his technical crew polish the enterprise to a brilliant lustre.

Herbert Marshall and Miriam Hopkins portray a pair of European society crooks, as deft and amoral at jewel thievery as they are at romantic dalliance. Their target here is Kay Francis, a wealthy Parisienne into whose life they smoothly intrude. Ex-lovers now in larcenous competition,

George Humbert, Miriam Hopkins, and Herbert Marshall

each manages to become a trusted member of her household, he as personal secretary and she as her maid. But their "progress" is constantly threatened by Edward Everett Horton, a past victim of Marshall's whose efforts to recall where they'd previously met provide a clever running gag. Romance develops between Francis and Marshall, but is it genuine on his part or merely an act? Lubitsch leads us astray more than once with his tongue-in-cheek direction of this deliciously witty satire.

Herbert Marshall, Kay Francis, and C. Aubrey Smith

Herbert Marshall, so often tiresomely dull in his screen performances, quite blossoms under Lubitsch's tutelage here, offering a performance that could not have been bettered—except perhaps by Ronald Colman. Miriam Hopkins's eternal Georgian accents may clash with Marshall's cultivated British, but her low-key comedy technique blends well, as does that of Kay Francis, so often cast elsewhere as a suffering clotheshorse. *Trouble in Paradise* offers her a charming role, and she responds with style and warmth.

Like many another smart comedy of the Thirties, *Trouble in Paradise* garnered no Oscars. But the National Board of Review named it among 1932's ten best, and its reputation has easily survived the years.

Katharine Hepburn and John Barrymore

David Manners and Katharine Hepburn

A BILL OF DIVORCEMENT

1932

CREDITS

A Radio Picture. Directed by George Cukor. *Produced by* David O. Selznick. *Screenplay by* Howard Estabrook *and* Harry Wagstaff Gribble. *Based on the play by* Clemence Dane. *Photographed by* Sid Hickox. *Edited by* Arthur Roberts. *Art direction by* Carroll Clark. *Costumes by* Josette De Lima. *Music by* Max Steiner. *Piano concerto composed by* W. Franke Harling. *Running time: 75 minutes.*

CAST

John Barrymore, *Hillary Fairfield;* Billie Burke, *Margaret Fairfield;* Katharine Hepburn, *Sydney Fairfield;* David Manners, *Kit Humphrey;* Henry Stephenson, *Dr. Alliot;* Paul Cavanagh, *Gray Meredith;* Elizabeth Patterson, *Aunt Hester;* Gayle Evers, *Bassett;* Julie Haydon, *Party guest.*

The 1932 filming of Clemence Dane's play *A Bill of Divorcement* is best recalled as the vehicle that marked Katharine Hepburn's motion picture bow. In it, the novice Hepburn took third billing, after Billie Burke and the film's only above-the-title star, John Barrymore. At fifty, the actor offered one of his finest screen characterizations, quite devoid of the familiar Barrymore mannerisms. Like her colleague, Burke had long been a stage star who had appeared in many silent pictures. But unlike him, she was here, aged forty-seven, making her talking picture bow, and that might account for some of the irritating fussiness of her mannered performance, compounded by the recent death of her husband, legendary showman Florenz Ziegfeld. Twenty-four-year old Katharine Hepburn, of course, provides the film's central focus, then as now, and the public reaction was anything but apathetic. Most of the critics were impressed with her angular beauty, her obvious intelligence, and that distinctive Bryn Mawr/New England–accented voice. But others found her manner abrasive and that voice harsh and grating.

A Bill of Divorcement has to date been filmed three times. In 1922, a year after its stage incarnation, the British produced a silent adaptation featuring Constance Binney, Malcolm Keen, and Fay Compton in the roles reprised a decade later by Hepburn, Barrymore, and Burke. In 1940, a subsequent American remake starred young Maureen O'Hara, Adolphe Menjou, and Fay Bainter. But director George Cukor's 1932 version provides the most lasting memories.

Because of its stagy plot, sentimentalized, declamatory dialogue, and old-fashioned theatrics, *A Bill of Divorcement* dates badly for today's audiences. This melodramatic story of double romance threatened (and, in one case, defeated) by the disclosure of family insanity precipitates a good deal of *Sturm und Drang* and noble sacrifices that seem hopelessly foreign, phony, even risible in the Eighties. But, with the strength and sincerity of their playing, Barrymore and Hepburn, in particular, help suspend disbelief, enacting the tentative first meeting of a "fatherless" daughter and the asylum-incarcerated parent who had never known his offspring.

Hepburn credits both Barrymore's on-set kindness and Cukor's behind-the-scenes care with making her screen debut a success. "He presented me to the public in a way calculated to make me seem fascinating," the actress recently recalled. "He used very shrewdly what I had to offer: my harsh voice . . . my skinny face . . . my eccentric ways. He made them seem like virtues."

Henry Stephenson, John Barrymore, Katharine Hepburn, and Billie Burke

Katharine Hepburn and John Barrymore

I AM A FUGITIVE
FROM A CHAIN GANG
(I Am a Fugitive)

1932

Paul Muni as James Allen

CAST

A Warner Bros. Picture. Directed by Mervyn LeRoy. *Produced by* Hal B. Wallis. *Screenplay by* Sheridan Gibney, Brown Holmes, *and (uncredited)* Howard J. Green. *Based on the book* I Am a Fugitive From a Georgia Chain Gang *by* Robert E. Burns. *Photographed by* Sol Polito. *Edited by* Bill Holmes. *Art direction by* Jack Okey. *Gowns by* Orry-Kelly. *Technical advisers:* S. H. Sullivan *and* Jack Miller. *Running time: 93 minutes.*

CAST

Paul Muni, *James Allen;* Glenda Farrell, *Marie Woods;* Helen Vinson, *Helen;* Preston Foster, *Pete;* Allen Jenkins, *Barney Sykes;* Edward Ellis, *Bomber Wells;* John Wray, *Nordine;* Hale Hamilton, *Rev. Allen;* Harry Woods, *Guard;* David Landau, *Warden;* Edward J. McNamara, *Second warden;* Robert McWade, *Ramsey;* Willard Robertson, *Prison commissioner;* Noel Francis, *Linda;* Louise Carter, *Mrs. Allen;* Berton Churchill, *Judge;* Sheila Terry, *Allen's secretary;* Sally Blane, *Alice;* James Bell, *Red;* Douglas Dumbrille, *District attorney;* Robert Warwick, *Fuller;* Charles Middleton, *Train conductor;* Jack La Rue, *Ackerman.*

In a decade heavy with films of an escapist nature, one studio—Warner Bros.—established a reputation for films of social conscience and comment. Movies like *Wild Boys of the Road* (1933), *Massacre* (1934), *Black Legion* (1936), and *They Won't Forget* (1937) mixed critical commentary with entertainment and won widespread approval. The fact that these stories were basically melodramas helped attract moviegoers. And sometimes they raised enough public consciousness to effect reform.

The movie perhaps most often brought to mind in this respect is *I Am a Fugitive From a Chain Gang,* based on the true-life experiences of an escapee who published his story under the pseudonym of Robert E. Burns. As adapted uncompromisingly to the screen by writers Sheridan Gibney, Brown Holmes, and Howard J. Green, Burns's harrowing story told how an honest World War I veteran returns to a clerical job he can't stand, leaves it to become an itinerant construction worker, and is implicated in a

Glenda Farrell and Paul Muni

Paul Muni and bit players

Paul Muni and Helen Vinson

holdup in a Southern town. As a result, he's sentenced to ten years' hard labor on a brutalized chain gang. A year later, he escapes and finds employment under an assumed name, eventually working his way up into a senior management position. But his landlady discovers his secret past and blackmails him into marriage. After he falls in love with another woman, the wife vindictively informs on him, and a press campaign seeking a pardon is mounted on his behalf. Tricked into returning to prison for a sixty-day sentence (with a promise of a pardon), he finds his case suspended and his hopes dashed. Again he escapes—to face a dubious future in which he must steal to survive.

I Am a Fugitive From a Chain Gang hit Depression-era audiences with the power of a sledgehammer. Powerful and uncompromising in its indictment of the law (especially with regard to carefully unnamed Southern communities), it was given a realistic, unvarnished production by Hal B. Wallis, straightforward direction by Mervyn LeRoy, and naturalistic, understated acting by its star Paul Muni, who had researched the film's background and subject matter with the dedication of a perfectionist. Largely because of his fine performance, this movie remains a powerful statement of social injustice. *I Am a Fugitive* (as it was more simply titled in re-release) earned widespread critical acclaim and Oscar nominations for Muni as Best Actor (Charles Laughton won for *The Private Lives of Henry VIII*) and Best Picture (that award went to *Cavalcade*). And the National Board of Review named it the year's best movie. Just how far this motion picture went to influence American prison reform has proven debatable. But as a hard-hitting comment on social ills, it remains a milestone.

THE MASK OF FU MANCHU

1932

CREDITS

A Metro-Goldwyn-Mayer Picture. Directed by Charles Brabin *and (uncredited)* Charles Vidor. *Screenplay by* Irene Kuhn, Edgar Allan Woolf, *and* John Willard. *Based on the novel by* Sax Rohmer. *Photographed by* Tony Gaudio. *Edited by* Ben Lewis. *Art direction by* Cedric Gibbons. *Costumes by* Adrian. *Running time: 72 minutes.*

CAST

Boris Karloff, *Dr. Fu Manchu;* Lewis Stone, *Nayland Smith;* Karen Morley, *Sheila Barton;* Charles Starrett, *Terrence Granville;* Myrna Loy, *Fah Lo See;* Jean Hersholt, *Prof. Von Berg;* Lawrence Grant, *Sir Lionel Barton;* David Torrence, *McLeod.*

In the Seventies, Fu Manchu, Sax Rohmer's erudite master of Oriental evil, was effectively impersonated in a series of modestly produced thrillers by Britain's Christopher Lee, who built a career on the masterful impersonation of movie monsters. But his Thirties counterpart, Boris Karloff, laid much of that groundwork with *Frankenstein* (1931), *The Mummy* (1932), and their various offshoots and sequels.

In 1932, Karloff lent his definitive, stately presence and commanding voice to *The Mask of Fu Manchu*, Metro-Goldwyn-Mayer's only foray into such comic-strip melodrama during that era. Taking over from Paramount, which had featured Warner Oland in both *The Mysterious Dr. Fu Manchu* in 1929 and *The Return of Dr. Fu Manchu* a year later, MGM's uncharacteristic thriller offered a curiously lurid yarn that just barely skirted the boundaries of traditional Metro taste and "class." But it left little doubt in sophisticated audience sensibilities as to its implications of sadistic torture and perverse pleasures. And while the *details* of physical persuasion and diabolic demise were mainly applied to such Caucasian character actors as Jean Hersholt (the threat of impalement) and Lewis Stone (lowered into a crocodile pit), the restlessly power-hungry Fu is given scant pause by the blonde beauty of Karen Morley.

Somewhat more sexually susceptible, however, is the megalomaniac scientist's exotic daughter Fah Lo See (Myrna Loy), whose erotic fascination with the ordered lashing of manacled hero Terrence Granville (Charles Starrett) is motivated by her all-too-obvious lust for his half-naked per-

son. Fu Manchu's own motivation, while equally ruthless, is somewhat more nebulous: world domination via ownership of the legendary Genghis Kahn's newly unearthed ceremonial sword and mask. His efforts to gain possession of these coveted relics spins the plot of this campy pulp-magazine movie, whose delicious villainy is carried out with tongue-in-cheek flair by Karloff and Loy (as the last of her many Oriental screen temptresses).

Metro's artisans were inspired to pull out all the proverbial stops for this one, from Cedric Gibbons's Art Deco torture chambers to Adrian's richly bizarre costume designs. As photographed by the soft-focus cameras of Tony Gaudio, its fantastic blend of racist plots and juvenile derring-do makes grand popular entertainment in the hands of Charles Brabin, who took over the directorial reins from Charles Vidor. Vidor reportedly shot the film's initial scenes only, until an otherwise-occupied Brabin was free to join the production.

Boris Karloff and Karen Morley

Boris Karloff, Charles Starrett, and Myrna Loy

Boris Karloff, Karen Morley, and Myrna Loy

HAUNTED GOLD

1932

Erville Alderson, Sheila Terry, John Wayne, Otto Hoffman, Blue Washington, and Harry Woods

John Wayne and Sheila Terry

CREDITS

A Warner Bros. Picture. Directed by Mack V. Wright. *Produced by* Leon Schlesinger. *Screenplay by* Adele Buffington. *Photographed by* Nick Musuraca. *Edited by* William Clemens. *Running time: 58 minutes.*

CAST

John Wayne, *John Mason;* Sheila Terry, *Janet Carter;* Erville Alderson, *Benedict;* Harry Woods, *Joe Ryan;* Otto Hoffman, *Simon;* Martha Mattox, *Mrs. Herman;* Blue Washington, *Clarence.*

John Wayne's starring debut, in Raoul Walsh's 1930 super-Western *The Big Trail,* was inauspicious. The movie wasn't popular, and nearly a decade passed before John Ford's 1939 *Stagecoach* finally pushed Wayne into his major career as a popular film star. In the years between these films, the actor had leading roles in some thirty-seven grade-B Westerns at various studios—not to mention his various serials and *non*-Westerns. Of the six cowboy films Wayne made under contract to Warner Bros., the first of them, *Haunted Gold,* is perhaps the best.

Like most of this series, it was shot in approximately seven days and derived from one of the many silents—1928's *The Phantom City*—that Ken Maynard had filmed for the same studio. In fact, much of *Haunted Gold*'s action footage is lifted directly from that Maynard silent, with Wayne's attire carefully duplicating his predecessor's. And one actor, "comic relief" Blue Washington, even plays the same role in both movies. Unfortunately, perhaps in an attempt to avoid audience detection of this patchwork approach to filmmaking, producer Leon Schlesinger permitted the 1928 footage to run at an unrealistically fast speed, thus eliciting audience laughter. But this tale of outlaw skullduggery over an abandoned gold mine haunted by a "phantom" is intriguingly established, and Mack V. Wright's no-lag direction keeps a tight rein on the proceedings, even when it appears that Wayne might be wasting valuable time dallying with his leading lady, Sheila Terry (later known as Sheila Bromley).

If *Haunted Gold* is little seen today (it was revived theatrically as late as 1962), it may well be due to its outmoded presentation of blacks as superstitious, eye-rolling objects of humor. In one scene, a subsidiary villain even makes a disparaging crack about actor Blue Washington's "watermelon accent"!

But the fledgling John Wayne presents a likable hero, and the mixture of action and mystery contributes to an entertaining fifty-eight minutes of old-fashioned sagebrush melodrama, well photographed by Nick Musuraca.

Edward G. Robinson and Bebe Daniels

SILVER DOLLAR

1932

CREDITS

A Warner Bros./First National Picture. Directed by Alfred E. Green. *Screenplay by* Carl Erickson *and* Harvey Thew. *Based on the book by* David Karsner. *Photographed by* James Van Trees. *Edited by* George Marks. *Running time: 84 minutes.*

CAST

Edward G. Robinson, *Yates Martin;* Bebe Daniels, *Lily Owens;* Aline MacMahon, *Sarah Martin;* Jobyna Howland, *Poker Annie;* De Witt Jennings, *Mine foreman;* Robert Warwick, *Col. Stanton;* Russel Simpson, *Hamlin;* Harry Holman, *Adams;* Charles Middleton, *Jenkins;* John Marston, *Gelsey;* Marjorie Gateson, *Mrs. Adams;* Emmett Corrigan, *President Chester A. Arthur;* Wade Boteler, William Le Maire, and David Durand, *Miners;* Lee Kohlmar, *Rische;* Theresa Conover, *Mrs. Hamlin;* Leon Waycoff/Ames, *Secretary;* Virginia Edwards, *Emma Abbott;* Christian Rub, *Hook;* Walter Rogers, *Gen. Grant;* Niles Welch, *William Jennings Bryan;* Bonita Granville, *Little girl in store.*

Horace Austin Warner Tabor (1830–1899) was·a Vermont-born Western prospector, familiarly known as "Silver Dollar" Tabor, who gained his considerable wealth mining silver from his Matchless Mine in Leadville, Colorado. In 1878, Tabor became Leadville's first mayor, served five years as Colorado's lieutenant governor, and briefly occupied a U.S. Senate seat. But before his death, Tabor lost his fortune, bequeathing his widow, Elizabeth "Baby Doe" Tabor, that Matchless Mine, which he vainly thought

Edward G. Robinson and Aline MacMahon

Edward G. Robinson and Bonita Granville

Edward G. Robinson, Bebe Daniels, and Emmett Corrigan

would yield additional riches.

Part of Tabor's change in fortune was attributable to society's refusal to accept his second wife, for scandal surrounded Tabor's affair with this vivacious young woman (some thirty years his junior), for whom the tycoon divorced the mother of his children. But "Baby Doe" Tabor remained faithful to Horace's memory, and when she died a recluse in 1935, it was in a shack near the mine. These events inspired the popular 1956 Douglas Moore–John Latouche opera, *The Ballad of Baby Doe.*

Little seen in recent years, this fine epic drama, attests to the superb range of Edward G. Robinson, whose *Little Caesar* remains that actor's most accessible early movie role. But a look at the more obscure *Silver Dollar* reveals by far the superior performance, for its dramatic scope alone.

As *Silver Dollar* was produced while Tabor's widow still lived, the well-crafted Carl Erickson–Harvey Thew screenplay changed the names of its protagonists, with the silver tycoon here rechristened "Yates Martin," his first wife Augusta now called "Sarah," and Mrs. Doe alias "Lily Owens." *Silver Dollar* remains faithful to the essence of Horace Tabor's story, albeit less so than the stirring opera, with a blonde-wigged Bebe Daniels as the rejuvenating second wife and Aline MacMahon in a superbly detailed characterization as the discarded Sarah/Augusta.

Perhaps *Silver Dollar* lacks the action and spectacle that might have kept this historical narrative before the movie public. But the consistent high quality of director Alfred E. Green's film, no matter how thinly disguised its facts, indicates the necessity of a reappraisal.

SHE DONE HIM WRONG

1933

Mae West as Lady Lou

Cary Grant and Mae West

Noah Beery and Cary Grant

CREDITS

A Paramount Picture. Directed by Lowell Sherman. *Produced by* William Le Baron. *Screenplay by* Harvey Thew *and* John Bright. *Based on the stage play Diamond Lil by* Mae West. *Photographed by* Charles Lang. *Edited by* Alexander Hall. *Art direction by* Bob Usher. *Music by* Ralph Rainger. *Songs:* "I Wonder Where My Easy Rider's Gone," "A Guy What Takes His Time," *and* "Frankie and Johnny." *Costumes by* Edith Head. *Running time: 66 minutes.*

CAST

Mae West, *Lady Lou;* Cary Grant, *Capt. Cummings/The Hawk;* Owen Moore, *Chick Clark;* Gilbert Roland, *Serge Stanieff;* Noah Beery, Sr., *Gus Jordan;* David Landau, *Dan Flynn;* Rafaela Ottiano, *Russian Rita;* Dewey Robinson, *Spider Kane;* Rochelle Hudson, *Sally Glynn;* Tammany Young, *Chuck Connors;* Grace La Rue, *Frances;* Fuzzy Knight, *Ragtime Kelly;* Robert E. Homans, *Doheney;* Louise Beavers, *Pearl;* Wade Boteler, *Pal;* Aggie Herring, *Mrs. Flaherty;* Arthur Houseman, *Barfly;* Tom Kennedy, *Big Bill;* James C. Eagle, *Pete;* Tom McGuire, *Mike;* Frank Moran, *Framed convict;* Lee Kohlmar, *Jacobson;* Harry Wallace, *Steak McGarry.* Mary Gordon, *Cleaning woman.*

Nowadays, Mae West's brand of sexuality seems quaint indeed, and it's difficult to comprehend what might once have caused offense and helped create a Hays Office that would lay down strict rules on what would (or not) be permissable in American movies. But Mae's suggestive screenplays, her raunchy songs, and her sex-slanted line-readings raised quite a stir in 1933. In that year alone, her two biggest film hits, *She Done Him Wrong* and *I'm No Angel,* hit the screen like a bombshell, creating a box-office sensation that put Paramount Pictures back on its once shaky corporate feet.

When West made her screen debut at the ripe age of thirty-nine in George Raft's 1932 *Night After Night,* she stole each of her several scenes with that undulating walk, frankly insinuating voice, and goodness-had-nothing-to-do-with-it humor. The woman was no beauty; her buxom figure could best be described as chunky, and she was sometimes even likened to a female impersonator. But her frank, good-natured sexual caricature was something new to the movies, and audiences *not* offended by her mildly salacious material loved Mae.

She Done Him Wrong offers the quintessential Mae West. After years as a prominent exponent of bawdy stage material, she enjoyed her first motion picture starring role in this slightly softened version of her 1928 play *Diamond Lil.* And although her singing saloon-keeper of the Gay Nineties Bowery retained that character's original lust for gems ("Diamonds is my career"), the lady's name was changed to "Lou," and all references to white slavery and the Salvation Army were clouded. Veteran actor Lowell Sherman directed, and both Mae and her off-color material (devoid of either guilt or sentiment) were held within tasteful boundaries. (Imagine what a permissive Eighties remake might look like!)

Rich in period atmosphere, *She Done Him Wrong* was shot in an astonishing eighteen days because Mae West retained control of her stage property, oversaw its changes, okayed its casting, and insisted on a full week of rehearsals prior to filming. Cary Grant was her leading man, supposedly because Mae spied him on the Paramount lot and fancied his dark good looks. And it's he who's the recipient of her oft-misquoted "Why don't you come up sometime—and see me?"

Mae West was a true original, easy to imitate but impossible to replace—as the continued popularity of this film and *I'm No Angel* attest.

Buster Crabbe and Frances Dee

KING OF
THE JUNGLE

1933

CREDITS

A Paramount Picture. Directed by H. Bruce Humberstone *and* Max Marcin. *Screenplay by* Philip Wylie *and* Fred Niblo, Jr. *Adaptation by* Max Marcin. *Based on The Lion's Way by* Charles Thurley Stoneham. *Photographed by* Ernest Haller. *Running time: 73 minutes.*

CAST

Buster Crabbe, *Kaspa the Lion Man;* Frances Dee, *Anne Rogers;* Sidney Toler, *Neil Forbes;* Nydia Westman, *Sue;* Robert Barrat, *Joe Nolan;* Irving Pichel, *Corey;* Douglas Dumbrille, *Ed Peters;* Sam Baker, *Gwana;* Patricia Farley, *Kitty;* Ronnie Cosby, *Kaspa at age three;* Warner Richmond, *Gus.*

On a 1979 TV show, Buster Crabbe recalled 1933's *King of the Jungle* as "the only A film I ever made," adding, "If I hadn't won the (Olympics) gold medal, Paramount would never have taken me for it."

A major swimming contender in both the 1928 and 1932 Olympics, Clarence Linden Crabbe had previously stunt-doubled for Joel McCrea in *The Most Dangerous Game* and had been tested for the role that made a film star of his swimming pal Johnny Weissmuller, MGM's *Tarzan the Ape Man.* But it was the 1932 Olympic Games, in which Buster (his nickname since childhood) broke (by four seconds) Weissmuller's record of 4:52 in the 400 that made him a sports hero. So it was only natural that Hollywood would turn to this good-looking athlete as well. The great popularity of Johnny's jungle hero inspired Paramount to rival Metro's ape-man thriller with the similarly themed *King of the Jungle.* Only *this* jungle-bred Caucasian, as impersonated by Crabbe, was a *lion* man, orphaned at three by explorer-parents who were killed by wild beasts during a photographic expedition.

Buster Crabbe as Kaspa the Lion Man

Nydia Westman, Frances Dee, and Buster Crabbe

The movie fails to explain how that little boy survived to become the healthy, well muscled Kaspa the Lion Man. Or how, abducted from his jungle habitat to the U.S. for circus exhibition, he so quickly masters English in the company of a pretty teacher (Frances Dee). But reality is not an important issue with *King of the Jungle*, an escapist entertainment directed, in obviously good-humored fun, by the fledgling team of H. Bruce Humberstone and Max Marcin. Paramount's handsome production expertise added to an interesting story line two exciting action sequences showing wild animals in mortal combat and a spectacular, realistic-looking circus-fire climax.

But *King of the Jungle*'s success is also very much due to the manly prowess and striking, barrel-chested physique of Buster Crabbe. As little more than a prize-winning athlete with no formal acting training, he carries off what must have been a difficult assignment with dignity and skill. Clothed throughout most of the footage in what he later called "the briefest G-string of any of them," Crabbe hadn't many lines to speak. But his role more than compensated in its rigorous physical demands, including repeated body contact with the big cats.

Having exploited the inevitable comparisons with Johnny Weissmuller in advertising *King of the Jungle*, Paramount must have had second thoughts about promoting Buster as a male sex symbol. Instead, the studio turned its efforts to the easier exploitation of Mae West. Crabbe's major claim to screen immortality would come three years later, with the first of his three *Flash Gordon* serials for Universal.

GOLD DIGGERS OF 1933

Ruby Keeler, Dick Powell, Aline MacMahon, Joan Blondell, Tammany Young, and Ned Sparks

1933

CREDITS

A Warner Bros. Picture. Directed by Mervyn LeRoy. *Screenplay by* Erwin Gelsey, James Seymour, David Boehm, *and* Ben Markson. *Based on the play The Gold Diggers by* Avery Hopwood. *Photographed by* Sol Polito. *Edited by* George Amy. *Dance numbers devised and staged by* Busby Berkeley. *Art direction by* Anton Grot. *Gowns by* Orry-Kelly. *Songs by* Harry Warren *and* Al Dubin: *"The Gold Diggers Song (We're in the Money),"* *"I've Got to Sing a Torch Song,"* *"Pettin' in the Park,"* *"The Shadow Waltz,"* *and* *"Remember My Forgotten Man."* *Running time: 96 minutes.*

CAST

Warren William, *J. Lawrence Bradford;* Joan Blondell, *Carol King;* Aline MacMahon, *Trixie Lorraine;* Ruby Keeler, *Polly Parker;* Dick Powell, *Brad Roberts;* Guy Kibbee, *Thaniel H. Peabody;* Ned Sparks, *Barney Hopkins;* Ginger Rogers, *Fay Fortune;* Clarence Nordstrom, *Gordon;* Robert Agnew, *Dance director;* Tammany Young, *Gigolo Eddie;* Sterling Holloway, *Messenger boy;* Ferdinand Gott-schalk, *Clubman;* Lynn Browning, *Gold Digger girl;* Charles C. Wilson, *Deputy;* Billy Barty, *"Pettin in the Park" baby;* Fred "Snowflake" Toones *and* Theresa Harris, *Negro couple;* Joan Barclay, *Chorus girl;* Wallace MacDonald, *Stage manager;* Wilbur Mack, Grace Hayle, *and* Charles Lane, *Society reporters;* Hobart Cavanaugh, *Dog salesman.*

Warner Bros. had realized such enthusiastic public response to their earlier 1933 musical, *42nd Street,* that they rushed into production a succession of black-and-white musicals, often juggling many of the same players. But the biggest star of these films was that inventive master showman of the musical production number, Busby Berkeley. With ingenious ideas, hordes of beautiful girls, and the technical resources of the Warner studio, Berkeley devised breathtaking, often amusing and kaleidoscopic dance numbers that astounded and delighted Depression-era audiences and thoroughly rejuvenated the movie musical.

The "Pettin' in the Park" production number

Joan Blondell, Dick Powell, and Warren William

"The Shadow Waltz" production number

Gold Diggers of 1933 had little innovation to offer in story content. Based on a 1919 Broadway play, *The Gold Diggers*, it had been initially filmed under that title in 1923, then again in 1929 as *Gold Diggers of Broadway*. But the 1933 edition had a sparkling Harry Warren–Al Dubin score, a talented cast headed by vivacious Joan Blondell, tap-clumping Ruby Keeler, and crooning tenor Dick Powell. Adding the spice were wise-cracking Aline MacMahon and Ginger Rogers (billed eighth but opening the movie with the extravagant "We're in the Money," costumed in gold coins and dancing amid giant coin replicas). The trivial backstage-Broadway story line merely serves as a bridge connecting big production numbers like the audacious "Pettin' in the Park" (the girls end up in armor, which

their admirers attack with giant can openers!), "Remember My Forgotten Man," that weird hymn to the Depression which Joan Blondell talk-sings (augmented by the voice of black songstress Etta Moten), and the spectacular "Shadow Waltz." For the latter number, Berkeley wired the girls with violins and neon tubes and had them dancing on a giant curved staircase with batteries controlling each violin.

This extravaganza was followed by such popular Warners musicals as *Dames, Footlight Parade,* and *Wonder Bar,* but their quality lessened as the Thirties waned. In 1951, the studio remade *Gold Diggers of 1933* as *Painting the Clouds with Sunshine,* a Technicolor package that could hardly compare with the lavish style set by Busby Berkeley in 1933.

101

Bruce Cabot, Fay Wray, Robert Armstrong, and bit players

KING KONG

1933

CREDITS

An RKO Radio Picture. Directed by Merian C. Cooper *and* Ernest B. Schoedsack. *Executive producer:* David O. Selznick. *Screenplay by* James Creelman *and* Ruth Rose. *Story by* Merian C. Cooper *and* Edgar Wallace. *Photographed by* Edward Linden, Verne Walker, *and* J. O. Taylor. *Edited by* Ted Cheesman. *Special effects by* Willis O'Brien, *assisted by* E. B. Gibson, Marcel Delgado, Fred Reefe, Orville Goldner, Carroll Shepphird, Mario Larrinaga, *and* Byron L. Crabbe. *Sound effects by* Murray Spivack. *Art direction by* Carroll Clark *and* Al Herman. *Music by* Max Steiner. *Running time: 100 minutes.*

CAST

Fay Wray, *Ann Darrow;* Robert Armstrong, *Carl Denham;* Bruce Cabot, *Jack Driscoll;* Frank Reicher, *Capt. Englehorn;* Sam Hardy, *Weston;* Noble Johnson, *Native chief;* James Flavin, *Second mate;* Steve Clemento, *Witch king;* Victor Long, *Lumpy;* Ethan Laidlaw, *Mate;* Dick Curtis *and* Charlie Sullivan, *Sailors;* Vera Lewis *and* Leroy Mason, *Theater patrons;* Paul Porcasi, *Apple vendor;* Lynton Brent *and* Frank Mills, *Reporters; and* King Kong, *the Eighth Wonder of the World.*

Forty-eight years after its initial theatrical release, *King Kong* stands high among the most imaginative and exciting of the American screen's adventure-fantasies, not only of the Thirties but of all time. Its visual effects have inspired endless imitations, sequels, and rip-offs—including a ridiculously overblown 1976 remake, whose multimillion-dollar budget failed to make it memorable. The 1933 original, long in meticulous production at a then costly $650,000, remains the unsurpassed classic.

Very much a collaborative effort, *King Kong* nevertheless owes most of its success to the expertise of special-effects wizard Willis O'Brien, who literally worked miracles with trick photography, miniatures, and animation that united live actors with ersatz prehistoric creatures, especially the gigantic ape of the film's title.

King Kong's story line is simple. A Manhattan-based film company journeys to an uncharted island off the African coast, where its ranks are reduced by the rampage of Kong, a giant ape that nevertheless takes a liking to their beautiful

leading lady (Fay Wray). The film's producer (Robert Armstrong) turns impresario by subduing the creature and bringing it back to civilization, where he presents Kong as the "Eighth Wonder of the World." But reporters' flashbulbs anger the monster, who breaks all restraining ties, runs amok through New York, and finally—in the most famous sequence—is destroyed by aircraft when cornered atop the Empire State Building.

This beauty-and-the-beast classic rescued RKO Radio Pictures from imminent bankruptcy and became the film for which movie showmen Merian C. Cooper and Ernest B. Schoedsack are best remembered. For blonde-bewigged, scantily clad Fay Wray, *King Kong* was the springboard to instant, screaming immortality. And she's never lived it down.

Miriam Hopkins and Jack La Rue

THE STORY OF TEMPLE DRAKE

1933

CREDITS

A Paramount Picture. Directed by Stephen Roberts. *Produced by* Benjamin Glazer. *Screenplay by* Oliver H. P. Garrett. *Based on the novel Sanctuary by* William Faulkner. *Photographed by* Karl Struss. *Running time: 72 minutes.*

CAST

Miriam Hopkins, *Temple Drake;* Jack La Rue, *Trigger;* William Gargan, *Stephen Benbow;* William Collier, Jr., *Toddy Gowan;* Irving Pichel, *Lee Goodwin;* Sir Guy Standing, *Judge Drake;* Elizabeth Patterson, *Aunt Jennie;* Florence Eldridge, *Ruby Lemar;* James Eagles, *Tommy;* Harlan E. Knight, *Pap;* James Mason, *Van;* Jobyna Howland, *Miss Reba;* Henry Hall, *Judge;* John Carradine, *Courtroom extra;* Frank Darien, *Gas station proprietor;* Clarence Sherwood, *Lunch wagon proprietor;* Oscar Apfel, *District attorney;* Kent Taylor and Clem Beauchamp, *Jellybeans;* Arthur Belasco, *Wharton;* Grady Sutton, *Bob;* George Pearce, *Doctor;* Hattie McDaniel, *Minnie.*

Dealing as it does with Southern decadence, sexual bondage, rape, and murder, William Faulkner's notorious 1931 novel *Sanctuary* seems an odd property to have been purchased for a major-studio motion picture in early-Thirties Hollywood. But Paramount had recently sponsored Mae West's outrageously suggestive *She Done Him Wrong.* So why not a restructured adaptation of *Sanctuary?* The book's title was changed to *The Story of Temple Drake* to cool any possible public protest and also to pacify Hollywood's nervous Hays Office, which advised the studio that no reference to *Sanctuary* would be permitted. Paramount conceded by simply crediting "a novel by William Faulkner."

Even in its whitewashed state, *The Story of Temple Drake* offers unusually perverse melodrama. In essence, and despite censorship restrictions, Oliver H. P. Garrett's screenplay adheres closely to his sordid source material. Temple Drake is the restless, neurotic granddaughter of a Southern judge who rejects the marriage proposal of an

Miriam Hopkins as Temple Drake

Miriam Hopkins, James Mason (the character actor), Irving Pichel, Florence Eldridge

upstanding young attorney, gets involved with a bootleg gang, is seduced by Trigger, a sadistic hood, who sets her up in his big-city brothel, eventually kills the gangster with his own gun, stands trial, and eventually comes to repent her moral degradation.

Temple Drake is a role of challenge and substance, and Miriam Hopkins gives it everything she's got. As she later told an interviewer, "I enjoy playing that sort of woman. They have the courage of the damned. They know what they want and they go right ahead." Jack La Rue, who replaced a reluctant George Raft as the sinister Trigger, delivers a chilling characterization. The movie's West Virginia–born director, Stephen Roberts, evinces a certain understanding of Southern decadence, and he and screenwriter Garrett frequently employ unspoken suggestion and understatement to fulfill Faulkner's original intent. And the artfully lit, soft-focus photography of Karl Struss goes far to diffuse the story's more harsh and shocking implications.

But the film's controversial literary origin could not be kept from the filmgoing public, and *The Story of Temple Drake* drew audiences on its notoriety alone. In 1961, under its original title, *Sanctuary* was unsuccessfully remade with Lee Remick and Yves Montand, incorporating Faulkner's 1951 sequel, *Requiem for a Nun*.

William Gargan, Miriam Hopkins, and Jack La Rue

Barbara Stanwyck as Lily Powers

BABY FACE

1933

CREDITS

A Warner Bros. Picture. Directed by Alfred E. Green. *Produced by* Ray Griffith. *Screenplay by* Gene Markey *and* Kathryn Scola. *Story by* Mark Canfield (Darryl F. Zanuck). *Photographed by* James Van Trees. *Edited by* Howard Bretherton. *Art direction by* Anton Grot. *Costumes by* Orry-Kelly. *Running time: 70 minutes.*

CAST

Barbara Stanwyck, *Lily Powers;* George Brent, *Mr. Trenholm;* Donald Cook, *Mr. Stevens;* Arthur Hohl, *Ed Sipple;* John Wayne, *Jimmy McCoy;* Henry Kolker, *Mr. Carter;* James Murray, *Brakeman;* Robert Barrat, *Nick Powers;* Margaret Lindsay, *Ann Carter;* Douglass Dumbrille, *Mr. Brody;* Theresa Harris, *Chico;* Renee Whitney, *The girl;* Nat Pendleton, *Stolvich;* Alphonse Ethier, *Cragg;* Harry Gribbon, *Doorman;* Arthur De Kuh, *Lutza;* Grady Sutton, *Personnel manager;* Toby Wing, *Secretary.*

Barbara Stanwyck had one of her best roles as Phyllis Dietrichson, the coldly calculating, amoral blonde of 1944's *Double Indemnity.* But that characterization had its genesis eleven years earlier in *Baby Face,* a 1933 film that caused a Hays Office censorship stir. In its review, *Variety* dubbed the movie "blue and nothing else," reporting, "This is reputed to be a remake of the first print, which was considered too hot." However "hot" the original cut of *Baby Face* may have been, there is nothing in the released version to worry anyone. And although Stanwyck's Lily Powers is obviously a heartless opportunist with many men in her life, her on-screen favors consist solely of seductive smiles.

Lily is patently a tough tart from the start. She's introduced reluctantly serving the patrons of her dad's small-town speakeasy, where she repels a politician's lustful hands with deftly spilled coffee. Scriptwriters Gene Markey and Kathryn Scola quickly dispatch Lily's unlamented father in an explosion, and she's off on a freight train to New York. Getting her first big-city job is a snap: asked whether she's had any experience, Lily answers, "Plenty!"—and starts her rapid rise in the offices of a bank. There, a cunning use of its male employees and executives (the movie's sound-

Barbara Stanwyck, Robert Barrat, Nat Pendleton

*George Brent and
Barbara Stanwyck*

track moans with "St. Louis Blues") soon installs her in the extramarital quarters of bank president Carter (Henry Kolker) while she continues a relationship with an executive, Stevens (Donald Cook), who, in turn, is engaged to Carter's daughter (Margaret Lindsay). All of which proves too much for Stevens, who shoots both Carter and himself, as the tabloids scream "DOUBLE TRAGEDY IN LOVE NEST!"

The bank's board of directors then attempts to prevent Lily's detailing her sordid affairs to a scandal sheet by offering her a payoff. Claiming she'll need $15,000 as a poor "victim of circumstances" and that she only wants a chance to earn an honest living, Lily is dismayed when the bank's new president, Trenholm (George Brent), arranges a job for her in their Paris branch. Lily now undergoes rehabilitation in his company, and when he suddenly loses his fortune, she saves him from suicide. At the film's end, the bank's board members are reading a letter informing us that the couple is "working out their happiness together" in Pittsburgh, where he's become a steelworker, no less!

The film never rings true, but it's directed at a typically fast Warner Bros. pace by Alfred E. Green and emerges as a key picture in the early Stanwyck career, for she's utterly fascinating to watch in the resourcefulness of her gold-digging tricks, mixing guile with wide-eyed innocence. This

was Stanwyck's first crack at an important bad-gal role, and with the clever aid of Orry-Kelly's costuming, stylish blonde wigs, and James Van Trees' photographic expertise, she alone makes us believe in the unbelievable.

Barbara Stanwyck and Henry Kolker

Grant Mitchell, George Baxter, Louise Closser Hale, Jean Harlow, Wallace Beery, Edmund Lowe, Karen Morley, and Billie Burke

DINNER AT EIGHT

1933

CREDITS

A Metro-Goldwyn-Mayer Picture. Directed by George Cukor. *Produced by* David O. Selznick. *Screenplay by* Frances Marion *and* Herman J. Mankiewicz, *with additional dialogue by* Donald Ogden Stewart. *Based on the play by* George S. Kaufman *and* Edna Ferber. *Photographed by* William Daniels. *Edited by* Ben Lewis. *Art direction by* Cedric Gibbons. *Gowns by* Adrian. *Running time: 113 minutes.*

Lionel Barrymore and Billie Burke

CAST

Marie Dressler, *Carlotta Vance;* John Barrymore, *Larry Renault;* Wallace Beery, *Dan Packard;* Jean Harlow, *Kitty Packard;* Lionel Barrymore, *Oliver Jordan;* Lee Tracy, *Max Kane;* Edmund Lowe, *Dr. Wayne Talbot;* Billie Burke, *Millicent Jordan;* Madge Evans, *Paula Jordan;* Jean Hersholt, *Jo Stengel;* Karen Morley, *Mrs. Wayne Talbot;* Louise Closser Hale, *Hattie Loomis;* Phillips Holmes, *Ernest de Graff;* May Robson, *Mrs. Wendel;* Grant Mitchell, *Ed Loomis;* Phoebe Foster, *Miss Alden;* Elizabeth Patterson, *Miss Copeland;* Hilda Vaughn, *Tina, Kitty's maid;* Harry Beresford, *Fosdick;* Edwin Maxwell, *Mr. Fitch, hotel manager;* John Davidson, *Mr. Hatfield, assistant manager;* Edward Woods, *Eddie;* George Baxter, *Gustave the butler;* Herman Bing, *The waiter;* Anna Duncan, *Dora the maid.*

Marie Dressler and Jean Harlow

The great success of 1932's *Grand Hotel* encouraged MGM to repeat the pattern with still another all-star comedy-drama, this time an adaptation of the witty George S. Kaufman–Edna Ferber play *Dinner at Eight.* Scenarists Frances Marion and Herman J. Mankiewicz remained essentially faithful to the Broadway original, while adapting for the camera a multisetting script that was always more screenplay than stage play anyway. And Donald Ogden Stewart's contribution was that brief but unforgettable exchange between Marie Dressler and Jean Harlow that capped the film's upbeat ending.

In a series of colorful vignettes, *Dinner at Eight* offers a rich character study of those involved in social-climbing hostess Billie Burke's plans for a fancy dinner party held to honor a pair of titled guests—who never turn up. Most of the film takes place during the hours prior to that eight o'clock gala, centering on a gruff, belligerent tycoon (Wallace Beery) and his flashy, wisecracking wife (Jean Harlow); her enamored doctor (Edmund Lowe); his long-suffering wife (Karen Morley); an alcoholic has-been actor (John Barrymore), romantically involved with the hostess's impressionable young daughter (Madge Evans); a worldly-wise, theatrical *grande dame* (Marie Dressler); and the evening's business-troubled host (Lionel Barrymore).

This cast could hardly have been better chosen, and George Cukor directed the felicitous blend of high comedy and melodramatic pathos with all the taste and style that have distinguished his lengthy film career. *Dinner at Eight* achieved great success with critics and public alike and, while winning no Oscars, it has continued to draw audiences half a century after its initial release. Yet 1933's Academy Award–winning Best Picture was the long-forgotten *Cavalcade.*

John Barrymore, Lee Tracy, and Madge Evans

Eddie Cantor, Alan Mowbray, and Edward Arnold

Gloria Stuart and Eddie Cantor

ROMAN SCANDALS

1933

CREDITS

United Artists release of a Samuel Goldwyn Production. Directed by Frank Tuttle. *Screenplay by* William Anthony McGuire, George Oppenheimer, Arthur Sheekman, *and* Nat Perrin. *Original story by* George S. Kaufman *and* Robert E. Sherwood. *Photographed by* Gregg Toland. *Edited by* Stuart Heisler. *Art direction by* Richard Day. *Costumes by* John Harkrider. *Production numbers staged by* Busby Berkeley. *Chariot sequence director:* Ralph Cedar. *Music direction by* Alfred Newman. *Songs:* "Rome Wasn't Built in a Day," "Build a Little Home," "Keep Young and Beautiful," *and* "No More Love" *by* Al Dubin *and* Harry Warren; "Tax on Love" *by* L. Wolfe Gilbert *and* Harry Warren. *Running time: 93 minutes.*

CAST

Eddie Cantor, *Eddie;* Ruth Etting, *Olga;* Gloria Stuart, *Princess Sylvia;* David Manners, *Josephus;* Veree Teasdale, *Empress Agrippa;* Edward Arnold, *Emperor Valerius;* Alan Mowbray, *Majordomo;* Jack Rutherford, *Manius;* Grace Poggi, *Slave dancer;* Willard Robertson, *Warren F. Cooper;* Harry Holman, *Mayor of West Rome;* Lee Kohlmar, *Storekeeper;* Stanley Fields, *Slave auctioneer;* Charles C. Wilson, *Police Chief Pratt;* Clarence Wilson, *Buggs, museum keeper;* Stanley Andrews, *Official;* Stanley Blystone, *Cop/Roman jailer;* Harry Cording, Lane Chandler, *and* Duke York, *Soldiers;* William Wagner, *Slave buyer;* Louise Carver, *Lady slave bidder;* Francis Ford, *Citizen;* Charles Arnt, *Caius, food tester;* Leo Willis, *Torturer;* Frank Hagney, *Lucius, aide;* Michael Mark, *Assistant cook;* Dick Alexander, *Guard;* Paul Porcasi, *Chef;* John Ince, *Senator;* Jane Darwell, *Beauty salon manager;* Billy Barty, *Little Eddie;* Irish Shunn/Meredith, *Girl;* Aileen Riggin, *Slave dancer;* Katharine Mauk, Rosalie Fromson, Mary Lange, Vivian Keefer, Barbara Pepper, Theo Plane, *and* Lucille Ball, *Slave girls;* Florence Wilson, Rose Kirsner, Genevieve Irwin, *and* Dolly Bell, *The Abbottiers.*

Of the six films starring Eddie Cantor under his Goldwyn contract, *Roman Scandals* and 1932's *The Kid From Spain* were the most popular and successful. But this one has the greater appeal, with its amusing (if supremely silly) comedy scenes and its exotic Busby Berkeley production numbers, featuring bevies of scantily clad Goldwyn Girls, (among them one Berkeley hired over Goldwyn's objections—Lucille Ball).

Eddie Cantor in the "Keep Young and Beautiful" production number

Roman Scandals bears a structural resemblance to *The Wizard of Oz*, opening and closing as it does in contemporary, rural America, while most of the action is confined to another world entirely—in this case, ancient Rome. But, with Eddie Cantor in the lead, low comedy is the order of the day, with satirical barbs aimed at such past epics as the silent *Ben-Hur,* with its chariot race, and DeMille's *The Sign of the Cross*. Plot transitions evolved out of Cantor's being cast as an Oklahoma delivery boy who dreams himself back into the Rome of wicked Emperor Valerius (Edward Arnold), where he's sold into slavery. Court intrigue mixes with star-crossed young love (Gloria Stuart and David Manners), all serving as a nonsensical framework for Cantorian humor, gags, and musical numbers—even including one in anachronistic blackface, a Cantor tradition.

Ruth Etting, then a popular torch singer, is billed second only to Cantor, but in the film's release print, she has only one number ("No More Love"). Fortunately, her dialogue footage is kept to a minimum, for it's very poorly delivered. This was dance director Busby Berkeley's last film for Goldwyn before going on to greater fame with Warner Bros. musicals like *42nd Street* and the *Gold Diggers* series.

David Manners and Eddie Cantor

Greta Garbo and John Gilbert

QUEEN CHRISTINA

1933

CREDITS

A Metro-Goldwyn-Mayer Picture. Directed by Rouben Mamoulian. *Produced by* Walter Wanger. *Screenplay by* Salka Viertel, H. M. Harwood, S. N. Behrman, *and (uncredited)* Ben Hecht. *From an original story by* Salka Viertel *and* Margaret P. Levine. *Photographed by* William Daniels. *Edited by* Blanche Sewell. *Art direction by* Alexander Toluboff *and* Edwin B. Willis. *Music by* Herbert Stothart. *Costumes by* Adrian. *Running time: 100 minutes.*

CAST

Greta Garbo, *Christina;* John Gilbert, *Don Antonio;* Ian Keith, *Magnus;* Lewis Stone, *Oxenstierna;* Elizabeth Young, *Ebba;* C. Aubrey Smith *Aage;* Reginald Owen, *Prince Charles;* Georges Renavent, *French ambassador;* Gustav von Seyffertitz, *General;* David Torrence, *Archbishop;* Ferdinand Munier, *Innkeeper;* Akim Tamiroff, *Pedro;* Cora Sue Collins, *Christina as a child;* Edward Norris, *Count Jacob;* Barbara Barondess, *Servant girl;* Paul Hurst, *Swedish soldier;* Ed Gargan, *Fellow drinker;* Wade Boteler, *Rabble-rouser;* Fred Kohler, *Member of the Court.*

Greta Garbo as Queen Christina

Greta Garbo had been away from the screen over a year when MGM released *Queen Christina*, near the close of 1933. The film had been tailored expressly for the star by her friend Salka Viertel, whose scenario had lured the enigmatic Swede back from a prolonged eighteen-month "vacation" in her native land. Garbo felt a particular spiritual affinity for the character of the Swedish monarch (1626–1689), and her stipulation that this be among the properties included in her new two-films-per-year Metro contract insured completion of a project MGM might otherwise have ignored. To vintage-film TV watchers, *Queen Christina* remains strangely obscure. Yet this might just be Garbo's greatest performance in her finest Hollywood motion picture. Of course, the movie owes a great deal to the taste and visual flair of director Rouben Mamoulian. But it also boasts a well-chosen supporting cast, handsome sets, and the beautifully lit cinematography of William Daniels, Garbo's favorite cameraman. As always, the star rivets the eye whenever she's on-screen. And Mamoulian's skill with the non-Garbo scenes, aided by that handsome MGM production polish, produces a fine movie that proudly stands the test of time. *Queen Christina* hasn't really dated in the years that have intervened. Nor was its lustre dimmed by an already forgotten but equally romanticized 1974 movie of Christina's life, *The Abdication*, which starred Liv Ullmann.

It is not difficult to view *Queen Christina* as the quintessential Garbo movie: she suffers, she laughs, she's strong and yet pliant, regal but approachable, masculine ("I shall die a bachelor") and feminine, all in one ambiguous, charismatic incarnation. Like the actress herself, her Christina inspires awe as much as adoration. It is a stunning performance, with her closing ship's-figurehead close-up probably Garbo's most immortal celluloid moment. Much has been written of how the twenty-six-year-old Laurence Olivier, initially selected by Garbo as her costar, was replaced by John Gilbert, her former romantic vis-a-vis, both on-screen and off. Gilbert's career as a big silent star had fallen on hard times with the transition to sound. *Queen Christina* provided him with a brief comeback of sorts, but one film and three years later, the former matinee idol was dead—at thirty-eight. *Queen Christina* met with widespread critical enthusiasm, as did Garbo's fine characterization of her countrywoman, but the film was by no means a box-office hit. Nor did it win the awards it merited.

Barbara Barondess, Greta Garbo, John Gilbert

Greta Garbo and Ian Keith

Arthur Hohl, Marjorie Rambeau, and Loretta Young

Spencer Tracy, Loretta Young, and Walter Connolly

MAN'S CASTLE

1933

CREDITS

A Columbia Picture. Directed by Frank Borzage. *Screenplay by* Jo Swerling. *Based on a play by* Lawrence Hazard. *Photographed by* Joseph August. *Edited by* Viola Lawrence. *Running time: 75 minutes.*

CAST

Spencer Tracy, *Bill;* Loretta Young, *Trina;* Glenda Farrell, *Fay LaRue;* Walter Connolly, *Ira;* Arthur Hohl, *Bragg;* Marjorie Rambeau, *Flossie;* Dickie Moore, *Crippled boy.*

Frank Borzage's *Man's Castle,* with its sensitive tale of romance among the unemployed in Depression-era Manhattan, stands in marked contrast to such harsher contemporary reflections of that era as King Vidor's semidocumentary drama *Our Daily Bread* and William Wellman's hard-hitting *Wild Boys of the Road.* As in Borzage's silent classic *Seventh Heaven,* here love triumphs over a downtrodden setting, and the Depression's torments are virtually ignored, rendering *Man's Castle* rather valueless as a social document. But as a compassionately romanticized love story of two unfortunate young people, Jo Swerling's engaging screenplay offers director Borzage the opportunity of recounting an intimate story with telling detail. All of this is photographed in exquisite soft focus by Joseph August, whose only failing appears to have been an inability to give verisimilitude to a street scene in which poor rear-projection literally dwarfs its two stars before the "giants" passing behind them on the process screen. But this is a minor complaint; *Man's Castle* is a lovely little film that seems unjustly neglected today.

Spencer Tracy and Loretta Young were already screen veterans, he of seventeen films and she of forty-one, when they were teamed for this venture. His style was, even then, low-key and naturalistic; hers was of quiet charm and an unspectacular big-eyed prettiness, enhanced by a toothy smile. Their styles blended well, unhampered by the fact that the two stars were then involved in a hopeless off-screen romance as well. Perhaps that accounts for their wonderful performances in *Man's Castle,* although, to judge from the equally fine supporting work of Marjorie Rambeau, Walter Connolly, and Arthur Hohl, it might

simply have been a happy blend of director, screenplay, and
casting.

In essence, this is the story of cynical Bill (Tracy), who
supports himself through odd jobs and who picks up
homeless waif Trina (Young), whom he shelters in the shan-
tytown hovel he inhabits beside New York's East River. The
stabilizing Trina makes their shack into a home, but Bill remains at heart a free spirit and resists being "tied down,"
maintaining that their live-in arrangement is only temporary. Her eventual pregnancy drives him to attempt a robbery, in which he's wounded. Now realizing just how much
Trina means to him, Bill returns for her, and they hop a
freight train together to confront an uncertain future.

Sentimental romantic drama was Frank Borzage's
speciality, and Tracy's gruff, reticent manliness plays very
well off of Young's ethereal loveliness. Watching her work
here makes one aware of how unappreciated an actress she
is today.

For its era, *Man's Castle* is rather matter-of-fact about its
lovers' living together without benefit of wedlock, and the
film even includes (but not on TV!) a brief, discreet flash of
nudity as Tracy dives into the river for a swim. Just a year
later, such innocent frankness would be ruled out by the
Production Code's notorious clamp-down. Most of this bog-
gles the mind in the permissive Eighties.

Spencer Tracy and Glenda Farrell

Phillips Holmes and Anna Sten

NANA

1934

CREDITS

A Samuel Goldwyn Production, released by United Artists. Directed by Dorothy Arzner. *Screenplay by* Willard Mack *and* Harry Wagstaff Gribble. *Suggested by* Emile Zola's *novel. Photographed by* Gregg Toland. *Edited by* Frank Lawrence. *Art direction by* Richard Day. *Costumes by* Travis Banton, John W. Harkrider, *and* Adrian. *Music by* Alfred Newman. *Song: "That's Love" by* Richard Rodgers *and* Lorenz Hart. *Running time: 87 minutes.*

CAST

Anna Sten, *Nana;* Lionel Atwill, *Col. Andre Muffat;* Mae Clarke, *Satin;* Richard Bennett, *Gaston Greiner;* Phillips Holmes, *Lt. George Muffat;* Muriel Kirkland, *Mimi;* Reginald Owen, *Bordenave;* Lawrence Grant, *Grand Duke Alexis;* Helen Freeman, *Sabine Muffat;* Jessie Ralph, *Zoe;* Ferdinand Gottschalk, *Finot;* Hardie Albright, *Lt. Gregory;* Branch Stevens, *Leon;* Barry Norton, *Louis;* Lauri Beatty, *Estelle Muffat;* Lucille Ball, *Chorus girl.*

Perhaps the most legendary Hollywood debacle of the Thirties centered on super-producer Samuel Goldwyn's unflagging efforts to make an American movie star of Russia's beautiful Anna Sten. Having been impressed with her fine performance in the 1931 German film *Der Morder Dimitri Karamasoff* (from Dostoevski's *The Brothers Karamazov*), Goldwyn wasted no time in signing the actress to a five-year contract. But her 1932 arrival in the American movie capital immediately gave Goldwyn pause, due to her now-*zaftig* appearance, nearly impenetrable English, and the constant interfering of her husband, Dr. Eugene Frenke. The Goldwyn minions went to work on her. But Sten's American-debut vehicle was a problem.

Finally meeting the requirements of a story which would accommodate her foreign accent, Goldwyn selected Emile Zola's classic *Nana* and assigned Willard Mack and Harry Wagstaff Gribble to write a screenplay. Unfortunately for *Nana*, a faithful treatment of this notorious literary whore and the men she ruins was impossible in an industry newly saddled with the restrictions of Will Hays and his Production Code.

Anna Sten's earthy glamour and forthright acting talents were well suited to Zola's *Nana*, but not to the bowdlerization of Mack and Gribble. With George Fitzmaurice directing, *Nana* began a tortuous production schedule. Apparently Sten found it difficult to coordinate pantomime and speech. And since she had learned her English dialogue by rote, there was none of the vital spontaneity that had so entranced Goldwyn in her German film. With *Nana* only half-completed, Goldwyn ordered a private screening—and decided it was unreleasable. Refusing to admit defeat, he fired Fitzmaurice, junked all the completed footage, and hired a new director, Dorothy Arzner. Arzner didn't much care for the script, but there was great rapport between her and Sten (whose husband was now banished from the set), and the production moved smoothly through to completion. The producer spent so much money publicizing his new star that *Nana*'s opening at New York's Radio City Music Hall broke all box-office records. The critics thought Anna Sten an interesting newcomer of peasantlike beauty and vivacity that reminded some of Dietrich. But her vehicle met with negative response.

Word of mouth was bad, and the Music Hall's poor second-day attendance was reflected in movie theaters all across the country. Undeterred, Sam Goldwyn presented Anna Sten in two better vehicles, *We Live Again* (1934) and *The Wedding Night* (1935). But the public wasn't buying. It was his greatest star-making defeat.

Anna Sten and Richard Bennett

Anna Sten and Lionel Atwill

Hardie Albright, Anna Sten, Mae Clarke, and Muriel Kirkland

MANDALAY

1934

CREDITS

A Warner Bros./First National Picture. Directed by Michael Curtiz. *Associate producer:* Robert Presnell. *Screenplay by* Austin Parker *and* Charles Kenyon. *Based on a story by* Paul Hervey Fox. *Photographed by* Tony Gaudio. *Edited by* Thomas Pratt. *Art direction by* Anton Grot. *Costumes by* Orry-Kelly. *Running time: 65 minutes.*

CAST

Kay Francis, *Tanya Borisoff/Spot White;* Ricardo Cortez, *Tony Evans;* Lyle Talbot, *Dr. Gregory Burton;* Warner Oland, *Nick;* Ruth Donnelly, *Mrs. Peters;* Reginald Owen, *Commissioner;* David Torrence, *Captain;* Etienne Girardot, *Mr. Abernathie;* Rafaela Ottiano, *Countess;* Lucien Littlefield, *Mr. Peters;* Halliwell Hobbes, *Col. Dawson Ames;* Bodil Rosing, *Mrs. Kleinschmidt;* Herman Bing, *Prof. Kleinschmidt;* Lillian Harmer, *Louisa Mae Harrington;* Torben Meyer, *Mr. Van Brinken;* Harry C. Bradley, *Henry P. Warren;* James Leong, *Ram Singh;* Shirley Temple, *Betty.*

Kay Francis, Warner Oland, and Ricardo Cortez

During her seven contract years at Warner Bros./First National (1932–1939), Kay Francis ground out twenty-seven movies for the matinee ladies, most of which titles have long since been forgotten by all but the most loyal of her fans. But in the Thirties, tall, handsome, and flat-chested Kay Francis wore chic wardrobes like a high-priced mannequin and suffered nobly in endless soap operas, with few classics among them (an exception was 1932's *One Way Passage*). She also commanded a high salary, which concerned her far more than the quality of her scripts.

Mandalay, the first of four Kay Francis vehicles released in 1934, is an exotic, often ridiculous (but entertaining) melodrama whose content would seem better suited to Marlene Dietrich than Kay (it had, in fact, already been rejected by Warners' other soap-opera queen, Ruth Chatterton). And its milieu, the streets and dives of Rangoon and a ship bound from that Eastern city to Mandalay, recalls the earlier Paramount creations of Josef von Sternberg. But, under the guidance of Warners' all-purpose director, Michael Curtiz, this unlikely tale of a mistreated lady's survival becomes an unintentionally amusing sixty-five minutes of constant drinking, smoking, and incredible conversation. Its statuesque star distracts her audience from her unpronounceable r's with an array of glamorous white frocks (and one knockout silver sheath). "If you touch my garter, I'll scweam," she warns a lustful gentleman early on. Sympathetic screenwriters usually helped Kay avoid these verbal pitfalls, but *Mandalay* scenarists Austin Parker and Charles Kenyon must have had a grudge against her; near the film's climax, they have her address costar Lyle Talbot with "Gwegowy, we awwive in Mandalay tomowwow. We ah two wecked people."

Lyle Talbot, Kay Francis

Mandalay's plot hardly deserves coverage. Kay is introduced as "Tanya Borisoff," the mistress and traveling companion of Ricardo Cortez, a munitions smuggler who abandons her in Nick's Place, a Rangoon establishment run by Charlie Chan–like Warner Oland. There she becomes the unattainable star-attraction, "Spot White." But then she meets a sympathetic but alcoholic doctor (Talbot), and they fall in love, a fact that's later complicated by the return of Cortez, whose drink Kay poisons, after which he conveniently falls overboard, unnoticed by anyone, as the brief but pithy movie reaches a happy-looking conclusion for the apparently reformed Francis and Talbot.

Mandalay offers pure, foolish escapism, and for 1934's Depression-weary moviegoers, what could have been more welcome?

Kay Francis as Tanya Borisoff

W. C. Fields and George Burns

Gracie Allen, Mary Boland, and George Burns

Irving Bacon, Charlie Ruggles, Mary Boland, Gracie Allen, and George Burns

SIX OF A KIND

1934

CREDITS

A Paramount Picture. Directed by Leo McCarey. *Screenplay by* Walter DeLeon *and* Harry Ruskin. *From an original story by* Keene Thompson *and* Douglas MacLean. *Photographed by* Henry Sharp. *Edited by* LeRoy Stone. *Art direction by* Hans Dreier *and* Robert Odell. *Music by* Ralph Rainger. *Running time: 65 minutes.*

CAST

Charlie Ruggles, *J. Pinkham Whinney;* Mary Boland, *Flora Whinney;* W. C. Fields, *Sheriff John Hoxley;* George Burns, *George Edwards;* Gracie Allen, *Gracie Devore;* Alison Skipworth, *Mrs. K. Rumford;* Bradley Page, *Ferguson;* Grace Bradley, *Trixie;* William J. Kelly, *Gillette;* Phil Tead, *Newspaper office clerk;* James Burke, *Sparks;* Dick Rush, *Steele;* Walter Long, *Butch;* Leo Willis, *Mike;* Lew Kelly, *Joe;* Alf P. James, *Tom;* Tammany Young, *Dr. Busby;* Irving Bacon, *Desk clerk.*

The idea of putting no fewer than six seasoned comedy actors into one movie was an inspired one for Paramount. Charlie Ruggles and Mary Boland were already a popular costarring duo at that studio; the hilarious radio team of straight-man George Burns and scatterbrained Gracie Allen were also giving films a try; Alison Skipworth was a formidable character actress for both comedy and drama, and W. C. Fields, with his nasal, descending-scale line readings, was a unique comedy attraction with a large, specialized following. Leo McCarey, their director on this occasion, had just survived one of the Marx Brothers' more fondly remembered vehicles, *Duck Soup.*

Wild gags, both visual and verbal, abound in *Six of a Kind,* with each of the aforementioned six performing their specialties in a Walter DeLeon–Harry Ruskin script that appropriately sets the scene for uninhibited farce.

Gracie Allen, W. C. Fields, George Burns, Charlie Ruggles, and Mary Boland

Ruggles and Boland, as J. Pinkham and Florence Whinney, are about to depart on a cross-country second honeymoon to Hollywood, for which they make the mistake of advertising for a companion couple. Enter Burns and Allen—along with their overbearing Great Dane, which more closely resembles a pony and growls when consigned to the car's back seat! With the scene already set for hilarity, scenarists DeLeon and Ruskin add a dash of suspense by having bank-employee Ruggles unwittingly carry along a suitcase containing $50,000 in stolen funds, stashed there by a collegue who plans to hold them up en route and escape with his loot. But an unexpected change in itinerary foils that plan, and the suitcase of money is further endangered by hobo-highwaymen, who scare off the Great Dane but overlook the $50,000. Finally, the sheriff (Fields) and innkeeper (Skipworth) of an upcoming Nevada town are tipped off about the travelers and their money suitcase,

resulting in additional hilarity, an arrest, and, finally, exoneration for Whinney. At the close, Burns and Allen have managed to foist themselves on still another unsuspecting couple, finally leaving Ruggles and Boland to enjoy that honeymoon revisited.

A short episodic farce, *Six of a Kind* isn't the comedy classic it might have been, but there are classic moments, including those involving that giant hound in the car, another sequence in which both Ruggles and Boland successively topple over a cliff (to be saved by the same tree), and, of course, those featuring Fields, whose relatively brief supporting role includes his celebrated billiards scene. But there's a little too much of Gracie Allen, at her most obnoxious, and one wishes that the writers might have distributed the balance of scenes with a bit more equality among its stars.

Robert Young and Loretta Young

George Arliss and Boris Karloff

THE HOUSE OF ROTHSCHILD

1934

CREDITS

A United Artists release of a Twentieth Century/Darryl F. Zanuck–Joseph M. Schenck Production. Directed by Alfred Werker. *Screenplay by* Nunnally Johnson. *Based on an unproduced play by* George Hembert Westley. *Photographed by* Peverell Marley. *Final sequence in Technicolor. Edited by* Alan McNeil *and* Barbara MacLean. *Music by* Alfred Newman. *Running time: 86 minutes.*

CAST

George Arliss, *Mayer Rothschild/Nathan Rothschild;* Boris Karloff, *Baron Ledrantz;* Loretta Young, *Julie Rothschild;* Robert Young, *Captain Fitzroy;* C. Aubrey Smith, *Duke of Wellington;* Arthur Byron, *Baring;* Helen Westley, *Gudula Rothschild;* Reginald Owen, *Herries;* Florence Arliss, *Hannah Rothschild;* Alan Mowbray, *Metternich;* Noel Madison, *Carl Rothschild;* Holmes Herbert, *Rowerth;* Paul Harvey, *Solomon Rothschild.*

Throughout the Thirties, biographical drama provided prestigious, award-winning movie showcases for two stage-trained actors, George Arliss and Paul Muni. The former, a man in his sixties during his Hollywood heyday, had gained a distinguished reputation through his portrayals of the title characters in *Alexander Hamilton* (1931) and *Voltaire* (1933) and had won a 1929–30 Best Actor Oscar for *Disraeli.* In *The House of Rothschild* he essayed the dual roles of Mayer, the founder, and his successor, Nathan, of that famed European banking family. These father/son characterizations, as written for the screen by Nunnally Johnson and directed by Alfred Werker, were carried off with such consummate Arliss artistry that many consider this the actor's greatest film performance. What might have seemed, in prospect, a dry portrait of accumulated wealth became instead a fascinating study in triumph over adversity and prejudice as the Jewish Rothschilds rise from their Frankfurt ghetto origins to provide the financial backing for England's battle against Napoleon.

The House of Rothschild was among the more successful productions of Darryl F. Zanuck, who had left Warner Bros. to establish his own independent Twentieth Century Productions, which was soon to merge with Fox as 20th Century-Fox. Zanuck's production genius enabled him to engage not only Arliss, who had himself just concluded a successful contract with Warners, but also a talented supporting cast headed by Boris Karloff (in the small but vivid role of Baron Ledrantz, the Rothschilds' anti-Semitic nemesis), Loretta Young and Robert Young (in an interracial love affair), and those irreplaceable character actors, C. Aubrey Smith and Helen Westley.

Produced one year prior to the first three-color Technicolor feature film (*Becky Sharp*), *The House of Rothschild* concluded its predominantly black-and-white continuity with a Technicolor sequence depicting the honoring at court of Nathan Rothschild by the Prince Regent. It was a decorative but unnecessary climax to a stirring human drama of the indomitable men and women behind that world-famed financial clan of the "red shield."

The New York Times listed *The House of Rothschild* among 1934's ten best films, and the Motion Picture Academy gave it a Best Picture nomination. But *It Happened One Night* was the victor.

George Arliss as Mayer Rothschild

Florence Arliss, George Arliss, Loretta Young, Robert Young, and C. Aubrey Smith

LITTLE MISS MARKER

1934

CREDITS

A Paramount Picture. Directed by Alexander Hall. *Produced by* B. P. Schulberg. *Screenplay by* William R. Lipman, Sam Hellman, *and* Gladys Lehman. *Based on the story by* Damon Runyon. *Photographed by* Alfred Gilks. *Edited by* William Shea. *Songs by* Leo Robin *and* Ralph Rainger: "I'm a Black Sheep Who Is Blue," "Low Down Lullabye," *and* "Laugh, You Son-of-a-Gun." *Running time: 80 minutes.*

CAST

Adolphe Menjou, *Sorrowful Jones;* Dorothy Dell, *Bangles Carson;* Charles Bickford, *Big Steve;* Shirley Temple, *Miss Marker;* Lynne Overman, *Regret;* Frank McGlynn, Sr., *Doc Chesley;* Jack Sheehan, *Sun Rise;* Garry Owen, *Grinder;* Willie Best, *Dizzy Memphis;* Puggy White, *Eddie;* Tammany Young, *Buggs;* Sam Hardy, *Bennie the Gouge;* Warren Hymer, *Sore Toe;* Frank Conroy, *Dr. Ingalls;* James Burke, *Reardon;* John Kelly, *Canvasback;* Ernie Adams and Don Brodie, *Bettors;* Stanley Price, *Bookie.*

American film has never known a child star of the enduring popularity enjoyed by Shirley Temple. Although the peak years of her fame and fortune were the Thirties, the enthusiasm of her fans has continued through the decades.

Shirley entered films at four in 1932 in "Baby Burlesk" shorts, but her big break came in Fox's revue-styled 1934 musical *Stand Up and Cheer,* in which the delightfully dimpled, golden-curled child created a sensation singing and dancing in the "Baby, Take a Bow" number. That studio then wisely put her under contract. At Fox, Shirley Temple would soon become a major moneymaker. But the movie that actually made her a star was filmed on loan-out to Paramount—the title role in Damon Runyon's *Little Miss Marker.* In the seasoned company of actors like Adolphe Menjou and Charles Bickford, little Shirley more than held her own. During its making, an impressed Menjou told an interviewer, "She's an Ethel Barrymore at six."

In Temple's opinion, *Little Miss Marker* is a "a real tear-

Lynne Overman, Shirley Temple, and Adolphe Menjou

Charles Bickford, Adolphe Menjou, and Dorothy Dell

Adolphe Menjou and Shirley Temple

jerker." Typical of Runyon's stories, it features a good hearted bunch of underworld hangers-on, bearing oddball names and spouting colorful dialogue. Shirley's the apparently nameless daughter of a gambler, who leaves her with bookie Sorrowful Jones (Menjou) as pawn (or "marker," hence the title) for his $20 bet. When her father commits suicide, "Marky" is left to be cared for by the reluctant Sorrowful and his club-singer girlfriend, Bangles Carson (Dorothy Dell). Complications involve Sorrowful's enemy, gangster Big Steve (Bickford), a racehorse, and a climax—a climax in which the little girl's life hangs in the balance—until she's saved through a sentimental gesture by Big Steve.

Little Miss Marker is an excellent adaptation of the Runyon fable, and wee Shirley Temple, not yet in full possession of those "cute" acting tricks she would later be known for, is quite adorable. But an excellent cast and solid direction by Alexander Hall *(Madame Racketeer, Torch Singer)* brighten a sometimes sluggish screenplay, and the movie became one of 1934's most popular. The Shirley Temple legend was now assured. Unfortunately for nineteen-year-old, Alice Faye–like Dorothy Dell, the potential shown in this film would never reach fulfillment, for she died in a tragic accident less than a month after its release.

This story's popularity is well illustrated by its numerous remakes: 1949's *Sorrowful Jones,* with Bob Hope and Lucille Ball; 1963's Runyon-uncredited *40 Pounds of Trouble,* with Tony Curtis and Suzanne Pleshette; and 1980's return to the original title, with Walter Matthau and Julie Andrews. But it's worthy of note that none of the child stars of these subsequent movies became another Shirley Temple.

OF HUMAN BONDAGE

1934

CREDITS

An RKO Radio Picture. Directed by John Cromwell. *Produced by* Pandro S. Berman. *Screenplay by* Lester Cohen. *Based on the novel by* W. Somerset Maugham. *Photographed by* Henry W. Gerrard. *Edited by* William Morgan. *Art direction by* Van Nest Polglase *and* Carroll Clark. *Music by* Max Steiner. *Running time: 83 minutes.*

CAST

Leslie Howard, *Philip Carey;* Bette Davis, *Mildred Rogers;* Frances Dee, *Sally Athelny;* Kay Johnson, *Norah;* Reginald Denny, *Harry Griffiths;* Alan Hale, *Emil Miller;* Reginald Owen, *Thorpe Athelny;* Reginald Sheffield, *Dunsford;* Desmond Roberts, *Dr. Jacobs;* Tempe Pigott, *Landlady.*

W. Somerset Maugham's now-classic 1915 novel, centering on a clubfooted medical student's obsessive infatuation with a selfish, wanton waitress, has been filmed three times, with ever-diminishing success. The first version, produced in 1934 with Leslie Howard and Bette Davis, now looks very dated. But, under the perceptive direction of John Cromwell, it remains the most satisfying. The 1946 remake, which has long been unavailable for reevaluation, boasts a strong performance by the underrated Eleanor Parker, but little else. And its 1964 adaptation offers Laurence Harvey at his least appealing and Kim Novak earnestly attempting to prove she could act.

Bette Davis has remarked that, because the pivotal role of Mildred was so unpleasant, none of Hollywood's established stars was interested in portraying her. But Davis became obsessed with getting the part. Then under "bondage" contract to Warner Bros., where she dutifully accepted every part assigned to her, the ambitious young actress knew that director Cromwell wanted her for his RKO film, and she mercilessly badgered Jack Warner until he consented to her loan-out. Davis then began slavishly preparing her interpretation and studying the low-class accent with a Cockney wardrobe woman. The resulting performance remains arresting and powerful, although Davis's British accent remains that of an American making a valiant effort to cope with foreign sounds.

Bette Davis as Mildred Rogers

Leslie Howard and Frances Dee

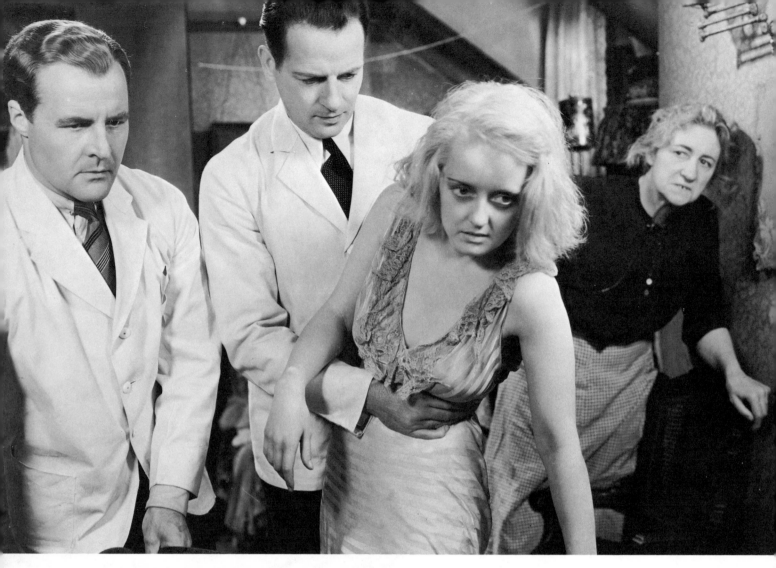

Reginald Sheffield, Reginald Denny, Bette Davis, and Tempe Pigott

The impact made by the blonde star's work in *Of Human Bondage* is suggested by the reactions of two prominent publications: Mordaunt Hall wrote in *The New York Times,* "Bette Davis provides what is easily her finest perfor-

mance"; *Life* ventured even further out on the critical limb by calling this "probably the best performance ever recorded on the screen by a U.S. actress." But a retrospective look at this 1934 movie only illustrates how much popular tastes have changed in styles of acting and directing.

Granted that Davis gives a bravura account of Mildred, but her intense, energetic delineation frequently ventures into overwrought mannerisms. And while her acting always holds the viewer's attention (often at the expense of Leslie Howard's appropriately quiet performance), her tirades tend to get out of control, making it difficult to comprehend how so well-bred a student-doctor could put up with such a guttersnipe.

RKO had gambled with the casting of Bette Davis. But *Of Human Bondage* proved both a popular and artistic triumph for the studio. An important career milestone for Davis, the picture inexplicably failed to garner her an Oscar nomination, which occasioned a protesting "write-in" campaign. Not that it did her any good: 1934's Best Actress Academy Award went to Claudette Colbert for *It Happened One Night.* Davis would cop the Oscar a year later for the inferior *Dangerous*—an award that is widely considered "consolation" for her neglect in 1934.

THE THIN MAN

1934

CREDITS

A Metro-Goldwyn-Mayer Picture. Directed by W. S. Van Dyke II. *Produced by* Hunt Stromberg. *Screenplay by* Albert Hackett *and* Frances Goodrich. *Based on the novel by* Dashiell Hammett. *Photographed by* James Wong Howe. *Edited by* Robert J. Kern. *Art direction by* Cedric Gibbons, David Townsend, *and* Edwin B. Willis. *Costumes by* Dolly Tree. *Music direction by* Dr. William Axt. *Running time: 91 minutes.*

CAST

William Powell, *Nick Charles;* Myrna Loy, *Nora Charles;* Maureen O'Sullivan, *Dorothy Wynant;* Nat Pendleton, *Lt. John Guild;* Minna Gombell, *Mimi Wynant;* Porter Hall, *MacCauley;* Henry Wadsworth, *Tommy;* William Henry, *Gilbert Wynant;* Harold Huber, *Nunheim;* Cesar Romero, *Chris Jorgenson;* Natalie Moorhead, *Julia Wolf;* Edward Brophy, *Joe Morelli;* Thomas Jackson, Creighton Hale, Phil Tead, Nick Copeland, *and* Dink Templeton, *Reporters;* Ruth Channing, *Mrs. Jorgenson;* Edward Ellis, *Clyde Wynant;* Gertrude Short, *Marion;* Clay Clement, *Quinn.*

Hollywood's most famed husband-wife detective team, Nick and Nora Charles, were originally considered a dim risk. Had it not been for the persistent convictions of the highly respected MGM director W. S. (Woody) Van Dyke II, William Powell and Myrna Loy might never have had the roles which did so much to elevate their stardom at the Metro studio.

Dashiell Hammett's best-selling 1932 mystery novel *The Thin Man* was among the MGM story acquisitions that interested Van Dyke. But no one else shared his enthusiasm for the property, contending that the detective-mystery genre had worn out and would no longer interest moviegoers. Persisting on his own, Van Dyke assigned writers Albert Hackett and Frances Goodrich to develop a succession of scenes emphasizing a cozy, bantering marital relationship between the mystery-prone Charleses, also involving their wire-haired terrier Asta. The results pleased studio boss Louis B. Mayer, although he was dubious about the casting of Powell and Loy, reasoning that they were *serious* actors, unsuited to the comedic content of *The Thin Man.*

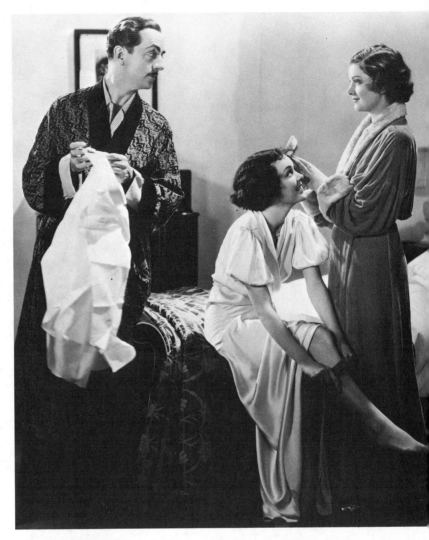

William Powell, Maureen O'Sullivan, and Myrna Loy

William Powell, Myrna Loy, and Asta

129

Thomas Jackson, William Powell, Creighton Hale, and Myrna Loy

Edward Ellis and Natalie Moorhead

Despite its sophisticated wit, tight narrative construction, and witty dialogue, the Hackett-Goodrich script inspired Van Dyke to improvise. Thus many of *The Thin Man*'s best scenes incorporate spontaneous bits of ''business'' conceived during the actual shooting: Myrna Loy's sprawling, package-laden entrance; Powell's shooting off of the Christmas tree ornaments with his airgun; the dog-walking sequence, shot only from the waist up, in which an unseen (but always scene-stealing) Asta's leash-jerks in the direction of passing lampposts generate sly humor. Nick and Nora Charles are here depicted as an imperfect ''perfect'' couple, bantering and bickering in their flippant, fun-loving relationship, fond of cocktails, and clearly in love. The *Thin Man* cast and crew apparently enjoyed unusual rapport working on this production—so much so that its filming was completed within a brief sixteen days, then quite unusual for a major-studio A picture.

Loy and Powell went on to make five sequels to this 1934 box-office hit, which won Oscar nominations for the contributions of Powell, Van Dyke, and its team of screenwriters. And *The Thin Man* was among the *twelve* films competing for Best Picture—an honor won by *It Happened One Night*.

Incidentally, the ''thin man'' of the title is not, as is so often surmised, detective Nick Charles, but, rather, Clyde Wynant (Edward Ellis), whose murder precipitates the story's plot.

BOLERO

1934

CREDITS

A Paramount Picture. Directed by Wesley Ruggles. *Associate producer:* Benjamin Glazer. *Screenplay by* Horace Jackson. *Based on a story by* Carey Wilson, Kubec Glasmon, *and* Ruth Ridenour. *Photographed by* Leo Tover. *Edited by* Hugh Bennett. *Music by* Ralph Rainger, *incorporating* Maurice Ravel's *"Bolero." Dance sequences staged by* LeRoy Prinz. *Running time: 85 minutes.*

CAST

George Raft, *Raoul De Baere;* Carole Lombard, *Helen Hathaway;* William Frawley, *Michael De Baere;* Frances Drake, *Leona;* Sally Rand, *Annette;* Raymond Milland, *Lord Robert Coray;* Gloria Shea, *Lucy;* Gertrude Michael, *Lady Claire D'Argon;* Del Henderson, *Theater Manager;* Frank G. Dunn, *Hotel manager.*

Carole Lombard and Ray Milland

George Raft, with his granite visage and hard-as-nails monotone, was a tough kid from the streets of New York City who had been a professional boxer, a gigolo, and a dancer in nightclubs and Broadway revues before entering films in 1929. In the late Fifties, he admitted, "I was born in a gang neighborhood, brought up with gangsters, and given a movie career by friends in the underworld." And it seemed only natural that Raft should gain fame as a screen gangster—most notably as the coin-flipping Guido Rinaldo in 1932's *Scarface.* Other mob-related roles followed at Paramount, where he was placed under contract. But Raft yearned for a change of pace that would utilize his dancing background, and in 1934 he was teamed with beautiful Carole Lombard (replacing Miriam Hopkins) in *Bolero,* the dramatic story of a perfectionist nightclub dancer with an aversion to any romantic involvements with his female partners. When he dumps one lady (Frances Drake) because she couldn't separate business from pleasure, Raft forms a professional alliance with an ex-Follies girl (Lombard), and together they reach the heights of success—until she falls for an attentive English lord (Ray Milland). This generates a jealous reaction from her dancing partner, and she ultimately leaves the act to marry her suitor. Raft enlists in World War I but emerges from service with a weakened heart. He's then driven to ignore doctors' advice and resume his dancing career, this time with a new partner (Sally Rand, who performs her famed fan dance).

Carole Lombard and George Raft

Carole Lombard and George Raft

George Raft, Carole Lombard, and William Frawley

The movie's climax is fraught with melodramatic coincidence: on opening night, Rand is too drunk to perform, but Raft's manager-brother (William Frawley) spots Lombard with Milland out front and persuades her to help Raft realize his dream by partnering him in the "Bolero." Just as a one-shot, she agrees. But afterwards, in his dressing room Raft collapses and dies before they can perform the encore demanded by an enthusiastic audience.

Bolero is episodic entertainment. But a good script, evenhanded direction by Wesley Ruggles, and effective casting help tremendously. Lombard had not yet gained her reputation for uninhibited comedy, but this was an early opportunity for her to play a role of personality and character, and she responded in kind. Raft was then going through his Latinate phase, and an unusual off-screen rapport with his costar carried over onto celluloid. Their chemistry made *Bolero* a very successful movie, and Paramount rushed them into a follow-up vehicle, *Rumba* (1935).

Although both stars were experienced dancers, some of *Bolero*'s more exacting adagio movements were performed by doubles, shot at a distance with clever lighting. Careful editing helped considerably. But Paramount executives had cared enough about the finished product to have contract director Mitchell Leisen reshoot the climactic dance number, performed to Ravel's throbbingly familiar "Bolero," after the movie was completed by Ruggles.

For Lombard, *Bolero* was an important career milestone; years later, Raft called it his favorite film.

132

THE GAY DIVORCEE

1934

Ginger Rogers and Fred Astaire

Ginger Rogers and Fred Astaire

Edward Everett Horton, Betty Grable, and Fred Astaire

CREDITS

An RKO Radio Picture. Directed by Mark Sandrich. *Produced by* Pandro S. Berman. *Screenplay by* George Marion, Jr., Dorothy Yost, *and* Edward Kaufman. *Based on the novel and Broadway musical Gay Divorce by* Dwight Taylor, Kenneth Webb, *and* Samuel Hoffenstein. *Photographed by* David Abel. *Edited by* William Hamilton. *Art direction by* Van Nest Polglase *and* Carroll Clark. *Musical direction by* Max Steiner. *Dance ensembles staged by* Dave Gould. *Costumes by* Walter Plunkett. *Songs: "Night and Day" by* Cole Porter; *"The Continental" and "A Needle in a Haystack" by* Con Conrad *and* Herb Magidson; *"Don't Let It Bother You" and "Let's K-nock K-neez" by* Harry Revel *and* Max Gordon. *Running time: 107 minutes.*

CAST

Fred Astaire, *Guy Holden;* Ginger Rogers, *Mimi Glossop;* Alice Brady, *Hortense Ditherwell;* Edward Everett Horton, *Egbert Fitzgerald;* Erik Rhodes, *Rodolfo Tonetti;* Eric Blore, *Waiter;* Lillian Miles, *Hotel guest;* Charles Coleman, *Guy's valet;* William Austin, *Cyril Glossop;* Betty Grable, *Dancer;* Paul Porcasi, *Nightclub proprietor;* E. E. Clive, *Customs inspector.*

Nearly fifty years after their supporting-role debut as a team in 1933's *Flying Down to Rio*, Fred Astaire and Ginger Rogers remain the most popular dance team in the history of American films. Oddly matched physically, the showgirl-pretty Rogers and skinny, plain-faced Astaire somehow produced the perfect blend. It has been reasoned that urbane Fred gave Ginger class, while she gave him sex appeal.

The Gay Divorcee provided the first Astaire-Rogers starring vehicle. On the screen, Cole Porter's stage musical *Gay Divorce* became *The Gay Divorcee* because of Hays Office objections that a divorce could not be depicted as gay (in the original sense of that word), while a divorcee could. In characteristic Hollywood fashion, the stage original underwent so many changes in its transition to the screen that, of its Porter score, only *one* song, the immortal "Night and Day," was retained! Instead, Con Conrad and Herb Magidson contributed the film's big production number, "The Continental," as well as the nimble Astaire solo, "A Needle in a Haystack." The team of Harry Revel and Mack Gordon wrote the Parisian showgirl number, "Don't Let It Bother You," and "Let's K-nock K-neez," the film's musical novelty, staged by Hermes Pan for Edward Everett Horton and a pre-stardom Betty Grable.

Oddly enough, *The Gay Divorcee's* 107-minute length includes only *ten minutes* of dance involving Astaire and Rogers. And much of *The Gay Divorcee's* mistaken-identity plot (Rogers assumes that dancer Astaire is the hired corespondent in her divorce suit) is foolish and tedious.

Fusspot Edward Everett Horton and dithering dowager Alice Brady have far too much footage, and their blatantly obvious comedic ploys, as directed by Mark Sandrich, sorely try audience patience. But the mustical sequences are worth the wait, and Dave Gould's choreography of the spectacular "The Continental" shows how much can be done with a simple but catchy tune.

Pandro S. Berman, the film's producer, claims respon-sibility for the repeated, but consistently reluctant, teaming of Fred and Ginger during their Thirties years at RKO. She, apparently, disliked taking second billing to Astaire and never really wanted to be a dancing comedienne. In Berman's words, "These two people were forced by circumstances to work together against their wills." And millions of moviegoers couldn't have been happier.

Ginger Rogers and Fred Astaire dance "The Continental"

Louise Beavers and Claudette Colbert

Warren William, Louise Beavers, and Claudette Colbert

IMITATION OF LIFE

1934

CREDITS

A Universal Picture. Directed by John M. Stahl. *Produced by* Carl Laemmle. *Screenplay by* William Hurlbut. *Based on the novel by* Fannie Hurst. *Photographed by* Merritt Gerstad. *Edited by* Phil Cahn. *Running time: 106 minutes.*

CAST

Claudette Colbert, *Beatrice Pullman;* Warren William, *Stephen Archer;* Ned Sparks, *Elmer;* Louise Beavers, *Delilah Johnson;* Baby Jane/Juanita Quigley, *Jessie Pullman at three;* Marilyn Knowlden, *Jessie at eight;* Rochelle Hudson, *Jessie at eighteen;* Sebie Hendricks, *Peola Johnson at four;* Dorothy Black, *Peola at nine;* Fredi Washington, *Peola at nineteen;* Alan Hale, *Martin, furniture man;* Clarence Hummel Wilson, *Landlord;* Henry Armetta, *Painter;* Henry Kolker, *Dr. Preston;* Wyndham Standing, *Butler;* Paulyn Garner; *Mrs. Ramsey;* Paul Porcasi, *Restaurant manager;* Alice Ardell, *French maid;* Walter Walker, *Hugh;* Noel Francis, *Mrs. Eden;* Franklin Pangborn, *Mr. Carven;* Alma Tell, *Mrs. Carven;* Joyce Compton, *Woman;* Fred "Snowflake" Toones and Hattie McDaniel, *Bit players at funeral.*

The year 1934 brought Claudette Colbert her only Academy Award—for her delightful comedy performance in Frank Capra's *It Happened One Night.* But she also displayed her versatility as the Egyptian queen in Cecil B. De Mille's spectacular *Cleopatra* and as the young widow who becomes a successful businesswoman in *Imitation of Life,* a tear-jerking adaptation of Fannie Hurst's popular 1933 novel. The varied excellence of these *three* characterizations is generally credited with deciding the 1934 Oscar vote for Colbert.

Imitation of Life required the twenty-nine-year-old actress to age fifteen years, ending up with a grown daughter (Rochelle Hudson) who threatens her mother's romantic happiness (with Warren William). It was an acting challenge that few of Colbert's contemporaries would have dared risk. But the movie also dealt more squarely with

Rochelle Hudson and Warren William

racial discrimination than any other film of its era, presenting a black woman as its second most important central character.

Louise Beavers, at thirty-two already a veteran of countless servant roles of the silent and early sound era, took fourth billing as Colbert's black counterpart, a widowed young mother of a light-skinned child. Circumstances launch them together into a storefront pancake business, which eventually becomes an empire, with their Aunt Delilah packaged mix. The Negro press didn't appreciate Fannie Hurst's having this character elect to become Colbert's lifelong *maid,* as well as business partner, rather than establish her *own* home with their considerable profits. Nor could black critics accept her advice to her tormented, teenaged daughter, Peola (a fine performance by Fredi Washington), who tried to pass for white: "Bow your head. You got to learn to take it." Already Beavers had successfully appealed to the NAACP to have the word "nigger" removed from William Hurlbut's screenplay, but she subsequently paid for her victory in humiliation by Universal's front-office personnel.

Beavers's warm and deeply affecting performance deserved an acting prize. But Claudette Colbert's role in the film's success must not be underrated. *Imitation of Life* is purest soap opera, no matter how superior its quality, and few such sob stories from so sentimental an era as the mid-Thirties would sustain its power as this one has, were it not for fine acting. Colbert brings considerable charm and integrity to this story, her naturalness and understated acting talents lending credibility to even the hokiest of plot turns. Without Colbert and Beavers, the 1934 *Imitation of Life* would now look as phony as its glossy 1959 remake with Lana Turner and Juanita Moore.

Of its three Oscar nominations, the most important was for Best Picture. But *Imitation of Life* lost that statuette to the film that swept away nearly all of 1934's top awards, *It Happened One Night.*

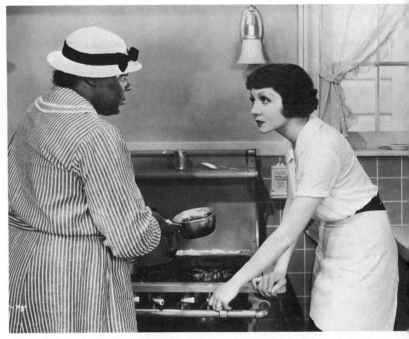

Louise Beavers and Claudette Colbert

Henry Armetta, Alan Hale, Louise Beavers, and Claudette Colbert

Charlie Ruggles, Charles Laughton, and Mary Boland

RUGGLES OF RED GAP

1935

CREDITS

A Paramount Picture. Directed by Leo McCarey. *Produced by* Arthur Hornblow, Jr. *Screenplay by* Walter DeLeon, Harlan Thompson, *and* Humphrey Pearson. *Based on the play and novel by* Harry Leon Wilson. *Photographed by* Alfred Gilks. *Edited by* Edward Dmytryk. *Art direction by* Hans Dreier *and* Robert Odell. *Costumes by* Travis Banton. *Music by* Ralph Rainger *and* Sam Coslow. *Running time: 90 minutes.*

CAST

Charles Laughton, *Ruggles;* Mary Boland, *Effie Froud;* Charlie Ruggles, *Egbert Froud;* ZaSu Pitts, *Mrs. Judson;* Roland Young, *George Vane Bassingwell;* Leila Hyams, *Nell Kenner;* Maude Eburne, *Ma Pettingill;* Lucien Littlefield, *Charles Belknap-Jackson;* Leota Lorraine, *Mrs. Belknap-Jackson;* James Burke, *Jeff Tuttle;* Dell Henderson, *Sam;* Baby Ricardo Lord Cezon, *Baby Judson;* Brenda Fowler, *Judy Ballard;* Augusta Anderson, *Mrs. Wallaby;* Sarah Edwards, *Mrs. Myron Carey;* Clarence Hummel Wilson, *Jake Henshaw;* Rafael Storm, *Clothing salesman;* George Burton, *Hank;* Victor Potel and Harry Bernard, *Cowboys;* Frank Rice, *Buck;* William J. Welsh, *Eddie;* Lee Kohlmar, *Red Gap jailer;* Alice Ardell, *Lisette;* Rolfe Sedan, *Barber;* Jack Norton, *Barfly;* Willie Fung, *Chinese servant.*

Charlie Ruggles, Mary Boland, Charles Laughton, Leila Hyams, and Roland Young

A retrospective look at Paramount's charming 1935 film reminds the viewer that performers like Charles Laughton, Mary Boland, Charlie Ruggles, ZaSu Pitts, Roland Young, and Maude Eburne are almost entirely absent from the cinema today. Actors whose talents many of us once took for granted are now sorely missed, and we aren't likely to enjoy their ilk again. So we return to the past and continue to appreciate movies like this gem from the mid-Thirties.

Laughton was ideally cast as Marmaduke Ruggles, the valet of a hard-luck Britisher, who is won in a poker game by his employer's nouveau-riche cousin from the States, where Ruggles responds to the blandishments of a democratic society, leaves service, and goes into the restaurant business. The actor had previously displayed his skills in U.S. films as the flamboyant Nero of De Mille's *The Sign of the Cross* and as the tyrannical father of Elizabeth Barrett Browning in *The Barretts of Wimpole Street*, and he was the first Briton to win a Hollywood Oscar, for *The Private Lives of Henry VIII*. But it is his low-key portrayal of Ruggles's triumphant, gradual emancipation from inhibited servant to master of his own future that dominates this comedy classic. The film's director, Leo McCarey, a recent veteran of the Marx Brothers' *Duck Soup*, was instrumental in helping Laughton as a comedian. The actor's characterization, in contrast to the sinister, exotic, and larger-than-life roles for which he was already so well known, is very human, very likable, and his climactic, drink-inspired recital of Lincoln's Gettysburg Address provides the film's high point.

Ruggles of Red Gap won no awards. But it did garner an Academy nomination in the Best Picture category—its Oscar taken by yet another Charles Laughton vehicle, *Mutiny on the Bounty.*

Harry Leon Wilson's 1915 novel about a British "gentleman's gentleman" adjusting to life in a pioneer town of the American West has proved a durable subject for motion picture comedy. Taylor Holmes had the title role in its 1918 silent-screen bow, and Edward Everett Horton succeeded him in a 1923 remake, followed by Charles Laughton in 1935's first talkie adaptation. Under the title *Fancy Pants*, it also provided an excellent vehicle for Bob Hope and Lucille Ball in 1950. But it seems unlikely that *Ruggles of Red Gap* could successfully be refilmed in the Eighties, because American movies no longer boast the fine roster of inimitable character actors they once had.

Mary Boland, Maude Eburne, Charlie Ruggles, Charles Laughton, Leota Lorraine, and Lucien Littlefield

Victor McLaglen, Joseph Sauers (Joe Sawyer), Preston Foster, Neil Fitzgerald, Donald Meek

THE INFORMER

1935

CREDITS

An RKO Picture. Directed by John Ford. *Produced by* Cliff Reid. *Screenplay by* Dudley Nichols. *Based on the novel by* Liam O'Flaherty. *Photographed by* Joseph H. August. *Edited by* George Hively. *Art direction by* Van Nest Polglase *and* Charles Kirk. *Set decoration by* Julia Heron. *Costumes by* Walter Plunkett. *Music by* Max Steiner. *Running time: 91 minutes.*

CAST

Victor McLaglen, *Gypo Nolan;* Heather Angel, *Mary McPhillip;* Preston Foster, *Dan Gallagher;* Margot Grahame, *Katie Madden;* Wallace Ford, *Frankie McPhillip;* Una O'Connor, *Mrs. McPhillip;* J. M. Kerrigan, *Terry;* Joseph Sauers/Joe Sawyer, *Bartly Mulholland;* Neil Fitzgerald, *Tommy Connor;* Donald Meek, *Peter Mulligan;* D'Arcy Corrigan, *The blind man;* Leo McCabe, *Donahue;* Gaylord Pendleton, *Dennis Daly;* Francis Ford, *Flynn;* May Boley, *Madame Betty;* Grizelda Harvey, *The lady;* Dennis O'Dea, *Streetsinger;* Jack Mulhall, *Man at wake.*

Liam O'Flaherty's 1925 novel is a masterful psychological study of Gypo Nolan, a dull-witted, impoverished Dubliner who, in the middle of the 1922 Sinn Fein Rebellion, turns stool pigeon during one event-filled night, revealing to police the whereabouts of Frankie McPhillip, a trusting friend and revolutionary who is wanted for murder. Gypo receives a reward of twenty pounds, while Frankie is tracked down by the authorities and takes his own life.

When Dan Gallagher, the revolutionaries' leader, seeks Frankie's informer, Gypo assuages his guilt with drink and carousing, placing blame on an innocent man. But before that night is over, Gypo's guilt is evident. While he's sleeping, Gypo's prostitute-girlfriend reveals his whereabouts, and he is seriously wounded. Gypo seeks refuge in a church where Mrs. McPhillip sits praying, and when he confesses his treachery to her, she grants him forgiveness as he falls dead.

The Informer had already been filmed by the British in 1929, and RKO reluctantly agreed to let Ford remake it with his assurance that it would be a low-budget movie. Reportedly, he brought it in for slightly over $200,000 on a

Margot Grahame and Victor McLaglen

three-week shooting schedule.

The results drew widespread critical acclaim, because of the skill and craftsmanship with which Ford and screenwriter Dudley Nichols had "humanized" O'Flaherty's grittily realistic book. One-dimensional characters now became more fully realized, and O'Flaherty's unattractive, degraded figures now attained dignity, while the overall story developed into epic tragedy.

In the strong hands of John Ford, *The Informer* is impassioned Irish melodrama, performed with all the stops out. Beautifully photographed in the mists and dark streets of the studio-built Dublin sets, Joseph H. August's photography coats the film with a striking overlay of distorted realism.

But *The Informer*'s most vivid image is that of its hulking, blustering central figure, as broadly portrayed by blustering, oafish Victor McLaglen in a performance that won him 1935's Best Actor Academy Award. Bluffing, slugging, and belting back Irish whiskey, McLaglen's Gypo Nolan emerges as a cowardly, despicable brute and a boozing liar, capable of any deceit to satisfy a whim or save his neck.

Ford's atmospheric direction brought him the first of his record four Academy Awards, with additional Oscars won by Dudley Nichols's screenplay and Max Steiner's relentless musical score.

In 1968, Jules Dassin directed an all-black cast in an unsuccessful remake entitled *Uptight!*

Joseph Sauers (Joe Sawyer), Mary Gordon, Una O'Connor, Heather Angel, and Victor McLaglen

Fred MacMurray and Claudette Colbert

THE GILDED LILY

1935

CREDITS

A Paramount Picture. Directed by Wesley Ruggles. *Produced by* Albert Lewis. *Screenplay by* Claude Binyon. *Story by* Melville Baker *and* Jack Kirkland. *Photographed by* Victor Milner. *Edited by* Otho Lovering. *Music by* Arthur Johnston. *Song: "Something About Romance" by* Sam Coslow *and* Arthur Johnston. *Costumes by* Travis Banton. *Running time: 80 minutes.*

CAST

Claudette Colbert, *Marilyn David;* Fred MacMurray, *Pete Dawes;* Raymond Milland, *Charles Gray/Granville;* C. Aubrey Smith, *Lord Granville;* Eddie Craven, *Eddie;* Luis Alberni, *Nate;* Donald Meek, *Hankerson;* Michelette Burani, *Marilyn's maid;* Claude King, *Boat captain;* Charles Irwin, *Oscar;* Ferdinand Munier, *Otto Bushe;* Rita Carlyle, *Proprietor's wife;* Forrester Harvey, *English inn proprietor;* Edward Gargan, *Guard;* Leonid Kinskey, *Vocal teacher;* Jimmy Aubrey, *Purser;* Charles Wilson, *Pete's editor;* Grace Bradley, *Daisy;* Tom Dugan, *Bum;* Warren Hymer, *Taxi driver;* Robert Dudley, *Shopkeeper.*

Between 1935 and 1949, Claudette Colbert and Fred MacMurray were teamed in seven motion pictures, of which all but one *(Maid of Salem)* were light comedies, a genre for which their collective natural charm, warmth, and timing made them a perfect match. When Paramount first brought them together in 1934 for *The Gilded Lily,* she was a screen veteran of twenty-nine and an important star, while his movie career rested on the juvenile lead in one minor May Robson vehicle at RKO called *Grand Old Girl.* But something clicked between the tall, strapping, twenty-seven-year-old newcomer and petite, tongue-in-cheek Colbert. On-screen they had true chemistry, and MacMurray has never stopped paying tribute to her for helping launch him into Hollywood's major league.

The Gilded Lily is probably their best film together, and certainly their scenes provide the highlight of Claude Binyon's amiably amusing screenplay. Claudette's a stenographer; Fred's a newspaper reporter. Their favorite

Ray Milland, Claudette Colbert, and Robert Dudley

Fred MacMurray, and Claudette Colbert

meeting place is a bench outside New York City's public library, where they argue such important issues as the snacking merits of peanuts versus popcorn. He loves her, but she's got her romantic sights set on a more ambitious Prince Charming—who happens along in the form of a handsome, wealthy, and titled young Englishman, Ray Milland. But a misunderstanding ensues between them and she turns down his proposal. Out of spite, MacMurray writes a story publicizing the situation and dubbing Colbert "The 'No' Girl." This leads to her being booked into a nightclub as a new singing sensation—and one of the movie's most delightful scenes when she makes her awkward debut, gowned to the nines, forgetting the words of her song, and attempting to cover her embarrassment with some gauche dance steps. But her ingenuous charm ("I'm just a freak!") wins them over, and she's an unexpected hit. There follows an unsuccessful attempt at enjoying the high life with the British nobleman, after which, having apparently come to her senses, she returns to settle down with her reporter-boyfriend.

In 1935, *The Gilded Lily* was fresh and diverting entertainment, engagingly played. Wesley Ruggles, who had directed Mae West's inimitable *I'm No Angel*, guided his skilled cast through this blend of whimsical humor and outright screwball nonsense with great success. *The Gilded Lily* enchanted Depression-era moviegoers and earned a prominent spot on the National Board of Review's list of 1935's ten best.

Colin Clive, Elsa Lanchester, Boris Karloff, and Ernest Thesiger

BRIDE OF FRANKENSTEIN

1935

CREDITS

A Universal Picture. Directed by James Whale. *Produced by* Carl Laemmle, Jr. *Screenplay by* John L. Balderston *and* William Hurlbut. *Based on the novel Frankenstein by* Mary Shelley. *Photographed by* John Mescall. *Edited by* Ted Kent. *Art direction by* Charles D. Hall. *Music by* Franz Waxman. *Makeup created by* Jack Pierce. *Special effects by* John P. Fulton. *Running time: 75 minutes.*

CAST

Boris Karloff, *The monster;* Colin Clive, *Henry Frankenstein;* Valerie Hobson, *Elizabeth Frankenstein;* Ernest Thesiger, *Dr. Pretorious;* Elsa Lanchester, *The bride/Mary Shelley;* O. P. Heggie, *The hermit;* Dwight Frye, *Karl;* Ted Billings, *Ludwig;* E. E. Clive, *Burgomaster;* Una O'Connor, *Minnie;* Anne Darling, *Shepherdess;* Douglas Walton, *Percy Shelley;* Gavin Gordon, *Lord Byron;* Neil Fitzgerald, *Rudy;* Reginald Barlow, *Hans;* Mary Gordon, *Hans's wife;* Gunnis Davis, *Uncle Glutz;* Tempe Pigott, *Aunt Glutz;* Lucien Prival, *Albert the butler;* Rollo Lloyd, Walter Brennan, and Mary Stewart, *Neighbors;* Billy Barty, *Baby;* John Carradine, *Hunter.*

*Elsa Lanchester
and Boris Karloff*

But *Bride of Frankenstein* "humanized" the monster to a degree that dismayed his interpreter; Karloff felt that allowing the creature to grunt words of dialogue weakened the character. Nevertheless, this sequel enjoyed as great a popularity as had its 1931 forerunner, and audiences reveled in its Gothic chills, macabre humor, and such flamboyant touches as character actor Ernest Thesiger's eccentric portrait of a mad doctor. Clive and Karloff both repeated their characterizations from the 1931 movie, but the distaff lead (Dr. Frankenstein's wife, Elizabeth) switched oddly from Mae Clarke to British-born Valerie Hobson.

Bride concludes with a cataclysmic lab-destroying sequence that eliminates both creatures—and just about everyone else. Of course, the apparently destroyed monster would surface again in 1939's *Son of Frankenstein*. But the 1935 *Bride*, with its marvelously atmospheric Franz Waxman score and inspired camerawork by John Mescall, remains the enduring classic and, arguably, Whale's horror masterpiece.

It took Universal four years to issue a sequel to 1931's popular *Frankenstein*. Fortunately, James Whale was retained to direct what is now considered the best of all the various Universal *Frankenstein* thrillers. For *Bride of Frankenstein* is a decided masterpiece of performance, photography, set design, and intelligent writing.

Frankenstein's monster (Boris Karloff) had seemed to perish in a burning mill at the close of the original film. But that problem was skirted by *Bride*'s screenwriters, John L. Balderston and William Hurlbut, with the explanation that the collapsing mill had deposited the creature in a flooded cellar beneath—from which he emerges in this sequel. It

seems that his creator, Dr. Frankenstein (Colin Clive), also survived the monster's previous efforts to destroy him. Whale employs a short prologue in which Elsa Lanchester, as authoress Mary Shelley, recounts the continuing saga. Lanchester also doubles in *Bride*'s title role, a sort of mechanical-spitfire Nefertiti/Betty Brillo, intended as a mate for the creature.

Valerie Hobson, Colin Clive, and Ernest Thesiger

Billie Burke, Helen Flint, Alison Skipworth, and Will Rogers

Frank Albertson, Ruth Warren, Will Rogers, and Billie Burke

DOUBTING THOMAS

1936

CREDITS

A Fox Film. Directed by David Butler. *Produced by* B. G. DeSylva. *Screenplay by* William Conselman. *Based on* George Kelly's *play The Torch Bearers, as adapted by* Bartlett Cormack. *Photographed by* Joseph Valentine. *Art direction by* Jack Otterson. *Gowns by* Rene Hubert. *Music by* Arthur Lange. *Running time: 73 minutes.*

CAST

Will Rogers, *Thomas Brown;* Billie Burke, *Paula Brown;* Alison Skipworth, *Mrs. Pampinelli;* Sterling Holloway, *Mr. Spindler;* Andrew Tombes, *Hossefrosse;* Gail Patrick, *Florence McCrickett;* Frances Grant, *Peggy Burns;* Frank Albertson, *Jimmy Brown;* Johnny Arthur, *Ralph Twiller;* Helen Flint, *Nelly Fell;* Fred Wallace, *Teddy;* T. Roy Barnes, *LaMaze;* Ruth Warren, *Jenny;* John Qualen, *Von Blitzen;* George Cooper, *Stagehand;* Helen Freeman, *Mrs. Sheppard;* William Benedict, *Caddie;* Lynn Bari, *Girl.*

Will Rogers, homely humorist and cowboy philosopher, was the essence of grassroots America and a great populist hero, especially during the Depression era. The entertainer's talent for wry, homespun self-expression encompassed radio, lecture tours, and a syndicated newspaper column, as well as motion pictures, and his untimely death at fifty-five, in a 1935 plane crash in Alaska, shocked the nation.

At the time of Roger's death, movie theaters were showing his *Doubting Thomas,* a movie somewhat atypical of his customary screen image, for this amusing comedy is hardly what could be termed a Rogers "vehicle." Despite occasional scenes in which the writing and direction spotlight its star philosophizing or reacting against the phonies who threaten to disrupt his home life, his big solo moment is the startling one in which he impersonates a middle-aged "crooner" with slicked-back hair and so much makeup that it's difficult to recognize him. This totally unexpected display of versatility comes as a refreshing surprise.

Doubting Thomas is little more than a slight expansion of *The Torch Bearers,* George Kelly's hilarious 1922 satire on

Gail Patrick, Fred Wallace, Helen Flint, Sterling Holloway, Frances Grant, Alison Skipworth, Andrew Tombes, Johnny Arthur, Billie Burke, and Will Rogers

amateur theatricals. Billie Burke portrays the repressed wife who always wanted to be an actress—and gets her chance when another woman is forced to bow out of the local production; Rogers is the disapproving husband who, having been out of town on business, discovers her thespian involvement too late to prevent it. Overseeing this community disaster is the large, self-important figure of Alison Skipworth, inimitably re-creating her original Broadway role as Mrs. Pampinelli, the director with the Delsarte touch.

The movie's high point, as in the play, comes when these hapless amateurs experience their opening (and closing) night before an audience that witnesses ill-prepared actors coping with forgotten lines, recalcitrant mustaches, and falling scenery—all to sidesplitting effect. Rogers isn't in this play-within-the-play, so he's shown in the audience, expressing disgust with his wife's hammy acting.

Doubting Thomas is more of an ensemble work than a Will Rogers picture. But, cast with expert character actors like Skipworth, Burke, Sterling Holloway, and Helen Flint, it's a most enjoyable light entertainment.

Sterling Holloway, Will Rogers, and Helen Flint

Douglass Montgomery and Evelyn Venable

HARMONY LANE

1935

CREDITS

A Republic Pictures release of a Mascot Production. Directed by Joseph Santley. *Produced by* Nat Levine. *Supervised by* Colbert Clark. *Screenplay by* Joseph Santley *and* Elizabeth Meehan. *Based on a story by* Milton Krims. *Photographed by* Ernie Miller *and* Jack Marta. *Edited by* Joseph Lewis *and* Ray Curtis. *Musical direction by* Arthur Kay. *Running time: 84 minutes.*

CAST

Douglass Montgomery, *Stephen Foster;* Evelyn Venable, *Susan Pentland;* Adrienne Ames, *Jane McDowell;* Joseph Cawthorn, *Kleber;* William Frawley, *Christy;* Clarence Muse, *Old Joe;* Gilbert Emery, *Mr. Foster;* Florence Roberts, *Mrs. Foster;* James Bush, *Morrison Foster;* David Torrence, *Mr. Pentland;* Victor DeCamp, *William Foster, Jr.;* Edith Craig, *Henrietta Foster;* Cora Sue Collins, *Marion;* Lloyd Hughes, *Andrew Robinson;* Ferdinand Munier, *Mr. Pond;* Mildred Gover, *Delia;* James B. Carson, *Proprietor;* Rodney Hildebrand, *Mr. Wade;* Mary McLaren, *Mrs. Wade;* Al Herman, *Tambo;* Earl Hodgins, *Mr. Bones;* Smiley Burnette, *Singer;* Hattie McDaniel, *Cook.*

In the years before 1956, when RKO became the first major studio to sell its old movies to television, TV film fare was heavy with minor-league pictures from the Thirties, many produced by the so-called Poverty Row studios like Majestic, Monogram, Liberty, and Chesterfield. Among these, Nat Levine's Mascot Pictures Corp. was best known for its serials, of which it turned out some thirty-one between 1927 and the close of 1935. Mascot pictures were known for being quickly and cheaply made, a situation which changed somewhat in 1935, the year Levine leased the old Mack Sennett Studios and merged with Republic Pictures. That year, he also turned out nine feature films, including this modest but attractively produced movie biography of nineteenth-century American composer Stephen Collins Foster (1826–1864).

None of Hollywood's three motion pictures about Foster (this one was followed in 1939 by the Technicolor *Swanee River,* with Don Ameche, and *I Dream of Jeanie,* a 1952 effort with Bill Shirley) has been faithful to historical fact. Each has romanticized the composer's sad life to fit sentimental bio-film traditions and to showcase the obligatory musical interludes. But, in many of its basic elements, *Har-*

Douglass Montgomery, Adrienne Ames, and Evelyn Venable

mony Lane resembles Foster's life: he did leave clerical duties for music, he did write Negro-oriented songs for the minstrel shows of E. P. Christy, and it's true that he died in poverty, after years of excessive drinking.

Mascot was fortunate in engaging Douglass Montgomery to portray Foster in this ambitious film, for that actor had previously associated himself only with the more Establishment likes of RKO, Universal, and Paramount. But his portrayal of Foster, given the often banal dialogue and situations of the Joseph Santley–Elizabeth Meehan screenplay, is quite commendable as he ranges from youthful enthusiasm and romantic courtship of his beloved Susan (Evelyn Venable) to ill-advised marriage (Adrienne Ames), following Susan's jilting him for another man, to dissipation and untimely death.

Harmony Lane is too modest in its production values and too quaintly naive as a movie biography to hold much interest for audiences of the Eighties. But, for undemanding, melody-minded mid-Thirties filmgoers, it offered a pleasant eighty-four-minute diversion.

Douglass Montgomery, William Frawley, and Joseph Cawthorn

149

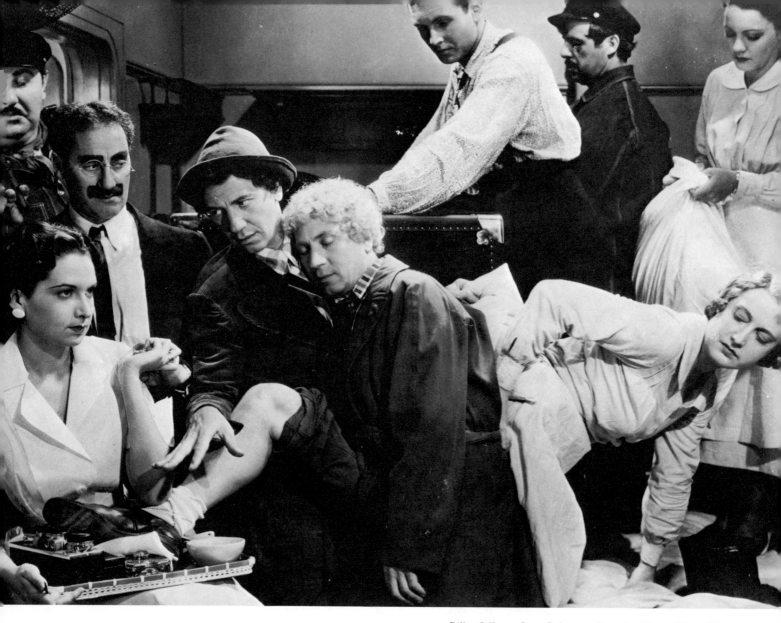

Billy Gilbert, Ines Palange, Groucho Marx, Chico Marx, Harpo Marx, Allan Jones, Frank Yaconelli, and bit players

A NIGHT AT THE OPERA

1935

CREDITS

A Metro-Goldwyn-Mayer Picture. Directed by Sam Wood. *Produced by* Irving Thalberg. *Screenplay by* George S. Kaufman *and* Morrie Ryskind. *Additional material by* Al Boasberg. *Original story by* James Kevin McGuinness. *Photographed by* Merritt B. Gerstad. *Edited by* William LeVanway. *Art direction by* Cedric Gibbons, Ben Carre, *and* Edwin B. Willis. *Music by* Herbert Stothart. *Opera scenes from* Leoncavallo's I Pagliacci *and* Verdi's Il Trovatore. *Songs:* "Alone" *by* Nacio Herb Brown *and* Arthur Freed; "Cosi-Cosa" *by* Bronislau Kaper, Walter Jurmann, *and* Ned Washington. *Running time: 96 minutes.*

CAST

Groucho Marx, *Otis B. Driftwood;* Harpo Marx, *Tomasso;* Chico Marx, *Fiorello;* Kitty Carlisle, *Rosa Castaldi;* Allan Jones, *Ricardo Baroni;* Siegfried "Sig" Rumann, *Herman Gottlieb;* Margaret Dumont, *Mrs. Claypool;* Walter Woolf King, *Rodolfo Lassparri;* Edward Keane, *The captain;* Robert Emmet O'Connor, *Henderson;* Gino Corrado, *Steward;* Purnell Pratt, *Mayor;* Frank Yaconelli, *Engineer;* Billy Gilbert, *Engineer's assistant/Peasant;* Sam Marx, *Extra on ship and at dock;* Claude Peyton, *Police captain;* Rita and Rubin, *Dancers;* Luther Hoobyar, *Ruiz;* Rodolfo Hoyos, *Count di Luna;* Olga Dane, *Azucena;* James J. Wolf, *Ferrando;* Ines Palange, *Maid;* Jonathan Hale, *Stage manager;* Otto Fries, *Elevator man;* William Gould, *Captain of police;* Leo White, Jay Eaton, *and* Rolfe Sedan, *Aviators.*

Allan Jones, Siegfried Rumann, Harpo Marx, Chico Marx, and Groucho Marx

The mad, anarchic screen world of the Marx Brothers was never better represented than in the hilarious first two movies they made, under Sam Wood's direction, for MGM: *A Night at the Opera* (1935) and *A Day at the Races* (1937). From 1929 to 1933, Groucho, Harpo, Chico, and Zeppo Marx had starred in five Paramount comedies, but when their material veered from mere outrageous lunacy to political satire in 1933's *Duck Soup*, neither critics nor audiences responded favorably, and Paramount dropped them.

The brothers were rescued by Metro's production chief Irving Thalberg, and the intial result (in addition to retiring straight man–brother Zeppo) was the very successful *A Night at the Opera*, whose elaborate gags were cannily pretested in a stage tour *(Scenes from a Night at the Opera)* prior to the start of filming. Some felt that the Marxes should not have had to concede so much footage to the film's romantic subplot and musical numbers involving singing actors Kitty Carlisle, Allan Jones, and Walter Woolf King. But this was more than compensated for by an episodically uproarious George S. Kaufman–Morrie Ryskind–Al Boasberg script that had the three brothers creating transatlantic havoc on an ocean liner (the celebrated stateroom scene) and, eventually, laying waste to an operatic performance of *Il Trovatore* with wildly alternating backdrops, backstage Marxian chaos, and an orchestra mixing Verdi with "Take Me Out to the Ballgame."

Always at the top of their unique form are the leering, cigar-flipping, wisecracking Groucho; mute, blond-wigged,

skirt-chasing Harpo; Italian-accented, piano-playing Chico; and their inevitable super-foil, the Wagnerian-proportioned Margaret Dumont, as another of her gullible and wealthy dowagers.

The Marx Brothers' lunatic movie legacy only totaled thirteen motion pictures as a team, but their inspired-nonsense humor continues to tickle the public's fancy. Unsurpassed, they remain in a comic class all thier own.

Margaret Dumont, Groucho Marx, and Gino Corrado

Charles Boyer and Claudette Colbert

PRIVATE WORLDS

1935

CREDITS

A Paramount Picture. Directed by Gregory La Cava. *Produced by* Walter Wanger. *Screenplay by* Lynn Starling. *Based on the novel by* Phyllis Bottome. *Photographed by* Leon Shamroy. *Edited by* Aubrey Scotto. *Running time: 84 minutes.*

CAST

Claudette Colbert, *Dr. Jane Everest;* Charles Boyer, *Dr. Charles Monet;* Joan Bennett, *Sally MacGregor;* Joel Mc-Crea, *Dr. Alex MacGregor;* Helen Vinson, *Claire Monet;* Esther Dale, *Matron;* Samuel Hinds, *Dr. Arnold;* Jean Rouverol, *Carrie;* Sam Godfrey, *Tom Hirst;* Dora Clement, *Bertha Hirst;* Theodore von Eltz, *Dr. Harding;* Stanley Andrews, *Dr. Barnes;* Guinn "Big Boy" Williams, *Jerry;* Maurice Murphy, *Boy in car;* Irving Bacon, *Male nurse.*

Because Depression audiences generally preferred the facile escapism of comedies, musicals, soap operas, and gangster stories to more serious-minded movies, it was considered quite daring in 1935 for a studio like Paramount to take a chance on *Private Worlds*. It was based on Phyllis Bottome's novel about a mental institution (inspired by her interest in the modified psychoanalytic system of Dr. Alfred Adler) and represented a formidable challenge for producer Walter Wanger. But a sound screen adaptation by Lynn Starling helped, and so did the cast. Claudette Colbert was the ruling queen of the lot, ironically because of her considerable popular and critical success the previous year in two films made on loan-out to *other* studios—*Imitation of Life* at Universal, and Columbia's *It Happened One Night*, which won her 1934's Best Actress Oscar. Having already made 1935 audiences laugh with *The Gilded Lily*, Colbert wisely selected this about face role of Dr. Jane Everest, a workaholic psychiatrist whose romantic proclivities are submerged by loving memories of a youth killed in World War I. With Colbert thus assuring box-office interest, Wanger added the fast-rising French actor Charles Boyer, contract ingenue Joan Bennett, and the personable Joel McCrea.

Boyer portrayed Dr. Charles Monet, an outsider who comes into immediate conflict with Colbert (he disapproves of female doctors) when he's appointed head of the asylum, a post young doctor McCrea had hoped to get. Thus frustrated, the latter takes up with Boyer's unstable, philandering sister (Helen Vinson), creating a breach between him and his pregnant wife (Joan Bennett). Later, Bennett loses her sanity, and the various crises of the institution break down the barriers between Colbert and Boyer, broadening their professional relationship into an emotional one.

Unfortunately, *Private Worlds* has drifted into obscurity over the years and is little seen today. Some of its impressive directorial and photographic touches (for example, tilted cameras to convey mental imbalance) may now seem cliched. But they weren't in 1935. And neither were the performances of a generally fine cast, working in extraordinary harmony for director Gregory La Cava. The distaff cast members, in particular, show to advantage, including Bennett, whose impressive mad scene raised her stock as a serious actress. Colbert's fine and sensitive acting earned her another Academy Award nomination, but the Oscar went to Bette Davis's unrestrained, flashier performance in *Dangerous*.

For the mid-Thirties, *Private Worlds* was admittedly a courageous groundbreaker in its genre, anticipating the psychological melodramas that would follow. But it would be thirteen years before a major studio, 20th Century-Fox, would take another chance on such hard-hitting drama, with *The Snake Pit*. Which says something for Hollywood's attitude toward serious social issues.

Joan Bennett and Claudette Colbert

Charles Boyer, Joel McCrea, and Claudette Colbert

Spring Byington, Bonita Granville, Frank Albertson, Eric
Linden, and Lionel Barrymore

Cecilia Parker and Eric Linden

AH, WILDERNESS!

1935

CREDITS

A Metro-Goldwyn-Mayer Picture. Directed by Clarence
Brown. *Produced by* Hunt Stromberg. *Screenplay by* Albert
Hackett *and* Frances Goodrich. *Based on the play by*
Eugene O'Neill. *Photographed by* Clyde De Vinna. *Edited
by* Frank E. Hull. *Art direction by* Cedric Gibbons *and*
William Horning. *Music by* Herbert Stothart. *Running
time: 101 minutes.*

CAST

Wallace Beery, *Sid Davis;* Lionel Barrymore, *Nat Miller;*
Aline MacMahon, *Lily Davis;* Eric Linden, *Richard Miller;*
Cecilia Parker, *Muriel McComber;* Spring Byington, *Essie
Miller;* Mickey Rooney, *Tommy Miller;* Charles Grapewin,
Mr. McComber; Frank Albertson, *Arthur Miller;* Edward
Nugent, *Wint Selby;* Bonita Granville, *Mildred Miller;*
Helen Flint, *Belle;* Helen Freeman, *Miss Hawley.*

Wallace Beery and Aline MacMahon

Ah, Wilderness! is totally uncharacteristic, in both spirit and subject matter, of the works of Eugene O'Neill, a playwright more often concerned with strong dramas of character and social criticism. But in this 1933 play, his only comedy, O'Neill etched a tender and affectionate portrait of a Connecticut family in 1906. "My purpose," he explained, "was to write a play true to the spirit of the American small town at the turn of the century . . . . It's the way I would have liked my boyhood to have been."

O'Neill is said to have written this wish-nostalgia excursion into Booth Tarkington country in a mere five weeks. With George M. Cohan as the family breadwinner, the play was an immediate hit, fostering a West Coast production with Will Rogers, who was to have repeated his stage role in MGM's movie version. But his sudden death in a 1935 plane crash necessitated his replacement by Lionel Barrymore.

In transferring O'Neill's play to the screen, producer Hunt Stromberg and the husband-and-wife writing team of Albert Hackett and Frances Goodrich shifted the emphasis somewhat from the father, Nat Miller, to his adolescent son Richard, thus affording twenty-five-year-old Eric Linden the best film role of his career. In the touching yet amusing scene in which Barrymore clumsily attempts to explain the "facts of life" to Linden, these actors are at their very best.

Ah, Wilderness! is episodic in structure, a character study of adolescence during one long-ago summer, as Richard struggles to reconcile his poetic nature with tendencies toward radicalism and emerging sexuality. Frustrated in his courtship of Muriel, whose father disapproves of the boy, Richard gets drunk and takes up with Belle, a tavern floozy, in the movie's amusing climax. The ending promises a happier future.

Clarence Brown, who had guided Greta Garbo through O'Neill's dramatic *Anna Christie,* directed, and the critics agreed that this was a felicitous wedding of production talent and ideal casting. In fact, only the top-billed Wallace Beery won disapproval, as the boozing Uncle Sid, for his overly broad display of familiar Beery tricks. But *Ah, Wilderness!* is a work of ensemble effort, and there are no "star turns" in this film. One and all have their moments, including Spring Byington's bustling mother, Aline Mac-Mahon's long-suffering Aunt Lily, Mickey Rooney's mischievous little brother, Cecilia Parker's pretty girl-next-door, and brattish sister Bonita Granville.

Ah, Wilderness! was joyously welcomed by 1935's Christmas moviegoing public. Thirteen years later, O'Neill's charming comedy would enjoy a delightful MGM-musical remake under the title *Summer Holiday.*

Eric Linden and Lionel Barrymore

Eric Linden and Helen Flint

Ronald Colman as Sydney Carton

A TALE OF TWO CITIES

1935

CREDITS

A Metro-Goldwyn-Mayer Picture. Produced by David O. Selznick. *Directed by* Jack Conway. *Revolutionary sequences directed by* Val Lewton *and* Jacques Tourneur. *Screenplay by* W. P. Lipscomb *and* S. N. Behrman. *Based on the novel by* Charles Dickens. *Photographed by* Oliver T. Marsh. *Edited by* Conrad A. Nervig. *Art direction by* Cedric Gibbons. *Music by* Herbert Stothart. *Costumes by* Dolly Tree. *Running time: 121 minutes.*

CAST

Ronald Colman, *Sydney Carton;* Elizabeth Allan, *Lucie Manette;* Edna May Oliver, *Miss Pross;* Blanche Yurka, *Mme. Defarge;* Reginald Owen, *Striver;* Basil Rathbone, *Marquis St. Evremonde;* Henry B. Walthall, *Dr. Manette;* Donald Woods, *Charles Darnay;* Walter Catlett, *Barsard;* Fritz Leiber, *Gaspard;* H. B. Warner, *Gabelle;* Mitchell Lewis, *Ernest Defarge;* Claude Gillingwater, *Jarvis Lorry;* Billy Bevan, *Jerry Cruncher;* Isabel Jewell, *Seamstress;* Lucile La Verne, *La Vengeance;* Tully Marshall, *Woodcutter;* Fay Chaldecott, *Lucie the daughter;* Eily Malyon, *Mrs. Cruncher;* E. E. Clive, *Judge in Old Bailey;* Lawrence Grant, *Prosecuting attorney in Old Bailey;* John Davidson, *Morveau;* Tom Ricketts, *Tellson, Jr.;* Donald Haines, *Jerry Cruncher, Jr.;* Ralph Harolde, *Prosecutor.*

Charles Dickens's stirring classic of seventeenth-century Paris and London and the events surrounding the French Revolution had already been brought to the silent screen on four separate occasions, twice each in Britain and the U.S., when David O. Selznick produced this definitive, painstaking adaptation for MGM. That company had scored a hit earlier in the year with Dickens's *David Copperfield*, and *A Tale of Two Cities*, released for Christmas 1935, displayed the Metro flair for literary classics with no expense spared—especially in the storming of the Bastille, a sequence filmed on one of Hollywood's largest sets ever, employing several thousand extras.

Jack Conway (in shirtsleeves) directs Reginald Owen, Ronald Colman, E. E. Clive, Edna May Oliver, Elizabeth Allan, Henry B. Walthall, and Claude Gillingwater on the Old Bailey set.

Fritz Leiber, Billy Bevan, Blanche Yurka, Lucille La Verne, Mitchell Lewis, and Donald Haines

Under Jack Conway's meticulous direction, *A Tale of Two Cities* offers memorable performances by a fine cast, including the marvelously hammy Blanche Yurka, vinegary Edna May Oliver, despicable Basil Rathbone, eloquent Henry B. Walthall, and, in a radical change of pace, Isabel Jewell, as the pathetic seamstress who accompanies Colman to the place of execution.

A Tale of Two Cities was remade by the British in 1958 and, for U.S. television, in 1980. But neither version could erase memories of their superior 1935 predecessor.

The film's top star, Ronald Colman, was initially reluctant to play the role of Sydney Carton, that charming but dissolute lawyer who commits the ultimate self-sacrifice when he trades places with the innocent aristocrat Charles Darnay (Donald Woods), en route to the guillotine. Colman balked at Selznick's original suggestion that he portray both Carton *and* Darnay (they resemble each other). But the actor was particularly opposed to tackling a role outside of his usual, debonair screen image, and it took great persuasion to make Colman shave off his trademark moustache for the movie. But once he had accepted these changes, the actor delivered perhaps his finest characterization in what he later declared was his favorite role.

Isabel Jewell, bit player, and Ronald Colman

*Herbert Marshall, Ann Harding, and
Margaret Lindsay*

THE LADY CONSENTS

1936

CREDITS

An RKO Picture. Produced by Edward Kaufman. *Directed by* Stephen Roberts. *Screenplay by* P. J. Wolfson *and* Anthony Veiller. *Based on the story The Indestructible Mrs. Talbot by* P. J. Wolfson. *Photographed by* J. Roy Hunt. *Art direction by* Van Nest Polglase. *Costumes by* Bernard Newman. *Running time: 76 minutes.*

CAST

Ann Harding, *Anne Talbot;* Herbert Marshall, *Dr. Michael Talbot;* Margaret Lindsay, *Jerry Mannerly;* Walter Abel, *Stanley Ashton;* Edward Ellis, *Jim Talbot;* Hobart Cavanaugh, *Yardley;* Ilka Chase, *Susan;* Paul Porcasi, *Joe;* Willie Best, *Sam;* Mary Gordon, *Apple lady.*

By late 1935, Ann Harding's Hollywood star had dimmed considerably, because of too many mediocre dramas like *The Right to Romance* and *The Flame Within.* *Enchanted April*'s stultifying efforts at comedy didn't help either. Unfortunately, not even Harding's fine performance in 1935's excellent *Peter Ibbetson* could stop her descent. To complete her RKO contract, she starred in *The Lady Consents,* a sophisticated comedy-drama, and finished with *The Witness Chair,* a sluggish courtroom mystery. Both were routine 1936 program pictures designed for the female audience that appeared most receptive to her warm, ladylike screen image.

The Lady Consents still holds up some forty-five years later, largely due to Stephen Roberts's sharp direction of a sophisticated, well-written P. J. Wolfson–Anthony Veiller screenplay. The basic story line concerns a middle-class doctor (Herbert Marshall) and his wife (Ann Harding), apparently wed happily for seven years, who are split apart by a predatory woman athlete (Margaret Lindsay). Wife then nobly steps aside for a divorce of the "civilized" variety, putting in an appearance at the wedding of ex-hubby and her rival. Commenting on all this from the sidelines is the doc's wryly observant father (Edward Ellis), who adores his

Walter Abel, Ann Harding, and Hobart Cavaugh

Herbert Marshall, Edward Ellis, and Ann Harding

ex-daughter-in-law and sees through the selfish pretensions of her successor. Ultimately, but tragically, he effects a reunion of doctor and first wife when he suffers a fatal accident that draws the couple back together.

Margaret Lindsay's "other woman" cleverly masks a ruthlessly self-deserving personality beneath a deceptively gracious, attractive facade, while the traditionally dull Herbert Marshall almost makes us sympathetic toward a rather stupid but likable man who is surely no match for either of his two wives. But Edward Ellis almost steals the picture with his scowling, cigar-chomping old codger, whom no phony emotion can fool. His deathbed scene's low-key power is as much a tribute to this fine character actor's ability as it is to Ann Harding's naturalistic, unmannered charm. The movie's only bigger-than-life performance is that of Ilka Chase, at her most obnoxiously obvious, as a gossipy "friend" to no one.

The Lady Consents represents movie-making of the most engaging sort, graced with wit and understatement and performed with the polish that somehow makes this woman's-magazine material interesting as well as credible.

Ann Harding, Herbert Marshall, and Edward Ellis

Charles Chaplin and Chester Conklin

Charles Chaplin and Sammy Stein

Charles Chaplin and Paulette Goddard

MODERN TIMES

1936

CREDITS

A United Artists release of a Charles Chaplin Production. Directed, written, and edited by Chaplin, *who also composed the music. Assistant directors:* Carter De Haven *and* Henry Bergman. *Photographed by* Rolland H. Totheroh *and* Ira Morgan. *Music direction by* Alfred Newman. *Running time: 89 minutes.*

CAST

Charles Chaplin, *A tramp;* Paulette Goddard, *A gamin;* Henry Bergman, *Cafe proprietor;* Chester Conklin, *Mechanic;* Stanley Sandford, *Big Bill;* Hank Mann and Louis Natheaux, *Assembly workers/Burglars;* Allen Garcia, *President of the steel company;* Murdock MacQuarrie, *J. Widdecombe Biddle;* Wilfred Lucas, *Juvenile officer;* Richard Alexander, *Tramp's cellmate;* Heinie Conklin and James C. Morton, *Assembly workers;* Lloyd Ingraham, *Diner;* Mira McKinney, *Minister's wife;* Walter James, *Assembly line foreman;* Sammy Stein, *Turbine operator;* Stanley Blystone, *Gamin's father;* Gloria De Haven, *Gamin's sister;* Fred Malatesta, *Waiter.*

Charles Chaplin, that prolific, brilliantly inventive tramp-clown of silent films, was given artistic pause by the advent of talking pictures. During the Thirties, Chaplin managed to produce only two motion pictures, 1931's *City Lights* and 1936's *Modern Times.* Each of these vintage comedy classics was long in the making—and both were silent (their soundtracks carried music and incidental sounds, but no synchronized spoken dialogue.)

Costing a then surprising $1.5 million, *Modern Times* enjoyed an unusually long shooting schedule (October 1934 to August 1935), after which Chaplin tinkered with the film for another five months. Some of the delay might be attributable to the filmmaker's careful grooming of his new leading lady, Paulette Goddard.

Paulette Goddard and Charles Chaplin

Prior to *Modern Times,* Goddard had played several feature film bits and had appeared in comedy shorts produced by Hal Roach. When she met Chaplin in 1932, she was a sophisticated, formerly married twenty-one and he a twice divorced forty-five. They soon became inseparable, as he took her under his wing, both personally and professionally. Chaplin bought up her Roach contract, announced that Goddard would costar in his next movie, and set about changing her image from hard-looking platinum blonde to charming, dark-haired ingenue. Decades later, a retired Paulette fondly spoke of Chaplin's "genius," recalling, "I loved working for him."

Modern Times is Charlie Chaplin's satiric comment on the machine age, embodied by his portrayal of a mild factory worker whose monotonous life style and assembly line job cause him to go berserk. The sentimental but episodic plot throws him into hospital, jail, and adventures with an impoverished teen-aged gamin (Goddard), culminating in their joint employment at a cheap cabaret, where she dances and he's a singing waiter (the only time Chaplin's voice is heard on the film's soundtrack). At fadeout, on the lam from juvenile-court authorities, the Little Tramp and his equally nameless girl trudge arm-in-arm into the sunset.

Modern Times drew mixed reviews in 1936. Not everyone understood its sociopolitical content—nor could they fathom Chaplin's wisdom in bringing forth a "silent" movie eight years into talkies. Its domestic engagements failed to earn *Modern Times* a profit.

Bing Crosby and Ethel Merman

ANYTHING GOES
(Tops Is the Limit)

1936

CREDITS

A Paramount Picture. Directed by Lewis Milestone. *Produced by* Benjamin Glazer. *Screenplay by* Howard Lindsay, Russel Crouse, Guy Bolton, *and* P. G. Wodehouse. *Photographed by* Karl Struss. *Edited by* Eda Warren. *Art direction by* Hans Dreier *and* Ernst Fegte. *Music and lyrics by* Cole Porter: *"Anything Goes," "You're the Top," "There'll Always Be a Lady Fair," and "I Get a Kick Out of You." Additional songs: "Moonburn" by* Hoagy Carmichael *and* Edward Heyman; *"Am I Awake?" "My Heart and I," "Hopelessly in Love," and "Shanghai-De-Ho" by* Frederick Hollander *and* Leo Robin; *"Sailor Beware" by* Richard Whiting *and* Leo Robin. *Running time: 92 minutes.*

CAST

Bing Crosby, *Billy Crocker;* Ethel Merman, *Reno Sweeney;* Charles Ruggles, *Rev. Dr. Moon/Moonface Martin;* Ida Lupino, *Hope Harcourt;* Grace Bradley, *Bonnie Le Tour;* Arthur Treacher, *Sir Evelyn Oakleigh;* Robert McWade, *Elisha J. Whitney;* Richard Carle, *Bishop Dodson;* Margaret Dumont, *Mrs. Wentworth;* Jerry Tucker, *Junior;* Edward Gargan, *Detective;* Matt Moore, *Ship's captain.*

Cole Porter's witty 1934 shipboard musical introduced to Broadway such timeless Porter standards as "You're the Top" and "I Get a Kick Out of You," performed by a cast starring Ethel Merman, William Gaxton, and Victor Moore. In 1936, *Anything Goes* reached the screen with Bing Crosby in the Gaxton part, Charles Ruggles replacing Moore, and Ethel Merman repeating her original role of nightclub singer Reno Sweeney. Characteristically, Paramount chose to retain only part of Porter's catchy score, substituting new songs that added little. The screenplay remained quite faithful to the Broadway version, with Crosby stowing aboard an ocean liner in pursuit of runaway English heiress Ida Lupino. He, in turn, is pursued by nightclub singer Merman. The trivial plot is heavy with mistaken-identity gimmicks and romantic misunderstandings, while a subplot offers Ruggles as the comic gangster Moonface Martin, here masquerading as a cleric oddly known as the Reverend Dr. Moon!

From a memorable Broadway show, this first movie version of *Anything Goes* remains little more thant pleasant, a typical Thirties vehicle for the blandly amiable singing talents of Bing Crosby and the dynamic trumpeting voice of Ethel Merman (somehow always better on stage than in films). It's amusing entertainment, but it should have been a more dynamic motion picture. Perhaps part of the fault lies with director Lewis Milestone, an odd selection for a musical comedy, since his most successful previous movies included such serious-themed dramas as *All Quiet on the Western Front, The Front Page,* and *Rain.*

Surprisingly vital for her routine ingenue role, teen-aged Ida Lupino—still several years away from recognition as a serious dramatic actress—is required to do little except register adoration while Crosby vocalizes. But during one of his numbers, "My Heart and I," an unusual thing happens: the camera lingers longer on ingenue Lupino's face than on big-star Crosby's—because, unlike the average pretty girl being sung to in a movie, this young lady is listening with interest and actually *reacting* to the lyrics.

In 1956, Paramount remade *Anything Goes,* again with Crosby, but with a much-altered screenplay. To avoid confusion on television, the 1936 film was meaninglessly retitled *Tops Is the Limit.*

Bing Crosby and Ethel Merman in the "Shanghai-De-Ho" production number

Ida Lupino and Bing Crosby

Ethel Merman, Arthur Treacher, and Charles Ruggles

ville, *Mary Tilford;* Marcia Mae Jones, *Rosalie Wells;* Carmencita Johnson, *Evelyn;* Mary Ann Durkin, *Joyce Walton;* Margaret Hamilton, *Agatha;* Marie Louise Cooper, *Helen Burton;* Walter Brennan, *Taxi driver.*

Lillian Hellman's powerful first play, *The Children's Hour,* had proved the sensation of the 1934–35 New York season. Set in a girls' school run by two young, unmarried women, the plot is set in motion by a spiteful student who maliciously spreads an unsupported rumor that the school's administrators are lesbian lovers. Her lie causes the closing of the school, a sensational libel case, and, finally, one teacher's suicide. Based on an early-nineteenth-century Scottish court scandal, the play struck Broadway like a thunderbolt, impressing the critics and playing to enthusiastic crowds for 691 performances.

Hays office watchdogs strongly disapproved, but producer Samuel Goldwyn paid $50,000 for the movie rights to Hellman's powerful drama, with the stipulation that he could use neither the play's title nor its plot. All Hollywood thought Goldwyn was demented, but that master showman proved not so dumb by employing Lillian Hellman, who turned out a strong screenplay (retitled *These Three*) that, while obfuscating the sexual aspects of her stage play to suggest *heterosexual* intrigue, nevertheless maintained its original thesis—the *power,* not the nature, of a lie.

Under William Wyler's superb direction (the first of his eight films for Goldwyn), Miriam Hopkins and Merle Oberon, as the two slandered teachers, gave what many consider the performances of their careers. Critic Graham Greene wrote: "I have seldom been so moved by any fictional film as by *These Three*. The more than human evil of the lying, sadistic child is suggested with quite shocking mastery by Bonita Granville."

In *The New York Times,* Frank S. Nugent called it, "one of the finest screen dramas in recent years." With praise for all concerned, he singled out Bonita and Marcia Mae Jones, who played her schoolgirl disciple. Nor could Hollywood overlook the malevolent power of Granville's performance, which won her an Oscar nomination as Best Supporting Actress (Gale Sondergaard was the winner for *Anthony Adverse*). *These Three* established Granville's career as a film brat, but the parallel role in Wyler's 1962 Audrey Hepburn–Shirley MacLaine remake (now allowed to be called *The Children's Hour* and tackle the play's original issues squarely) did nothing for strident, twelve-year-old Karen Balkin.

Goldwyn opted for a gratuitous "happy" ending that had Merle Oberon and her doctor-fiance, Joel McCrea, reunited in Vienna. But, because of Wyler's deft handling, this denouement never quite spoils what has gone before. *These Three* remains among Hollywood's best dramatic films of the Thirties.

Margaret Hamilton, Bonita Granville, and Alma Kruger

THESE THREE

1936

CREDITS

A United Artists release of a Samuel Goldwyn Production. Directed by William Wyler. *Screenplay by* Lillian Hellman, *based on her play The Children's Hour. Photographed by* Gregg Toland. *Edited by* Daniel Mandell. *Art direction by* Richard Day. *Costumes by* Omar Kiam. *Music by* Alfred Newman. *Running time: 93 minutes.*

CAST

Miriam Hopkins, *Martha Dobie;* Merle Oberon, *Karen Wright;* Joel McCrea, *Dr. Joseph Cardin;* Catherine Doucet, *Mrs. Lily Mortar;* Alma Kruger, *Mrs. Tilford;* Bonita Gran-

Marcia Mae Jones, Alma Kruger, Bonita Granville, Merle Oberon, and Miriam Hopkins

Merle Oberon and Miriam Hopkins

Allan Jones and Irene Dunne sing "Make Believe."

SHOW BOAT

1936

CREDITS

A Universal Picture. Directed by James Whale. *Produced by* Carl Laemmle, Jr. *Screenplay and songs by* Oscar Hammerstein II *and* Jerome Kern. *Based on their stage musical and the novel by* Edna Ferber. *Photographed by* John J. Mescall *and* John P. Fulton. *Edited by* Ted Kent *and* Bernard Burton. *Art direction by* Charles D. Hall. *Musical direction by* Victor Baravelle. *Musical arrangements by* Robert Russell Bennett. *Dance direction by* LeRoy Prinz. *Songs:* "Cotton Blossom," "Cap'n Andy's Ballyhoo," "Where's the Mate for Me?" "Make Believe," "Ol' Man River," "Can't Help Lovin' Dat Man," "I Have the Room Above Her," "Gallivantin' Around," "You Are Love," "Ah Still Suits Me," "Bill," "Good-Bye, Ma Lady Love," *and* "After the Ball." *Costumes by* Doris Zinkeisen *and* Vera West. *Running time: 110 minutes.*

CAST

Irene Dunne, *Magnolia Hawks;* Allan Jones, *Gaylord Ravenal;* Charles Winninger, *Cap'n Andy Hawks;* Paul Robeson, *Joe;* Helen Morgan, *Julie;* Helen Westley, *Parthy Ann Hawks;* Queenie Smith; *Ellie;* Sammy White, *Frank;* Donald Cook, *Steve;* Hattie McDaniel, *Queenie;* Francis X. Mahoney, *Rubber Face;* Marilyn Knowlden, *Kim as a child;* Sunnie O'Dea, *Kim at sixteen;* Arthur Hohl, *Pete;* Charles Middleton, *Vallon;* J. Farrell MacDonald, *Windy;* Clarence Muse, *Sam;* Charles Wilson, *Jim;* Patricia Barry, *Kim as a baby;* Stanley Fields, *Backwoodsman;* Stanley J. "Tiny" Sandford, *Zebe;* May Beatty, *Landlady;* Dorothy Granger, Barbara Pepper, *and* Renee Whitney, *Chorus girls;* Forrest Stanley, *Theater manager;* Selmer Jackson, *Hotel clerk;* Ernest Hilliard, Jack Mulhall, *and* Brooks Benedict, *Race fans;* Elspeth Dudgeon, *Mother Superior;* E. E. Clive, *Englishman;* Helen Jerome Eddy, *Reporter;* Don Briggs, *Press agent;* Eddie "Rochester" Anderson, *Young Negro;* LeRoy Prinz, *Dance director.*

Francis X. Mahoney, Queenie Smith, Sammy White, Donald Cook, Irene Dunne, Charles Winninger, Helen Morgan, and Helen Westley

Paul Robeson, Hattie McDaniel, Sammy White, Irene Dunne, and Charles Winninger

Helen Morgan and Irene Dunne

Allan Jones, Helen Westley, Charles Winninger, Forrest Stanley, and Irene Dunne

With its immortal Jerome Kern–Oscar Hammerstein II score, *Show Boat,* based on Edna Ferber's 1926 novel, thrilled Broadway audiences a year later, and has reached the screen on three separate occasions. Its 1929 Universal version was only a partial talkie that adhered more closely to Ferber's sobering plot than its successors. In 1936 Universal's generation-spanning remake reached the screen with a cast chiefly composed of singing actors who had already performed it on various stages. And, in 1951, MGM gave it the full-fledged Technicolor treatment in the Kathryn Grayson–Howard Keel–Ava Gardner version most frequently seen today.

But its best incarnation, in the estimation of film buffs, critics, and historians, is the one released in 1936 with an incomparable cast topped by Irene Dunne, Allan Jones, Charles Winninger, Paul Robeson, and the unforgettable Helen Morgan. Universal made it their big film of that year, re-creating the nineteenth-century Mississippi River towns and that paddle-wheeled, floating theater on their backlot. Oddly enough, James Whale, an Englishman who had never directed a musical and was best known for his horror movies (*Frankenstein, The Old Dark House*), was chosen to direct. But few had reservations about the final results; the movie was immensely popular with both press and audiences. And, with one exception, all of *Show Boat*'s unforgettable, enduring melodies are included. That exception, the lilting duet "Why Do I Love You?" was filmed but deleted just before the movie's release to shorten what Universal considered an overlong running time. Cut to a rich 110 minutes, this near-definitive *Show Boat* became one of the year's top moneymakers.

THE GENERAL
DIED AT DAWN

1936

Madeleine Carroll, Dudley Digges, Gary Cooper, and J. M. Kerrigan

Madeleine Carroll and Gary Cooper

Akim Tamiroff and Gary Cooper

CREDITS

A Paramount Picture. Directed by Lewis Milestone.
Produced by William Le Baron. *Screenplay by* Clifford
Odets. *Based on an unpublished novel by* Charles G. Booth.
Photographed by Victor Milner. *Edited by* Eda Warren. *Art
direction by* Hans Dreier *and* Ernst Fegte. *Music by* Werner
Janssen. *Costumes by* Travis Banton. *Running time: 97
minutes.*

CAST

Gary Cooper, *O'Hara;* Madeleine Carroll, *Judy Perrie;* Akim
Tamiroff, *General Yang;* Dudley Digges, *Mr. Wu;* Porter
Hall, *Peter Perrie;* William Frawley, *Brighton;* J. M. Ker-
rigan, *Leach;* Philip Ahn, *Oxford;* Lee Tung Foo, *Mr. Chen;*
Leonid Kinskey, *Stewart;* Van Duran, *Wong;* Willie Fung,
Bartender; Hans Fuerberg, *Yang's military adviser;* Sarah
Edwards and Paul Harvey, *American couple;* Spencer Chan,
Killer; Barnett Parker, *Englishman;* Clifford Odets, John
O'Hara, Sidney Skolsky, and Lewis Milestone, *Reporters.*

In the Thirties, the patrician loveliness of British-born
Madeleine Carroll frequently caused her to be known as
Hollywood's most beautiful blonde. But her many bland
roles in forgettable pictures often left only the vivid memory
of that matchless glamour. Among the few exceptions were
Alfred Hitchcock's British-made *The Thirty-Nine Steps* and
Lewis Milestone's *The General Died at Dawn*—both times
as young women of some mystery who, it turns out, are not
quite what they seem.

The General Died at Dawn, based on an unpublished
work of pulp fiction by Charles G. Booth, represents the
first Hollywood work of controversial, proletarian Broadway
playwright Clifford Odets, whose efforts to make this script
politically significant were somewhat mitigated during production. The result is an interesting, occasionally slow-
moving melodrama bearing inescapable similarities to Josef
von Sternberg's 1932 *Shanghai Express.* It was especially
evident in the moody, artfully lit cinematography of Victor
Milner, who won an Academy Award nomination for this
movie.

Like the von Sternberg film, *The General Died at Dawn* is
rife with intrigue and the conflict between Oriental cunning
versus Occidental courage. Its hero (Gary Cooper) is a drifting champion of the social underdog who accepts a com-
mission to smuggle gold so that Chinese peasants can buy
ammunition to fight a tyrannical warlord (Akim Tamiroff, in
an Oscar-nominated performance). But Cooper is lured into
a trap set by the general, with the cooperation of Carroll
and her self-serving father (Porter Hall). At the exciting
climax of a thick and tenuous plot, the protagonists are
hostages aboard Tamiroff's junk, in danger of imminent execution. But, in a duel of wits with the stabbed and dying
Tamiroff, Cooper secures freedom for himself and Carroll
by persuading the weakening tyrant that the world can
never know of his greatness unless *they* are freed to spread
the word of his "noble" demise.

Lewis Milestone was not particularly proud of this film,
deferring credit to its cast and technicians. But, granted the
dated aspects of its script, *The General Died at Dawn* still
holds interest as an entertaining example of exotic mid-
Thirties melodrama.

Gail Patrick, Ernie Adams, Alice Brady, Carole Lombard, and William Powell

MY MAN GODFREY

1936

CREDITS

A Universal Picture. Produced and directed by Gregory La Cava. *Screenplay by* La Cava, Morrie Ryskind, *and* Eric Hatch. *Based on a story by* Hatch. *Photographed by* Ted Tetzlaff. *Edited by* Ted Kent. *Art direction by* Charles D. Hall. *Music direction by* Charles Previn. *Running time: 95 minutes.*

CAST

William Powell, *Godfrey Smith;* Carole Lombard, *Irene Bullock;* Alice Brady, *Angelica Bullock;* Eugene Pallette, *Alexander Bullock;* Gail Patrick, *Cornelia Bullock;* Alan Mowbray, *Tommy Gray;* Jean Dixon, *Molly;* Mischa Auer, *Carlo;* Robert Light, *George;* Pat Flaherty, *Mike;* Robert Perry, *Hobo;* Franklin Pangborn, *Scorekeeper;* Selmer Jackson, *Blake;* Ernie Adams, *Forgotten man;* Phyllis Crane, *Party guest;* Grady Sutton, *Von Ronkel;* Jack Chefe,

Headwaiter; Eddie Fetherston, *Process server;* Edward Gargan and James Flavin, *Detectives;* Art Singley, *Chauffeur;* Reginald Mason, *Mayor;* Bess Flowers, *Mrs. Meriwether;* Jane Wyman, *Girl at party.*

Jean Dixon and William Powell

171

William Powell, Eugene Pallette, Carole Lombard, Alice Brady, Gail Patrick, and Edward Gargan

Carole Lombard and William Powell

Between the opening credits of *My Man Godfrey* and its traditional boy-gets-girl conclusion, this typically mid-Thirties "screwball" comedy exposes the mindless artificiality of some Fifth Avenue socialites with sparkling verve and wit. The wit derives from a well-crafted screenplay by Morrie Ryskind, Eric Hatch, and Gregory La Cava, and the verve is easily attributable to the inspired guidance of comedy expert La Cava, a director known for his penchant for improvisation. And, in this whimsical tale of a well-born down-and-out who's engaged as butler for a family of wealthy loonies (whom he later saves from financial ruin), the fun lies in the development of character as the Bullock clan's fortunes change for the worse and they learn a few lessons in humanity.

As in most such escapades, this wacky social farce relies on the comic expertise of its cast. In the title role, William Powell is completely at home with Godfrey Smith's wry humor and unflappable reactions to the unpredictable chaos all around him. Carole Lombard, as a heroine less vivid than in 1934's *Twentieth Century* or 1937's *Nothing Sacred,* is as zany as she is beautiful. But her calculating on-screen sister, Gail Patrick, frequently manages to steal the scenes they share and ultimately leaves the more indelible impression. As their mother, Alice Brady once again portrays a fluttering, falsetto-voiced flibbertigibbet with scattered brains and inane dialogue ("If you're going to be rude to my daughter, you might as well at least take your hat off"). But because of a superior script, she never becomes the irritant that she did in *The Gay Divorcee* two years earlier. Basement-voiced Eugene Pallette, as the Bullocks' failing breadwinner, is, as always, inimitble, while Mischa Auer's ape-mimicking Brady protege almost makes the nuttiest of the clan look sane. And, finally, mention must be made of the marvelous Jean Dixon, with her exquisite comic timing, as Molly the all-wise household maid—a role too brief for her talents.

Despite its immense popularity and six nominations, *My Man Godfrey* won no Oscars for 1936. But it fostered inferior imitations like 1938's *Merrily We Live* and an uninspired 1957 *Godfrey* remake with David Niven and June Allyson.

Ruth Chatterton and Walter Huston

DODSWORTH

1936

CREDITS

A United Artists release of a Samuel Goldwyn Production. Directed by William Wyler. *Associate producer:* Merritt Hulburd. *Screenplay by* Sidney Howard, *based on his stage play and the novel by* Sinclair Lewis. *Photographed by* Rudolph Maté. *Edited by* Daniel Mandell. *Art direction by* Richard Day. *Music by* Alfred Newman. *Costumes by* Omar Kiam. *Running time: 90 minutes.*

CAST

Walter Huston, *Sam Dodsworth;* Ruth Chatterton, *Fran Dodsworth;* Paul Lukas, *Arnold Iselin;* Mary Astor, *Edith Cortright;* David Niven, *Capt. Clyde Lockert;* Gregory Gaye, *Baron Kurt von Obersdorf;* Maria Ouspenskaya, *Baroness von Obersdorf;* Odette Myrtil, *Mme. Renée de Penable;* Kathryn Marlowe, *Emily McKee;* John Howard Payne, *Harry McKee;* Spring Byington, *Matey Pearson;* Harlan Briggs, *Tubby Pearson;* Charles Halton, *Hazzard;* Gino Corrado, *American Express clerk;* Ines Palange, *Edith's housekeeper.*

Mary Astor and Walter Huston

Ruth Chatterton and Maria Ouspenskaya

Taste and integrity enabled independent producer Samuel Goldwyn to continue, year after year, bringing fine entertainment to the moviegoing public. *Dodsworth*, based on Sidney Howard's stage adaptation of the 1929 Sinclair Lewis novel, could not possibly have seemed a hot box-office prospect to Goldwyn, dealing as it did with middle-age marital problems. But the master showman came up with an excellent and critically lauded motion picture, because he hired the best available actors and technicians and because he brought Lewis's book to the screen without compromise.

Director William Wyler drew great performances from a uniformly fine cast, headed by Walter Huston (re-creating his successful 1934 Broadway role), waning Ruth Chatterton (in her last Hollywood film), and the charming Mary Astor, then suffering the notoriety of a marital scandal. Paul Lukas and David Niven led a distinguished supporting cast, highlighted by the scene-stealing movie debut of stage actress and drama teacher Maria Ouspenskaya, who made the most of one telling scene.

Dodsworth's bittersweet plot centers on a Midwestern auto manufacturer and his self-centered wife. Fran Dodsworth has engineered his factory's sale to suit her fear-of-aging restlessness, and it is Sam's love for her that makes him agree to retire so that they can travel in Europe. Subsequently, Fran indulges in covert flirtations with adventurers, encouraging Sam to go home without her. Later, he returns to Europe to find her in love with a baron and eager for a divorce. Despondent, Sam travels to Italy, where he runs into expatriate Edith Cortright (Astor), a charming widow he first encountered aboard ship. Together, Sam and Edith appear to have found solace for their mutual loneliness.

Dodsworth drew excellent notices for nearly everyone concerned and aided the faltering film careers of Astor and Huston, who won that year's Best Actor nod from the New York Film Critics. But his performance drew only a nomination from the motion picture Academy, whose only *Dodsworth* Oscar went to art director Richard Day. Among the film's other nominations; Best Picture, director Wyler, supporting actress Ouspenskaya, screenwriter Sidney Howard, and sound technician Oscar Lagerstrom.

Walter Huston and Mary Astor

BORN TO DANCE

1936

CREDITS

A Metro-Goldwyn-Mayer Picture. Directed by Roy Del Ruth. *Produced by* Jack Cummings. *Screenplay by* Jack McGowan *and* Sid Silvers. *Based on an original story by* McGowan, Silvers, *and* B. G. "Buddy" De Sylva. *Photographed by* Ray June. *Edited by* Blanche Sewell. *Dances by* Dave Gould. *Musical direction by* Alfred Newman. *Music and lyrics by* Cole Porter. *Songs:* "Rolling Home," "Rap-Tap on Wood," "Hey, Babe, Hey," "I'm Nuts About You," "Love Me, Love My Pekinese," "Easy to Love," "I've Got You Under My Skin," *and* "Swingin' the Jinx Away." *Running time: 108 minutes.*

CAST

Eleanor Powell, *Nora Paige;* James Stewart, *Ted Barker;* Virginia Bruce, *Lucy James;* Una Merkel, *Jenny Saks;* Sid Silvers, *Gunny Saks;* Frances Langford, *Peppy Turner;* Raymond Walburn, *Capt. Dingby;* Alan Dinehart, *McKay;* Buddy Ebsen, *Mush Tracy;* Juanita Quigley, *Sally Saks;* Reginald Gardiner, *Policeman;* Georges and Jalna, *Themselves;* Barnett Parker, *Floorwalker;* Helen Troy, *Phone girl;* and The Foursome, *J. Marshall Smith, L. Dwight Snyder, Ray Johnson, Del Porter;* Bud Flanagan/Dennis O'Keefe, *Bit player.*

Eleanor Powell and James Stewart

Buddy Ebsen, Frances Langford, Eleanor Powell, James Stewart, Sid Silvers, and Una Merkel

Eleanor Powell's flashing legs and machine-gun tapping feet were to late-Thirties MGM musicals what Ann Miller's were to Metro films of the late Forties and Fifties. And, while her tap-dancing Warner Bros. counterpart, Ruby Keeler, displayed a winning personality and somewhat klutzy talent, Powell's terpsichorean professionalism, perfect balance, and acrobatic skills made her one of the finest fast-stepping hoofers ever to grace the American screen.

Born to Dance, her third movie, gave her top billing, an unlikely song-and-dance costar in gangling Jimmy Stewart, and an absolute knockout of a production number to Cole Porter's "Swingin' the Jinx Away," in which spangled showgirls fraternize with sailors on the deck of a grandiose ship only Hollywood could construct. That finale, which understandably continues to draw enthusiastic applause in movie-revival theaters, garnered an Oscar nomination for its choreographer, Dave Gould.

But the film is more than just a vehicle for Eleanor Powell's educated feet and sparkling smile. It's also a fast-moving package of songs, comedy, silly romantic cliches, and specialty turns like Reginald Gardiner's pantomimic "orchestra conducting," Buddy Ebsen's humorously eccentric dancing, and Barnett Parker's gay-decorator monologue in a gratuitous honeymoon-cottage sequence. With a large and talented cast of singers, dancers, and comedians, director Roy Del Ruth carries this potentially cumbersome enterprise like a master juggler, with an original Cole Porter score as the icing on the cake. Of the seven songs here introduced, two of them ("Easy to Love," rendered by the game but untrained tenor of Jimmy Stewart, and "I've Got You Under My Skin," smoothly sung by Virginia Bruce) have become standard favorites.

With comedy experts like the screenplay's coauthor Sid Silvers, Una Merkel, and Raymond Walburn, *Born to Dance* constantly amuses its audience. But it is that dynamic demon-on-taps, Eleanor Powell, with her charming grin and striking physique, that lingers in the Porter-tuned memory.

Rosalind Russell as Harriet Craig

CRAIG'S WIFE

1936

CREDITS

A Columbia Picture. Directed by Dorothy Arzner. *Produced by* Edward Chodorov. *Screenplay by* Mary C. McCall, Jr. *Based on the play by* George Kelly. *Photographed by* Lucien Ballard. *Edited by* Viola Lawrence. *Running time: 75 minutes.*

CAST

Rosalind Russell, *Harriet Craig;* John Boles, *Walter Craig;* Billie Burke, *Mrs. Frazier;* Jane Darwell, *Mrs. Harold;* Dorothy Wilson, *Ethel Landreth;* Alma Kruger, *Miss Austen;* Thomas Mitchell, *Fergus Passmore;* Raymond Walburn, *Billy Birkmire;* Robert Allen, *Gene Fredricks;* Elisabeth Risdon, *Mrs. Landreth;* Nydia Westman, *Mazie;* Kathleen Burke, *Adelaide Passmore;* Frankie Vann, *Cab driver.*

Rosalind Russell was under contract to MGM, where she had played a succession of crisply intelligent "other woman" roles in A pictures and leading ladies in a few B's, when she was chosen by director Dorothy Arzner for Columbia's remake of *Craig's Wife.* George Kelly's 1925 play was an incisive study of a dominating, self-absorbed woman who treasures her home above husband, family, and friends. A thoroughly disagreeable shrew, Harriet Craig manages to drive one and all from her house—and her life—before the drama's denouement. "People who live to themselves are generally left to themselves," theorized playwright Kelly.

On Broadway, *Craig's Wife* ran for 360 performances and won a Pulitzer Prize. In 1928, it reached the silent screen, starring Irene Rich and Warner Baxter. For its second screen incarnation, Columbia Pictures boss Harry Cohn wisely entrusted this "women's picture" to the capable Dorothy Arzner, then Hollywood's only important woman director. With women in charge of both script (Mary C. McCall, Jr.) and editing (Viola Lawrence), Arzner was assured of a certain consistency of viewpoint. But George Kelly was not pleased that she elected to "distort" his play by presenting the henpecked Walter Craig as mother-dominated.

Craig's Wife could not have seemed like a hot box-office

Alma Kruger and Rosalind Russell

Jane Darwell, John Boles, and Rosalind Russell

prospect in 1936. But Arzner convinced Cohn by assuring him that she could turn out "an A picture for B-picture money." And so she did, operating on a four-week shooting schedule and a budget of $280,000. The film gave a prestigious boost to Rosalind Russell's career. At twenty-eight, the actress was really too young for the part (Joan Crawford was all of forty-six when she starred in Columbia's 1950 third version, *Harriet Craig*). But Russell's height, regal bearing, and natural sophistication enabled her to be convincing as a woman of maturity. Arzner's reason for choosing Russell was that she "did not want an actress the audience loved." And it's to Rosalind Russell's credit that her Harriet Craig is a woman not even a *mother* could love as she dominates the film with what *The New York Times*'s Frank S. Nugent accurately termed "a viciously eloquent performance." In supporting roles, words of praise must be added for the professional expertise of blandly handsome John Boles's husband, of motherly Jane Darwell's faithful housekeeper, of Billie Burke's friendly neighbor, and of Alma Kruger's all-too-knowing aunt. But, under Arzner's firm hand, *Craig's Wife* is really Rosalind Russell's movie all the way.

Rosalind Russell, Dorothy Wilson, and Frankie Vann

Jean Arthur and Gary Cooper

Porter Hall, Gary Cooper, Fred Kohler

THE PLAINSMAN

1937

CREDITS

A Paramount Picture. Produced and directed by Cecil B. De Mille. *Associate producer:* William H. Pine. *Screenplay by* Waldemar Young, Harold Lamb, *and* Lynn Riggs. *Adapted by* Jeanie McPherson *from information in the stories "Wild Bill Hickok" by* Frank J. Wilstach *and "The Prince of Pistoleers" by* Courtney Ryley Cooper *and* Grover Jones. *Photographed by* Victor Milner *and* George Robinson. *Edited by* Anne Bauchens. *Art direction by* Hans Dreier *and* Roland Anderson. *Set decoration by* A. E. Freudenman. *Music by* George Antheil. *Costumes by* Natalie Visart, Dwight Franklin, *and* Joe De Young. *Special camera effects by* Gordon Jennings, Farciot Edouart, *and* Dewey Wrigley. *Running time: 115 minutes.*

CAST

Gary Cooper, *Wild Bill Hickok;* Jean Arthur, *Calamity Jane;* James Ellison, *Buffalo Bill Cody;* Charles Bickford, *John Latimer;* Porter Hall, *Jack McCall;* Helen Burgess, *Louisa Cody;* John Miljan, *Gen. George Armstrong Custer;* Victor Varconi, *Painted Horse;* Paul Harvey, *Chief Yellow Hand;* Frank McGlynn, Sr., *Abraham Lincoln;* Granville Bates, *Van Ellyn;* Purnell Pratt, *Capt. Wood;* Pat Moriarty *Sgt. McGinnis;* Charles Judels, *Tony the barber;* Anthony Quinn, *Cheyenne warrior;* George MacQuarrie, *Gen. Merritt;* George "Gabby" Hayes, *Breezy;* Fuzzy Knight, *Dave;* George Ernest, *Urchin;* Fred Kohler, *Jack;* Frank Albertson, *Young soldier;* Harry Woods, *Quartermaster sergeant;* Francis McDonald, *Gambler on boat;* Francis Ford, *Veteran;* Irving Bacon, *Soldier;* Edgar Dearing, *Custer's messenger;* Edwin Maxwell, *Stanton;* Charlie Stevens, *Injun Charlie;* Arthur Aylesworth, Douglas Wood, *and* George Cleveland, *Van Ellyn's associates;* Lona Andre, *Southern belle;* Leila McIntyre, *Mary Todd Lincoln.*

Hollywood's unparalleled master showman Cecil B. De Mille spent much of his forty-three-year career producing and directing spectacular films with historical, Biblical, or Western themes. His *Cleopatra* (1934) offered Claudette Colbert in an eye-filling extravaganza of great popularity, followed by *The Crusades* (1935), an epic failure that lost more than $700,000.

Helen Burgess, Gary Cooper, Jean Arthur, and James Ellison

Cooper and Arthur had just scored a great success of another kind in Frank Capra's 1936 comedy *Mr. Deeds Goes to Town*. But in this Western setting, Cooper loses his characteristic awkwardness, and Arthur responds enthusiastically to boots, trousers, and a man-taming bullwhip with aplomb—although De Mille presents her as a far too glamorous Calamity Jane, with lipstick, mascaraed eyelids, and perfect grooming, despite her masculine attire. But it's all in line with De Mille's epic view of history, recycled in the name of entertainment. Replete with sterotyped Hollywood Indians (1200 Montana Cheyennes were employed) and sentimentalized distortion of fact, *The Plainsman* remains as stirring and entertaining today as it was forty-five years ago, an inferior 1966 remake notwithstanding.

The Plainsman, representing something of a "comeback" for De Mille, was a frank distortion of historical facts surrounding the Western legends of Wild Bill Hickok, Calamity Jane, and Buffalo Bill Cody. Faithful biography was never De Mille's intent. Instead, he chose to synthesize the romance and adventure of pioneer America, serving up the results in a stirring blend of folklore and movie-star glamour that restored his movies to popularity and reinforced the public appeal of Gary Cooper and Jean Arthur.

Jean Arthur as Calamity Jane

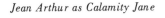

Ginger Rogers, Constance Collier, and Katharine Hepburn

STAGE DOOR

1937

CREDITS

An RKO Radio Picture. Directed by Gregory La Cava. *Produced by* Pandro S. Berman. *Screenplay by* Morrie Ryskind, Anthony Veiller, *and (uncredited)* La Cava. *Based on the play by* Edna Ferber *and* George S. Kaufman. *Photographed by* Robert De Grasse. *Edited by* William Hamilton. *Art direction by* Van Nest Polglase *and* Carroll Clark. *Set decoration by* Darrell Silvera. *Music by* Roy Webb. *Song: "Put Your Heart Into Your Feet and Dance" by* Hal Borne *and* Mort Greene. *Costumes by* Muriel King. *Running time: 92 minutes.*

Ginger Rogers and Lucille Ball

CAST

Katharine Hepburn, *Terry Randall;* Ginger Rogers, *Jean Maitland;* Adolphe Menjou, *Anthony Powell;* Gail Patrick, *Linda Shaw;* Constance Collier, *Catherine Luther;* Andrea Leeds, *Kaye Hamilton;* Samuel S. Hinds, *Henry Sims;* Lucille Ball, *Judy Canfield;* Pierre Watkin, *Richard Carmichael;* Franklin Pangborn, *Harcourt;* Elizabeth Dunne, *Mrs. Orcutt;* Phyllis Kennedy, *Hattie;* Grady Sutton, *Butcher;* Jack Carson, *Milbank;* Fred Santley, *Dunkenfield;* William Corson, *Bill;* Frank Reicher, *Stage director;* Eve Arden, *Eve;* Ann Miller, *Annie;* Jan Rhodes, *Ann Braddock;* Margaret Early, *Mary;* Jean Rouverol, *Dizzy;* Norma Drury, *Olga Brent;* Peggy O'Donnell, *Susan;* Harriett Brandon, *Madeline;* Katherine Alexander, Ralph Forbes, Mary Forbes, and Huntley Gordon, *Cast of play.*

For half a century, the unique Katharine Hepburn has been offering arresting performances on the screen, and one of her best was as the smug society girl determined to barge her way into a Broadway acting career in *Stage Door.* Originally a New York theatrical hit of 1936 with Margaret Sullavan, this Edna Ferber–George S. Kaufman comedy-drama about theatrical hopefuls in a Manhattan boardinghouse was extensively reworked for the movies—so much so that Kaufman quipped, "It should be called *Screen Door.*" But the team of Morrie Ryskind and Anthony Veiller (with uncredited help from director Gregory La Cava and a characteristically meddlesome Hepburn) turned a mediocre stage work into a sparkling screenplay. Its use of naturalistic, overlapping theater-talk is partially explained by actress Andrea Leeds: "La Cava had all of us girls in the movie come to the studio for two weeks before the shooting started and live as though we were in the lodging house itself. He had a script girl take down our conversations and he would adapt these into dialogue."

The movie's climax is a sure-fire tear-jerker: Hepburn learns, on opening night of her first Broadway lead, that her boardinghouse friend (Leeds) has killed herself in despair. She then plays the role with more feeling than she'd ever shown at rehearsals, scores a triumph, and delivers a humble curtain speech that moves her audience to tears: "The person you should be applauding died a few hours ago. I hope that wherever she is she knows and understands and forgives."

Hepburn had suffered a spate of unsuccessful costume pictures which even her fine performance in 1935's *Alice Adams* had scarcely alleviated, and her popularity had

Katharine Hepburn as Terry Randall

Ginger Rogers, Katharine Hepburn, and Adolphe Menjou

declined. So RKO producer Pandro Berman worked closely with his star, his director, and the screenwriters to make sure that everything about *Stage Door* was just right. Produced at a cost of $900,000, it opened at New York's prestigious Radio City Music Hall and was an immediate success, eventually grossing over $2 million. *Stage Door* went on to win the New York Film Critics Award for La Cava and Oscar nominations for his direction, screenwriters Ryskind and Veiller, supporting actress Leeds, and the film itself.

This movie made RKO appreciate Hepburn's "surprise" flair for comedy, while showing costar Ginger Rogers to be as good a dramatic actress as she was a wisecracking ballroom dancer. Among those similarly inspired to do their best work for La Cava were Adolphe Menjou, Lucille Ball, Eve Arden, Gail Patrick, and Constance Collier. Forty-five years later, *Stage Door* continues to sparkle as one of the Thirties' best motion pictures.

Katharine Hepburn and Andrea Leeds

YOU ONLY LIVE ONCE

1937

CREDITS

A United Artists Picture. Directed by Fritz Lang. *Produced by* Walter Wanger. *Screenplay by* Gene Towne *and* Graham Baker. *Photographed by* Leon Shamroy. *Edited by* Daniel Mandell. *Art direction by* Alexander Toluboff. *Music by* Alfred Newman. *Song: "A Thousand Dreams of You" by* Louis Alter *and* Paul Francis Webster. *Running time: 86 minutes.*

CAST

Henry Fonda, *Eddie Taylor;* Sylvia Sidney, *Joan "Jo" Graham;* Barton MacLane, *Stephen Whitney;* Jean Dixon, *Bonnie Graham;* William Gargan, *Father Dolan,* Warren Hymer, *Muggsy;* Charles "Chic" Sale, *Ethan;* Margaret Hamilton, *Hester;* Guinn Williams, *Rogers;* Jerome Cowan, *Dr. Hill;* John Wray, *Warden;* Jonathan Hale, *District attorney;* Ward Bond, *Guard;* Wade Boteler, *Policeman;* Henry Taylor, *Kozderonas;* Jack Carson, *Gas station attendant.*

Sylvia Sidney and Henry Fonda

Sylvia Sidney, Henry Fonda, William Gargan, and Barton MacLane

The theme of man against his fate is, by Austrian-born director Fritz Lang's own admission, the central characteristic of all his motion pictures. And that motif is nowhere more evident than in his Thirties films of social protest, *Fury* (1936) and *You Only Live Once* (1937). Almost as powerful now as they were when first released, both stand among the cinematic masterpieces of their decade.

In each film, mistaken identity and/or circumstantial evidence implicates an innocent man in crime. But in *You Only Live Once* the protagonist (Henry Fonda) is already a three-time loser, having served that many prison terms for robbery. Desperate to go straight, Fonda finds a job and takes a bride (Sylvia Sidney). But their future plans are doomed when he's fired for lateness and, on the sole evidence of a hat bearing his initials, is convicted of a bank robbery–murder and sentenced to death. New evidence then results in an eleventh-hour pardon, but Fonda is by then involved in a prison break. Thinking that the prison

Sylvia Sidney and Henry Fonda

Charles "Chic" Sale, Margaret Hamilton, and Henry Fonda

chaplain is trying to trick him, the confused escapee accidentally kills him. Now guilty of murder, convict and wife take it on the lam for Canada. But authorities have been tipped off; in a grim finale, they shoot them down.

The Gene Towne–Graham Baker screenplay for this Depression-era melodrama leans heavily on contrivance, but the painstaking Fritz Lang's direction of a fine cast compensates for these shortcomings. And the exceptionally honest acting of Fonda and Sidney is enough to ensure audience empathy and the suspension of disbelief.

The well-staged impact of such key sequences as the rain-drenched armored-car holdup, the prison break in the fog, and the final wilderness flight from justice are imaginatively influenced by Lang's solid background in the Impressionist German cinema of the Twenties, with its striking deployment of light and shadow. To this end, Lang was fortunate in having the expertise of cameraman Leon Shamroy, who found working under the perfectionist director as irritating as did Henry Fonda. "Lang was fantastically meticulous," reports Shamroy. "We worked every night until three o'clock." Fonda has summed up the experience as "a tortured nightmare."

You Only Live Once received critical acclaim but proved too downbeat for 1937 audiences apparently not interested in seeing the love team of 1936's *The Trail of the Lonesome Pine* meet so depressing a fate.

Luise Rainer and Paul Muni

THE GOOD EARTH

1937

CREDITS

A Metro-Goldwyn-Mayer Picture. Directed by Sidney
Franklin. *Associate directors (uncredited):* Sam Wood, Vic-
tor Fleming, George Hill, Fred Niblo, *and* Andrew Marton.
Produced by Irving G. Thalberg. *Associate producer:* Albert
Lewin. *Screenplay by* Talbot Jennings, Tess Schlesinger,
Claudine West, *and (uncredited)* Frances Marion. *Based on
the novel by* Pearl S. Buck *and its stage adaptation by* Owen
and Donald Davis. *Photographed by* Karl Freund. *Edited
by* Basil Wrangell. *Art direction by* Cedric Gibbons, Harry
Oliver, Arnold Gillespie, *and* Edwin B. Willis. *Montage by*
Slavko Vorkapich. *Costumes by* Dolly Tree. *Music by*
Herbert Stothart. *Running time: 138 minutes.*

Jessie Ralph, Paul Muni, and Walter Connolly

CAST

Paul Muni, *Wang Lung;* Luise Rainer, *O-Lan;* Walter Connolly, *Uncle;* Tilly Losch, *Lotus;* voice dubbed by Lotus Lui; Charley Grapewin, *Old Father;* Jessie Ralph, *Cuckoo;* Soo Yong, *Aunt;* Keye Luke, *Elder son;* Roland Lui, *Younger son;* Suzanna Kim, *Little Fool;* Chingwah Lee, *Ching;* Harold Huber, *Cousin;* Olaf Hytten, *Liu, grain merchant;* William Law, *Gateman;* Mary Wong, *Little Bride;* Charles Middleton, *Banker;* Philip Ahn, *Captain.*

Nobel Prize winner Pearl S. Buck was best known for her novels about Chinese life, especially 1931's *The Good Earth,* which was awarded a Pulitzer Prize. Its 1932 Broadway adaptation starred Claude Rains and Alla Nazimova as the restless peasant farmer, who moves up from poverty to become a wealthy landowner, and his patient wife.

Mrs. Buck's popular novel reached the screen early in 1937 at a cost of $2,816,000—then a whopping sum for a black-and-white motion picture. Its producer, Irving Thalberg, dedicated the last three years of his life to seeing this project through its difficult birth pangs. But he died of pneumonia in 1936, at the age of thirty-seven, six months before the movie's release. Consequently, *The Good Earth* carries a frame that reads: "To the Memory of Irving Grant Thalberg, We Dedicate This Picture—His Last Great Achievement."

And great it was. Forty-five years after its completion, a retrospective look at *The Good Earth* continues to impress the viewer with its epic power, its fine performances, and the virtuosity of its technical accomplishments. On what was then termed "the world's largest set," five hundred acres of San Fernando Valley land were purchased and turned into a replica Chinese farm. Almost two million feet of atmospheric location footage was shot in China, some of which was used in the complex, technically amazing locust-plague sequence—which remains a masterpiece of montage and special-effects artistry.

As the devoted farm couple who age through the years until death claims the wife, Paul Muni and Luise Rainer offered dedicated performances that garnered Academy Award nominations. And the beatific-faced Rainer surprised many of her colleagues by copping 1937's Best Actress Oscar, despite the competition of Greta Garbo's *Camille.* But Muni, dedicated technician though he was, considered himself miscast in this movie and never liked his performance.

The Good Earth was immensely popular and earned a half-million dollars profit. Aside from Rainer, it won cinematographer Karl Freund a deserved Oscar. But its nominations for Best Picture and Best Director lost out, respectively, to *The Life of Emile Zola* (another Muni film) and *The Awful Truth's* Leo McCarey.

Luise Rainer and Paul Muni

Luise Rainer and Paul Muni

Thomas Mitchell, Fay Bainter, and Beulah Bondi

MAKE WAY
FOR TOMORROW

1937

CREDITS

A Paramount Picture. Produced and directed by Leo Mc-Carey. *Screenplay by* Viña Delmar. *Based on the novel The Years Are So Long by* Josephine Lawrence *and its dramatization by* Helen *and* Nolan Leary. *Photographed by* William C. Mellor. *Edited by* LeRoy Stone. *Art direction by* Hans Dreier *and* Bernard Herzbrun. *Music by* Victor Young *and* George Antheil. *Title song by* Leo Robin, Sam Coslow, *and* Jean Schwartz. *Age makeup by* Wally Westmore. *Running time: 92 minutes.*

CAST

Victor Moore, *Barkley Cooper;* Beulah Bondi, *Lucy Cooper;* Fay Bainter, *Anita Cooper;* Thomas Mitchell, *George Cooper;* Porter Hall, *Harvey Chase;* Barbara Read, *Rhoda Cooper;* Maurice Moscovitch, *Max Rubens;* Elisabeth Risdon, *Cora Payne;* Minna Gombell, *Nellie Chase;* Ray Mayer, *Robert Cooper;* Ralph Remley, *Bill Payne;* Louise Beavers, *Mamie;* Louis Jean Heydt, *Doctor;* Gene Morgan, *Carlton Gorman;* Dell Henderson, *Auto salesman;* Ruth Warren, *Secretary;* Paul Stanton, *Hotel manager;* Ferike Boros, *Mrs. Rubens;* Granville Bates, *Mr. Hunter;* Nick Lukats, *Boyfriend.*

Old age and such attendant problems as disability, financial insolvency, and senility have, understandably, never been good box-office. But in 1937, Paramount took a

Beulah Bondi and Victor Moore

chance with Leo McCarey's *Make Way for Tomorrow*, which landed on that year's ten-best lists of both *The New York Times* and the National Board of Review of Motion Pictures—even though its box-office record was disastrous.

As the story opens, Bark and Lucy Cooper (Victor Moore and Beulah Bondi) are about to lose their home to the bank, a situation revealed only at the eleventh hour to their gathered offspring, none of whom has the means, the space, or the willingness to accommodate *both* elderly Mother and Dad. As a temporary solution, their New York City son and daughter-in-law agree to take Lucy, and Bark goes to stay with a small-town daughter hundreds of miles from Manhattan.

In a series of well-structured scenes, Viña Delmar's relatively unsentimentalized screenplay unfolds the nearly insoluble story of a "typical" American family whose midlife crisis with the predicament of what-to-do-with-the-old-folks proves an irritating burden. A lifetime of self-centered pursuits, lack of interfamily communication, and avoidance of responsibility cannot, of course, be solved in a matter of weeks or even months. As *Make Way for Tomorrow* reaches its climax, Moore and Bondi enjoy an afternoon together in the setting of their honeymoon, before parting—probably forever—at the train station. She is bound for an Eastern old women's home, while he (whose health requires a warmer climate) will go to the California home of an estranged daughter. It's a heartbreaking conclusion, and because of the talent and restraint of its acting and direction, this motion picture never fails to move its audience.

Comedian Victor Moore was sixty when he took on this (for him) rare serious role. It's a flawless performance, equaled every step of the way by the simple honesty of Beulah Bondi, then only forty-six, but an established character actress whose face lent itself easily to the makeup skills of Wally Westmore.

The painful beauty of its profound truths are the very factors that prevented *Make Way for Tomorrow* from winning widespread audience acceptance. Nor did the Academy of Motion Picture Arts and Sciences bother even to *nominate* artists here offering perhaps the finest work of their careers. As fate would have it, Leo McCarey *did* win the 1937 Best Director Oscar—but for a *popular* success, *The Awful Truth*.

Beulah Bondi

MAYTIME

1937

CREDITS

A Metro-Goldwyn-Mayer Picture. Directed by Robert Z. Leonard. *Produced by* Hunt Stromberg. *Screenplay by* Noel Langley. *Based on the operetta by* Rida Johnson Young *and* Sigmund Romberg. *Photographed by* Oliver T. Marsh. *Edited by* Conrad A. Nervig. *Musical direction by* Herbert Stothart. *Opera sequences staged by* William von Wymetal. *Art direction by* Cedric Gibbons, Fredric Hope, *and* Edwin B. Willis. *Costumes by* Adrian. *Musical numbers:* "Sweetheart" *and* "Maytime Finale" *by* Romberg *and* Young; "Virginia Ham and Eggs" *and* "Vive L'Opéra" *by*

Jeanette MacDonald in the "Czarita" opera sequence

Stothart, Bob Wright, *and* Chet Forrest; *"Student Drinking Song" by* Stothart; *"Carry Me Back to Old Virginny" by* James A. Bland; *"Czarita," based on* Tchaikovsky's Fifth Symphony, *libretto by* Wright *and* Forrest; *"Reverie," based on* Romberg *airs; "Jump Jim Crow," "Road to Paradise," and "Dancing Will Keep You Young" by* Romberg, Young, *and* Cyrus Wood; *"Maypole" by* Ed Ward; *"Street Singer" by* Wright, Forrest, *and* Stothart; *and adaptations of music by* Delibes, Wagner, Bellini, *and* Meyerbeer. *Running time: 132 minutes.*

CAST

Jeanette MacDonald, *Marcia Mornay/Miss Morrison;* Nelson Eddy, *Paul Allison;* John Barrymore, *Nicolai Nazaroff;* Herman Bing, *August Archipenko;* Tom Brown, *Kip;* Lynne Carver, *Barbara Roberts;* Rafaela Ottiano, *Ellen;* Charles Judels, *Cabby;* Paul Porcasi, *Trentini;* Sig Rumann, *Fanchon;* Walter Kingsford, *Rudyard;* Edgar Norton, *Secretary;* Guy Bates Post, *Emperor Louis Napoleon;* Iphigenie Castiglioni, *Empress Eugénie;* Anna Demetrio, *Mme. Fanchon;* Frank Puglia, *Orchestra conductor;* Russell Hicks, *M. Bulliet;* Harry Davenport, Harry Hayden, Howard Hickman, and Robert C. Fischer, *Opera directors;* Harlan Briggs, *Bearded director;* Billy Gilbert, *Drunk;* Ivan Lebedeff, *Empress's dinner companion;* Leonid Kinskey, *Student in bar.*

The immense popularity of Jeannette MacDonald and Nelson Eddy, those vocally modest singing sweethearts of the screen operetta, began with 1935's *Naughty Marietta* and ended six years—and seven films—later with the disappointing *I Married an Angel.* For their legion of loyal fans, MacDonald and Eddy could do no wrong—as long as they performed *together* (their films with other costars were less successful).

Maytime, their third such collaboration, was immensely popular with the filmgoing public, and it is quite likely the best of the eight MacDonald-Eddy motion pictures. But it bears little resemblance to Sigmund Romberg's 1917 stage hit, which first reached the silent screen six years later, featuring Ethel Shannon and Harrison Ford.

In 1936 Metro began a remake of *Maytime* in Technicolor, with MacDonald and Eddy supported by Paul Lukas and Frank Morgan, under the direction of Edmund Goulding. But the untimely death of MGM production chief Irving Thalberg brought the movie to a costly halt while the studio reconnoitered. When production resumed, there were extensive script revisions, a new producer (Hunt Stromberg), and another director (Robert Z. Leonard). Lukas and Morgan were replaced, respectively, by John Barrymore and Herman Bing, and nearly all of Goulding's Technicolor footage was discarded, including the song "Farewell to Dreams" and scenes from the opera *Tosca.* As an economy move, black-and-white photography replaced

Nelson Eddy and Jeanette MacDonald

Jeanette MacDonald, John Barrymore

color, and still the completed *Maytime,* running a lengthy 132 minutes, cost a then surprising $1.5 million.

This lavishly handsome, sentimental tale of tragic romance involving two opera singers in a love triangle with the Svengali-like impresario she married, was a great audience pleaser that the critics also admired.

Barbara Stanwyck as Stella Dallas

STELLA DALLAS

1937

CREDITS

A Samuel Goldwyn Production for United Artists. Directed by King Vidor. *Screenplay by Sarah Y. Mason and* Victor Heerman. *Based on the novel by* Olive Higgins Prouty. *Adaptation by* Harry Wagstaff Gribble *and* Gertrude Purcell. *Photographed by Rudolph Mate. Edited by* Sherman Todd. *Art direction by* Richard Day. *Music by* Alfred Newman. *Costumes by* Omar Kiam. *Running time: 105 minutes.*

CAST

Barbara Stanwyck, *Stella Martin Dallas;* John Boles, *Stephen Dallas;* Anne Shirley, *Laurel Dallas;* Barbara O'Neill, *Helen Morrison;* Alan Hale, *Ed Munn;* Marjorie Main, *Mrs. Martin;* Edmund Elton, *Mr. Martin;* George Walcott, *Charlie Martin;* Gertrude Short, *Carrie Jenkins;* Tim Holt, *Richard Grosvenor III;* Ann Shoemaker, *Margaret Phillibrown;* Nella Walker, *Mrs. Grosvenor;* Bruce Saterlee, *Con Morrison as a child;* Jimmy Butler, *Con Morrison;* Jack Egger, *Lee Morrison;* Dickie Jones, *John Morrison;* Lillian Yarbo, *Gladys;* Laraine Johnson/Day, *Schoolgirl.*

Samuel Goldwyn produced two highly acclaimed screen versions of Olive Higgins Prouty's popular, tear-jerking 1922 novel, *Stella Dallas:* a silent film starring Belle Bennett in 1925, under Henry King's direction, and its closely followed 1937 remake, with King Vidor directing Barbara Stanwyck in her best-remembered Thirties performance. Oddly enough, she wasn't Goldwyn's first choice for Stella. He had first tried, unsuccessfully, to engage Ruth Chatterton (who considered the character "too unpleasant"), then Gladys George for Prouty's well-meaning but unfortunate heroine. The producer had considered Stanwyck too young and dramatically lightweight for the part. But actor Joel McCrea's intercession and a test she reluctantly made with director Vidor and Anne Shirley (cast as Stella's daughter Laurel) helped change Goldwyn's mind.

The role *is* a demanding one; Stella Martin is a girl of lower-class background who connives to ensnare and marry well-born Stephen Dallas, then loses him through her un-

Barbara Stanwyck and Anne Shirley

*Barbara Stanwyck
and Alan Hale*

couth selfishness. But she's also a devoted mother to their child, whom she *un*selfishly wants to have all the advantages that *she* never had—even at the eventual sacrifice of her own ambitions. Finally Stella realizes that, although she's never managed to rise above her own origins, young Laurel has acquired the taste and breeding to realize a marriage into society. At the story's famed conclusion, wistful Stella must be content to remain a silent, self-ostracized witness to that wedding.

In *The Saturday Evening Post's* series on "The Role I Liked Best," Stanwyck later said of *Stella Dallas:* "There was unusual stimulation in the dual nature of the part; it was like playing two different women simultaneously. Always Stella had to be shown both in her surface commonness and in her basic fineness. Each scene was delicately constructed, often with tragedy and comedy very close."

But despite its fine cast and direction and the excellence of so many of its parts, *Stella Dallas* occasionally fails to ring true. In the sequence in which Stella, overdressed to the nines, sashays among the country-club set looking for Laurel—and in which Laurel is humiliated to overhear the comment "It's not a woman; it's a Christmas tree!"—director Vidor permits Stanwyck's bravura performance to verge on parody. But her self-sacrificing confrontation scene with Barbara O'Neill (as the understandable object of Boles's affections) and her final scene with Anne Shirley's beautifully played Laurel more than compensate for any such lapse.

Stella Dallas won Barbara Stanwyck her first Oscar nomination. A sorely disappointed loser (to Luise Rainer for *The Good Earth*), she admitted at the time, "I really poured my blood into it!"

John Boles and Barbara Stanwyck

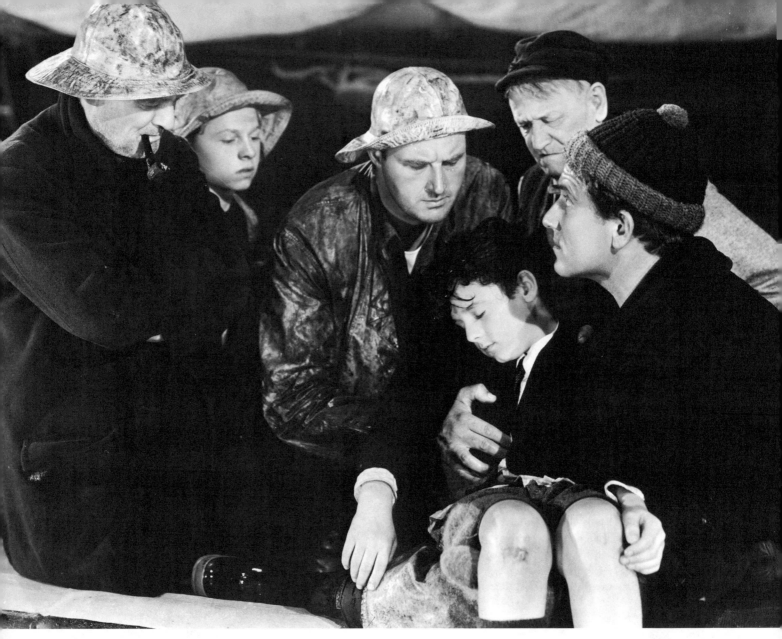

Lionel Barrymore, Mickey Rooney, Oscar O'Shea, Freddie Bartholomew, Charley Grapewin, and Spencer Tracy

CAPTAINS COURAGEOUS

1937

CREDITS

A Metro-Goldwyn-Mayer Picture. Directed by Victor Fleming. *Produced by* Louis D. Lighton. *Screenplay by* John Lee Mahin, Marc Connelly, *and* Dale Van Every. *Based on the novel by* Rudyard Kipling. *Photographed by* Harold Rosson. *Edited by* Elmo Vernon. *Art direction by* Cedric Gibbons, Arnold Gillespie, *and* Edwin B. Willis. *Marine direction by* James Havens. *Music by* Franz Waxman. *Lyrics by* Gus Kahn. *Running time: 116 minutes.*

CAST

Freddie Bartholomew, *Harvey Cheyne;* Spencer Tracy, *Manuel;* Lionel Barrymore, *Capt. Disko Troop;* Melvyn Douglas, *Mr. Cheyne;* Mickey Rooney, *Dan Troop;* Charley Grapewin, *Uncle Salters;* Christian Rub, *Old Clement;* Walter Kingsford, *Dr. Finley;* Donald Briggs, *Tyler;* Sam McDaniel, *Doc;* Dave Thursby, *Tom;* John Carradine, *Long Jack;* William Stack, *Elliott,* Leo G. Carroll, *Burns;* Charles Trowbridge, *Dr. Walsh;* Richard Powell, *Steward;* Billy Burrud, *Charles;* Jay Ward, *Pogey;* Kenneth Wilson, *Alvin;* Roger Gray, *Nate Rogers;* Jack La Rue, *Priest;* Oscar O'Shea, *Cushman;* Gladden James, *Sec. Cobb;* Katherine Kenworthy, *Mrs. Troop;* Murray Kinnell, *Minister;* Frank Sully, *Taxi driver;* Billy Gilbert, *Soda steward;* Charles Coleman, *Butler;* Wade Boteler, *Skipper of the* Blue Gill.

Spencer Tracy, Lionel Barrymore, and Freddie Bartholomew

The year 1937 was an especially rich one for Hollywood moviemaking and a fortuitous one for Spencer Tracy, who took away the first of his two Oscars for a role he hadn't wanted to play—that of the Portuguese fisherman Manuel in MGM's freely adapted production of Rudyard Kipling's *Captains Courageous.* Manuel was nothing like any of Tracy's previous characterizations, and he had serious misgivings about speaking with a foreign accent, having his hair curled, singing two sea chanteys solo. "I used to pray that something would happen to halt production," the actor later admitted. "I was positive I was doing the worst job of my life."

Captains Courageous was also a 1937 box-office favorite. Freddie Bartholomew, the precocious, London-born youngster who had reached fame as *David Copperfield* in 1935, was billed *above* both Tracy and Lionel Barrymore. Yet the child star's fame would not survive the decade (years later, he would become executive producer of the CBS-TV soap opera *As the World Turns*).

As *Captains Courageous* begins, young Bartholomew is a bit hard to take, so repellent is his delineation of Harvey Cheyne, a spoiled, bossy rich boy. But the film's story is of how this pint-sized monster becomes not only human but likable, after he falls from a cruise liner near the Grand Banks and is rescued by the fishing vessel of Captain Troop (Lionel Barrymore). Aboard the *We're Here,* this obnoxious lad quickly alienates everyone but Manuel (Tracy), whose kindly simplicity wins the boy over and gradually teaches him discipline and honor. The boy, in turn, adores his mentor, and when Manuel is killed in a tragic maritime accident, Harvey is heartbroken. At the film's close, the boy is returned to his tycoon-father (Melvyn Douglas) a changed person.

Captain Courageous lost 1937's Best Picture Oscar to *The Life of Emile Zola* but boasted the year's Best Actor award for Spencer Tracy, who deservedly nosed out *Zola's* Paul Muni for that honor. In 1977, a TV-movie remake starring Jonathan Kahn, Ricardo Montalban, and Karl Malden in the respective Bartholomew, Tracy, and Barrymore roles did little to dim the memory of MGM's 1937 classic.

Freddie Bartholomew, Spencer Tracy, and John Carradine

Mischa Auer, Adolphe Menjou, and Deanna Durbin

Deanna Durbin and Mischa Auer

Eugene Pallette, Billy Gilbert, Deanna Durbin, and Adolphe Menjou

ONE HUNDRED MEN AND A GIRL

1937

CREDIT

A Universal Picture. Directed by Henry Koster. *Produced by* Joe Pasternak *and* Charles R. Rogers. *Screenplay by* Bruce Manning, Charles Kenyon, *and* James Mulhauser. *Story by* Hans Kraly. *Photographed by* Joseph Valentine. *Edited by* Bernard W. Burton. *Musical direction by* Charles Previn. *Songs: "It's Raining Sunbeams" by* Frederick Hollander *and* Sam Coslow; *and "A Heart That's Free" by* Alfred G. Robyn *and* Thomas T. Railey. *Interpolated music: "Hungarian Rhapsody No. 2" by* Liszt; *"Alleluja" from* Exsultate Jubilate *by* Mozart; *Act 3 Prelude from* Lohengrin *by* Wagner; *"Brindisi" from* La Traviata *by* Verdi; *and* Finale *from "Symphony No. 5" by* Tchaikovsky. *Running time: 84 minutes.*

CAST

Deanna Durbin, *Patricia Cardwell;* Leopold Stokowski, *Himself;* Adolphe Menjou, *John Cardwell;* Mischa Auer, *Michael Borodoff;* Alice Brady, *Mrs. Frost;* Eugene Pallette, *John G. Frost;* Billy Gilbert, *Garage owner;* Alma Kruger, *Mrs. Tyler;* Jack/J. Scott Smart, *Stage doorman;* Jed Prouty, *Bitters;* Jameson Thomas, *Russell;* Howard Hickman, *Johnson;* Frank Jenks, *Taxi driver;* Christian Rub, *Gustave Brandstetter;* Gerald Oliver Smith, *Stevens;* Jack Mulhall, *Rudolph;* Mary Forbes, *Theater patron;* Bess Flowers, Rolfe Sedan, Charles Coleman, *and* Hooper Atchley, *Party guests;* Leonid Kinskey, *Pianist.*

Deanna Durbin has been called "probably the most agreeable child who ever starred in movies." Introduced, along with fellow fourteen-year-old Judy Garland, in the 1936 MGM two-reel short *Every Sunday,* she displayed an astonishingly rich, full soprano voice for so young a girl. But she initially lacked the confidence already possessed by Judy. Metro elected to retain Garland's services, while letting Durbin go, and Universal gambled by casting her as one of the *Three Smart Girls* in producer Joe Pasternak's 1936 comedy feature. The public took quickly to Deanna's

Deanna Durbin and Leopold Stokowski

combination of personality, warmth, and vocal ability, and the $2 million that the movie earned has been credited with pulling that studio out of debt.

Cognizant of Durbin's moneymaking potential, Universal raised her salary and gave Pasternak carte blanche with her first starring picture, *One Hundred Men and a Girl*. This charming Thirties fairy tale focused on a hundred out-of-work musicians and their trombonist's enterprising little girl, who temporarily solves the unemployment problem by engineering a benefit concert with no less than conductor Leopold Stokowski! In a seriously depressed decade, this was a nice, feel-good piece of escapist entertainment. Nowadays, the film's sentimental moments tend to cloy, and Durbin's non-stop falsetto prattle and ebullient charm

become irritating. But there remains the undeniable quality of that unusually mature voice, soaring through, among others, Mozart's difficult "Alleluja" and Verdi's drinking song from *La Traviata*.

In 1937 *One Hundred Men and a Girl* drew Academy Award nominations for Best Picture, original story, sound recording, editing, and music score, but its only Oscar went to Charles Previn for his musical supervision.

The following year, sixteen-year-old Deanna and Mickey Rooney won miniature Academy statuettes "for their significant contribution in bringing to the screen the spirit and personification of youth, and as juvenile players setting a high standard of ability and achievement."

THE AWFUL TRUTH

1937

CREDITS

A Columbia Picture. Produced and directed by Leo McCarey. *Associate producer:* Everett Riskin. *Screenplay by* Vina Delmar. *Based on the play by* Arthur Richman. *Photographed by* Joseph Walker. *Edited by* Al Clark. *Art direction by* Stephen Gooson *and* Lionel Banks. *Interior decoration by* Babs Johnstone. *Costumes by* Kalloch. *Musical direction by* Morris Stoloff. *Song: "My Dreams Have Gone With the Wind" by* Ben Oakland *and* Milton Drake. *Running time: 90 minutes.*

CAST

Irene Dunne, *Lucy Warriner;* Cary Grant, *Jerry Warriner;* Ralph Bellamy, *Daniel Leeson;* Alexander D'Arcy, *Armand Duvalle;* Cecil Cunningham, *Aunt Patsy;* Molly Lamont, *Barbara Vance;* Esther Dale, *Mrs. Leeson;* Joyce Compton, *Dixie Belle Lee/Toots Binswanger;* Robert Allen, *Frank Randall;* Robert Warwick, *Mr. Vance;* Mary Forbes, *Mrs. Vance;* Claud Allister, *Lord Fabian;* Zita Moulton, *Lady Fabian;* Scott Colton, *Mr. Barnsley;* Wyn Cahoon, *Mrs. Barnsley;* Paul Stanton, *Judge;* Leonard Carey, *Butler;* Byron Foulger, *Secretary;* Bess Flowers, *Viola Heath.*

A rich vein of comedy ran through Hollywood motion pictures during the Thirties. But the genre that relates most closely to that decade is the so-called "screwball" variety, with its round of wacky families, freesheeling playboys, and scatterbrained heroines—often played by Claudette Colbert, Carole Lombard, Jean Arthur, or Irene Dunne.

Dunne had warmth, beauty, charm, expert timing, and a tongue-in-cheek sense of humor that elicited empathetic amusement from her audiences. In 1936's *Theodora Goes Wild* she's hilarious as a young woman who writes a novel that scandalizes her home town. And in *The Awful Truth,* she and Cary Grant are ideally matched for laughter as a

Cary Grant and Irene Dunne

Cary Grant, Irene Dunne, Esther Dale, and Ralph Bellamy

couple involved in marital misunderstandings, mistaken identity, and masquerades. On the verge of divorce, they indulge in custody battle over their pet terrier, Mr. Smith (Asta of *Thin Man* fame), but eventually reconcile for the slyly amusing finale.

Rich with wit, farcical tomfoolery, and inspired clowning by an expert cast, *The Awful Truth* owes much of its success to its improvisation-prone producer-director, Leo McCarey. Yet when shooting began, none of the cast even had a *script* to work from! "But," reports Irene Dunne, "as the filming progressed, Cary and I fell happily into step with Leo's breezy let's-try-anything style of filmmaking, and we grew to love and turst his wonderfully hilarious inventiveness." Ralph Bellamy recalls, "We shot that in less than six weeks, without a script. Leo knew all the time what he was going to do, but he was the only one who did."

The Awful Truth derives from a 1922 play by Arthur Richman that became a 1925 silent film with Agnes Ayers and Warner Baxter which was remade as a talkie in 1929 with Ina Claire and Henry Daniell. Originally *The Awful Truth* was purely a comedy of manners. But in its 1937 incarnation, McCarey's cunning sense of fun replaced the old *bon mot* with uninhibited pantomimic farce so clever that he won the year's Best Director Oscar. The movie garnered nominations for Best Picture, actress Dunne, supporting actor Bellamy, and, most ironic of all, Vina Delmar for her "screenplay." In 1953, Columbia remade *The Awful Truth* with Jane Wyman and Ray Milland as *Let's Do It Again*. The results were negligible.

Irene Dunne, Alexander D'Arcy, and Cary Grant

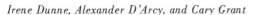

Andy Devine, Brian Donlevy, Tyrone Power, Alice Faye, and bit players

IN OLD CHICAGO

1938

CREDITS

A 20th Century-Fox Picture. A Darryl F. Zanuck Production. Directed by Henry King. *Associate producer:* Kenneth Macgowan. *Screenplay by* Lamar Trotti *and* Sonya Levien. *Based on the story "We, the O'Learys" by* Niven Busch. *Photographed by* Peverell Marley. *Edited by* Barbara McLean. *Special effects sequences staged by* Fred Sersen, Ralph Hammeras, *and* Louis J. Witte. *Special effects director:* H. Bruce Humberstone. *Special effects photographer:* Daniel B. Clark. *Art direction by* William Darling *and* Rudolph Sternad. *Set decoration by* Thomas Little. *Costumes by* Royer. *Music direction by* Louis Silvers. *Songs:* "In Old Chicago" *by* Mack Gordon *and* Harry Revel; "I've Taken a Fancy to You," "I'll Never Let You Cry," *and* "Take a Dip in the Sea" *by* Lew Pollack *and* Sidney D. Mitchell; *and* "Carry Me Back to Old Virginny" *by* James A. Bland. *Sound by* Eugene Grossman *and* Roger Heman. *Running time: 110 minutes.*

CAST

Tyrone Power, *Dion O'Leary;* Alice Faye, *Belle Fawcett;* Don Ameche, *Jack O'Leary;* Alice Brady, *Molly O'Leary;* Andy Devine, *Pickle Bixby;* Brian Donlevy, *Gil Warren;* Phyllis Brooks, *Ann Colby;* Tom Brown, *Bob O'Leary;* Sidney Blackmer, *Gen. Phil Sheridan;* Berton Churchill, *Senator Colby;* June Storey, *Gretchen O'Leary;* Paul Hurst, *Hitch;* Tyler Brooke, *Specialty singer;* J. Anthony Hughes, *Patrick O'Leary;* Gene Reynolds, *Dion as a boy;* Bobs Watson, *Bob as a boy;* Billy Watson, *Jack as a boy;* Madame Sul-Te-Wan, *Hattie;* Spencer Charters, *Beavers;* Rondo Hatton, *Warren's bodyguard;* Gustav von Seyffertitz and Russell Hicks, *Men in Jack's office;* Harry Hayden, *Secretary;* Vera Lewis, *Marriage witness;* Minerva Urecal, *Frantic mother.*

Don Ameche, Alice Faye, and Tyrone Power

Most celebrated for a climactic fire sequence that lasted twenty minutes, *In Old Chicago* was a favorite project of Darryl F. Zanuck and, at a production cost of $1 million, one of the Thirties' most costly movies. Its large cast and epic scope lodge it prestigiously among such popular entries in a disaster-film cycle highlighted by *San Francisco* (1936), *The Hurricane* (1937), and *The Rains Came* (1939).

Chicago's great fire of 1871 and the fabled account of how a certain Mrs. O'Leary's cow started the holocaust (by kicking over a lantern) provided the basis for this fictional Lamar Trotti–Sonya Levien screenplay, based on a Niven Busch story. Of course, the conflagration footage (masterfully staged by a separate production unit under H. Bruce Humberstone) was the picture's main attraction. But Zanuck saw to it that a fine cast, headed by Tyrone Power, Alice Faye (with five song numbers), and Don Ameche, was already involved in an interesting story of romance, political chicanery, and family conflicts *before* the film turned into the exciting epic it eventually becomes, with the disaster serving as a reforming device for the charming blackguard portrayed by Power.

In Old Chicago, released in the spring of 1938, inexplicably competed in 1937's Academy Award race, losing the Best Picture Oscar to *The Life of Emile Zola.* But it did win statuettes for Best Assistant Director Robert Webb (now a long-obsolete nomination category) and Best Supporting Actress Alice Brady, at forty-five unexpectedly cast as the feisty, Gaelic-accented *mother* of Tyrone Power, Don Ameche, and Tom Brown!

With its heavy doses of Irish sentiment and epic philosophy ("Nothing can lick Chicago," states fire-survivor Power, clasping a besmudged Faye to his chest), *In Old Chicago* clearly belongs to another era. But its technical expertise alone assures it a worthy place in the history of Hollywood "disaster" films.

Alice Brady and Tyrone Power

JEZEBEL

1938

CREDITS

A Warner Bros. Picture. Directed by William Wyler. *Executive producer:* Hal B. Wallis. *Associate producer:* Henry Blanke. Screenplay by Clements Ripley, Abem Finkel, John Huston, *and (uncredited)* Robert Buckner. *Based on the play by* Owen Davis, Sr. *Photographed by* Ernest Haller. *Edited by* Warren Low. *Art direction by* Robert Haas. *Music by* Max Steiner. *Songs:* "*Jezebel*" *by* Johnny Mercer *and* Harry Warren; "*Raise a Ruckus*" *by* Al Dubin *and* Harry Warren. *Costumes by* Orry-Kelly. *Running time: 104 minutes.*

CAST

Bette Davis, *Julie Marsden;* Henry Fonda, *Preston Dillard;* George Brent, *Buck Cantrell;* Margaret Lindsay, *Amy Bradford Dillard;* Fay Bainter, *Aunt Belle Massey;* Richard Cromwell, *Ted Dillard;* Donald Crisp, *Dr. Livingstone;* Henry O'Neill, *Gen. Theopholus Bogardus;* John Litel, *Jean Le Cour;* Gordon Oliver, *Dick Allen;* Janet Shaw, *Molly Allen;* Spring Byington, *Mrs. Kendrick;* Margaret Early, *Stephanie Kendrick;* Georgia Caine, *Mrs. Petion;* Irving Pichel, *Huger;* Georges Renavent, *De Lautrec;* Fred Lawrence, *Bob;* Ann Codee, *Mme. Poulard;* Lew Payton, *Uncle Cato;* Eddie Anderson, *Gros Bat;* Stymie Beard, *Ti Bat;* Theresa Harris, *Zette;* Sam McDaniel, *Driver;* Trevor Bardette, *Sheriff at plantation;* Jac George, *Orchestra leader;* Jack Norton, *Drunk.*

Bette Davis and Fay Bainter

For her fine acting in *Jezebel,* Bette Davis won her second Academy Award, an accolade she really deserved (the Oscar given her for 1935's *Dangerous,* an overmannered performance in an inferior movie, was obviously a consolation prize for *Of Human Bondage*). Filmed amid the highly publicized and lengthy preproduction planning of *Gone With the Wind,* this Warner Bros. drama about a willful and conniving daughter of the antebellum South drew inevitable comparisons with Scarlett O'Hara, a role which Davis had desperately wanted to play. *Jezebel,* of course, is not in the epic class of Margaret Mitchell's Civil War saga. But, thanks to intelligent scripting by a team of writers and brilliant direction by William Wyler, this 1938 costume picture vastly improved upon the unsuccessful 1933 Owen Davis stage play with Miriam Hopkins.

Jezebel is a handsomely produced movie that easily withstands the passage of years, because of the care and craftsmanship accorded it by Wyler and executive producer Hal B. Wallis. But due to Wyler's painstaking perfec-

George Brent, Fay Bainter, Richard Cromwell, Henry O'Neill, Margaret Lindsay, and Bette Davis

Bette Davis, Henry Fonda, and Jac George

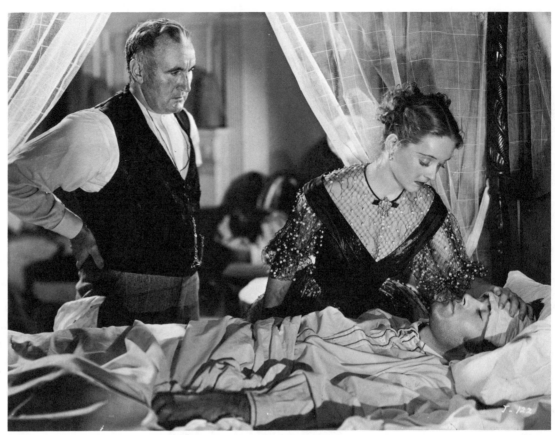

Donald Crisp, Bette Davis, and Henry Fonda

tionism, the picture fell behind its schedule, and Bette Davis successfully appealed to studio boss Jack Warner to keep the director from being replaced. ("I knew . . . Julie had a chance of making me an honest-to-goodness box-office star, because of the great direction I was receiving from Wyler.")

It was Davis's best performance to that date. Wyler kept her nervous, kinetic mannerisms in careful check, while encouraging her to explore other areas of her considerable talent: the controlled flamboyance of her early scenes; her later moments of subdued quiet; and the well-deserved humiliation she suffers when shunned at the white-gowned ball where she flaunts an outrageous scarlet dress. Bette Davis worked long and hard hours for Wyler and admits, "I earned the Oscar I won for *Jezebel*." The actress also has great praise for Fay Bainter, who won 1938's Best Supporting Actress award as the sympathetic Aunt Belle: "Julie would never have been as great a success for me without her."

Jezebel pleased most of its critics, and the public made it a popular hit. By 1939, Bette Davis had joined Shirley Temple, Alice Faye, and Sonja Henie among the nation's top box-office female stars.

Olivia de Havilland and Errol Flynn

THE ADVENTURES OF ROBIN HOOD

1938

CREDITS

A Warner Bros./First National Picture. Directed by Michael Curtiz *and* William Keighley. *Produced by* Hal B. Wallis. *Associate producer:* Henry Blanke. *Screenplay by* Norman Reilly Raine, Seton I. Miller, *and (uncredited)* Rowland Leigh. *Photographed in Technicolor by* Sol Polito, Tony Gaudio, *and* W. Howard Greene. *Edited by* Ralph Dawson. *Art direction by* Carl Jules Weyl. *Costumes by* Milo Anderson. *Music by* Erich Wolfgang Korngold. *Technical adviser:* Louis Van Den Ecker. *Archery supervisor:* Howard Hill. *Fencing master:* Fred Cravens. *Jousting scenes directed by* B. Reeves Eason. *Running time: 102 minutes.*

CAST

Errol Flynn, *Robin Hood;* Olivia de Havilland, *Maid Marian Fitzwalter;* Basil Rathbone, *Sir Guy of Gisbourne;* Claude Rains, *Prince John;* Patric Knowles, *Will Scarlett;* Eugene Pallette, *Friar Tuck;* Alan Hale, *Little John;* Melville Cooper, *High Sheriff of Nottingham;* Ian Hunter, *King Richard the Lion-Heart;* Una O'Connor, *Bess;* Herbert Mundin, *Much;* Montagu Love, *Bishop of the Black Canons;* Leonard Willey, *Sir Essex;* Robert Noble, *Sir Ralf;* Kenneth Hunter, *Sir Mortimer;* Robert Warwick, *Sir Geoffrey;* Colin Kenny, *Sir Baldwin;* Lester Matthews, *Sir Ivor;* Harry Cording, *Dickon Malbete;* Howard Hill, *Captain of the archers;* Ivan Simpson, *Proprietor of Kent Road Tavern;* Lionel Belmore, *Humility Prin.*

In a 1977 nationwide poll of television program directors, *TV Guide* reported that 1938's *The Adventures of Robin Hood* was tabulated fifth among their viewers in the roster of the most perennially popular movies. The reason is not difficult to fathom, for this wonderful Technicolor adventure yarn, derived from the fifteenth-century Robin Hood legends of that Sherwood Forest rogue who robbed the wealthy to benefit the poor, typifies the sort of movie "they don't make anymore."

Melville Cooper, Basil Rathbone, Olivia de Havilland, Claude Rains, and Errol Flynn

Basil Rathbone and Errol Flynn

Not only has Hollywood seemingly lost its knack with this sort of exhilarating escapist fare, but the old, established "studio system" has vanished, and with it many of the technical skills of direction, production design, cinematography, and editing that once flourished and marked a motion picture with the particular characteristics of its studio. Nor do we have actors versed in the flair and style of a cast like this one. There are no more dashing heroes like Errol Flynn, no villains as dastardly as Basil Rathbone and Claude Rains, and no heroines possessed of Olivia de Havilland's special blend of beauty, warmth, and spirit. And there never has been another composer of rousingly melodic film music quite like Erich Wolfgang Korngold.

The Adventures of Robin Hood, filmed at a cost of some $2 million, was an expensive production by 1938 standards. But producer Hal B. Wallis, then a Warner Bros. mainstay, knew his audiences, and he knew how to vary a movie's dramatic pace with scenes of archery prowess, swordplay, horseplay, and (briefly) innocent romantic dalliance.

The film was begun on location by director William Keighley, who staged many of the forest scenes. But studio boss Jack Warner wanted more sweep and epic action, so Keighley was replaced with Michael Curtiz. The resultant film pleased the critics and proved a huge box-office hit. Nominated for 1938's Best Picture Academy Award, it lost out to the farcical *You Can't Take It With You* but won Oscars for art direction, editing, and Korngold's colorful score.

Errol Flynn as Robin Hood

Franchot Tone, Robert Young, and Robert Taylor

THREE COMRADES

1938

CREDITS

A Metro-Goldwyn-Mayer Picture. Produced by Joseph L. Mankiewicz. Directed by Frank Borzage. Screenplay by F. Scott Fitzgerald, Edward E. Paramore, and (uncredited) David Hertz, Waldo Salt, Lawrence Hazzard, and Joseph L. Mankiewicz. Based on the novel by Erich Maria Remarque. Photographed by Joseph Ruttenberg. Edited by Frank Sullivan. Art direction by Cedric Gibbons. Music by Franz Waxman. Running time: 100 minutes.

CAST

Robert Taylor, *Erich Lohkamp;* Margaret Sullavan, *Patricia Hollman;* Franchot Tone, *Otto Koster;* Robert Young, *Gottfried Lenz;* Guy Kibbee, *Alfons;* Lionel Atwill, *Franz Breuer;* Monty Woolley, *Dr. Jaffe;* Henry Hull, *Dr. Heinrich Becker;* George Zucco, *Dr. Plauten;* Charley Grapewin, *Local doctor;* Spencer Charters, *Herr Schultz;* Sarah Padden, *Frau Schultz;* Ferdinand Munier, *Burgomaster;* Morgan Wallace,

Lionel Atwill, Margaret Sullavan, and   Robert Taylor

Robert Taylor, Margaret Sullavan, and Franchot Tone

By the late 1930s, the once-popular novelist F. Scott Fitzgerald was working on Hollywood movie scripts, for none of which he received any credit—until engaged by MGM producer Joseph L. Mankiewicz to adapt Erich Maria Remarque's international best-seller, *Three Comrades.* Ironically, this was the only film for which Fitzgerald was given screenwriting credit, although Mankiewicz admits that only about one-third of the novelist's work was in the final shooting script. Due largely to the movie's female star, Margaret Sullavan (who complained that much of her role was, literally, unspeakable), the producer quickly engaged several other writers to revise Fitzgerald's screenplay. The result, influenced by both Breen Office censorship suggestions and Louis B. Mayer's disinclination to risk offending the German export market, was a heavily sentimental film about the deeper meanings of friendship, love, and death in post–World War I Germany. But all sources of possible "offense" were deleted, and any inference of Naziism was obscured.

Those who hold affection for this film generally cherish its showcasing of the unique Margaret Sullavan in one of her best Hollywood roles. It was a part already turned down by Joan Crawford, who reasoned that she would be overshadowed by the story's male characters. But Sullavan, with her throaty voice and poignant style, proved that this role was worth accepting—and the dialogue worth fighting over—by winning fine notices, an Oscar nomination, and the New York Film Critics' accolade as 1938's Best Actress.

The story concerns a trio of German soldiers (Robert Taylor, Franchot Tone, and Robert Young), war veterans and old friends, trying to adjust to postwar life and united in their affection for a tubercular, dying girl. Comic horseplay mixes with moments of deep sentiment as the comrades variously experience love, joy, and sadness against the background of an ominously changing world. Nazi/Jewish differences are never specifically aired, but suggestions are frequently unavoidable. Despite the flashes of social commentary hovering just beyond its screenplay, *Three Comrades* is mostly schmaltzy entertainment for sentimentalists, and Frank Borzage was certainly the appropriate director. But surmounting the script's pitfalls and providing unforgettable memories long after the rest of *Three Comrades* is forgotten is the irreplaceable Margaret Sullavan, at her best.

Margaret Sullavan, Robert Taylor,
Franchot Tone, and Robert Young

HOLIDAY

1938

CREDITS

A Columbia Picture. Directed by George Cukor. *Produced by* Everett Riskin. *Screenplay by* Donald Ogden Stewart *and* Sidney Buchman. *Based on the play by* Philip Barry. *Photographed by* Franz Planer. *Edited by* Otto Meyer *and* Al Clark. *Art direction by* Stephen Gooson *and* Lionel Banks. *Set decoration by* Babs Johnstone. *Music by* Sidney Cutner. *Costumes by* Kalloch. *Running time: 94 minutes.*

CAST

Katharine Hepburn, *Linda Seton;* Cary Grant, *Johnny Case;* Doris Nolan, *Julia Seton;* Lew Ayres, *Ned Seton;* Edward Everett Horton, *Nick Potter;* Henry Kolker, *Edward Seton;* Binnie Barnes, *Laura Cram;* Jean Dixon, *Susan Potter;* Henry Daniell, *Seton Cram;* Charles Trowbridge, *Banker;* George Pauncefort, *Henry;* Charles Richman, *Thayer;* Mitchell Harris, *Jennings;* Bess Flowers, *Countess.*

Katharine Hepburn and Cary Grant had teamed with director George Cukor in 1935's failed attempt at eccentric humor, *Sylvia Scarlett,* and, to hilarious advantage, in Howard Hawks's wacky 1938 farce, *Bringing Up Baby. Holiday* provides a charming balance to the latter, with its delightful excursion into a subtler form of humor—the comedy of manners.

Philip Barry's 1928 stage hit satirizing the futility of wealth had first reached the screen in 1930 with Ann Harding, Robert Ames, Mary Astor, and Monroe Owsley in the parts now played by Hepburn, Grant, Doris Nolan, and Lew Ayres. In both versions the role of the hero's friend, "Nick Potter," is portrayed by the ageless Edward Everett Horton, in one of his more ingratiating characterizations.

Holiday afforded Hepburn an opportunity to play the Broadway role she had understudied a decade earlier, that of the free-thinking socialite who finds a soulmate in her snobbish sister's unconventional fiance, eventually convincing him that he's better suited to *her.* Introduced to these socially prominent aristocrats in their Fifth Avenue habitat, the young man (Grant) sets them on their stuffy heels with his theory that a man should enjoy a "holiday" from

Katharine Hepburn, Doris Nolan, and Henry Kolker

Cary Grant and Katharine Hepburn

regular employment while in his prime to discover life and enjoy himself, returning to the work force in his later years.

Donald Ogden Stewart's adaptation of the Barry play (director Cukor has divulged that studio politics alone account for Sidney Buchman's sharing undeserved credit for this script) bore such style and wit that Cukor and a handpicked cast could scarcely fail. Hepburn and Grant are at the top of their considerable form here, followed closely by Jean Dixon and Horton as Grant's wise old pals. Doris Nolan brings more sympathetic dimension to the losing sister than is customary in Hollywood films, and Henry Kolker is perfection as the girls' stuffy, rigid father, who would have his prospective son-in-law employed in the family bank.

George Cukor recalls that *Holiday* was "a very happy picture to make," and the movie's continued success with revival-house audiences over forty years later passes the test of time. Literate, amusing, thought-provoking, and often very moving, *Holiday* is vintage Thirties comedy, and its failure to win even an Academy Award *nomination* in 1938 is difficult to fathom.

Cary Grant, Doris Nolan, and Katharine Hepburn

Hedy Lamarr and Joseph Calleia

ALGIERS

1938

Charles Boyer, Stanley Fields, Charles D. Brown, and Gene Lockhart

CREDITS

A United Artists release of a Walter Wanger Production. Directed by John Cromwell. *Screenplay by* John Howard Lawson *and* James M. Cain. *Based on the French screenplay* Pepe le Moko *by* Julien Duvivier *and* Roger D'Ashelbe *and the novel by* D'Ashelbe. *Photographed by* James Wong Howe. *Edited by* Otho Lovering *and* William Reynolds. *Music by* Vincent Scotto *and* Muhammed Ygner Buchen. *Art direction by* Alexander Toluboff. *Costumes by* Omar Kiam *and (for Hedy Lamarr)* Irene. *Running time: 95 minutes.*

CAST

Charles Boyer, *Pépé le Moko;* Sigrid Gurie, *Inés;* Hedy Lamarr, *Gaby;* Joseph Calleia, *Slimane;* Gene Lockhart, *Régis;* Johnny Downs, *Pierrot;* Alan Hale, *Grandpére;* Mme. Nina Koshetz, *Tania;* Joan Woodbury, *Aicha;* Claudia Dell, *Marie;* Robert Greig, *Giroux;* Stanley Fields, *Carlos;* Charles D. Brown, *Max;* Ben Hall, *Gil;* Armand Kaliz, *French police sergeant;* Leonid Kinsky, *L'Arbi;* Walter Kingsford, *Louvain;* Paul Harvey, *Janvier;* Bert Roach, *Bertier.*

American audiences attuned to gangster films were used to settings like New York and Chicago for their crime yarns. But not such exotic locales as the labyrinthine alleys of the Casbah, that mysterious refuge of underwold characters in French Algiers.

This moody melodrama is an extremely close English-language remake of Julien Duvivier's 1937 French film *Pépé le Moko,* so faithfully paralleled by producer Walter Wanger and director John Cromwell that all character names are retained, the same music score is utilized, and ace cinematographer James Wong Howe incorporated atmospheric footage from the realistic Gallic original with the more glamorously lit sets for this version.

Algiers revolves about Pépé, a charming fugitive from the law, and his battle of wits with Slimane, the police chief dedicated to luring him from the safety of the Casbah. Into this milieu wanders a group of curiosity-seeking Parisian tourists, including the sensuously beautiful Gaby. Pépé is immediately drawn to her, and she to him, to the dismay of Inés, the Algerian girl whose love for him is unreciprocated. Ultimately, his love for the Frenchwoman draws Pépé out of his refuge, and he's gunned down by his nemesis as Gaby's ship leaves the harbor bound for France.

In the roles earlier enacted by Jean Gabin, Line Noro, and Mireille Balin, *Algiers* offered Charles Boyer, Sigrid Gurie, and, in her American debut, Viennese-born Hedy Lamarr. Gurie never quite captured the public's fancy. But Boyer, already a Hollywood romantic fixture, now became a major movie sex symbol. And the gorgeous Lamarr (never

Charles Boyer and Hedy Lamarr

better cast than as this faintly shady adventuress) caused a sensation—especially in her love scenes with Boyer.

Algiers is basically an exotic study of character, and the skill of its narrative reflects upon director Cromwell, as well as the economy of its John Howard Lawson—James M. Cain screenplay. Among the great box-office pictures of 1938, *Algiers* won no awards, but it drew nominations for Boyer, supporting actor Gene Lockhart (as the informer who suffers underworld vengeance), cameraman Howe, and art director Alexander Toluboff, whose skill gave his sets the look of actual locations.

A decade later, this story was remade as *Casbah,* with Tony Martin, Yvonne De Carlo, and Marta Toren. But there was little room for comparison. *Casbah* is now all but forgotten; *Algiers* remains a classic.

Joseph Calleia and Charles Boyer

Rosalind Russell and Robert Donat

THE CITADEL

1938

CREDITS

A Metro-Goldwyn-Mayer Picture. Directed by King Vidor. *Produced by* Victor Saville. *Screenplay by* Ian Dalrymple, Frank Wead, Elizabeth Hill, *and* Emlyn Williams. *Based on the novel by* A. J. Cronin. *Photographed by* Harry Stradling. *Edited by* Charles Frend. *Art direction by* Lazare Meerson *and* Alfred Junge. *Music by* Louis Levy. *Running time: 110 minutes.*

CAST

Robert Donat, *Andrew Manson;* Rosalind Russell, *Christine Manson;* Ralph Richardson, *Denny;* Rex Harrison, *Dr. Lawford;* Emlyn Williams, *Owen;* Penelope Dudley Ward, *Toppy Leroy;* Francis L. Sullivan, *Ben Chenkin;* Mary Clare, *Mrs. Orlando;* Cecil Parker, *Charles Every;* Nora Swinburne, *Mrs. Thornton;* Edward Chapman, *Joe Morgan;* Athene Seyler, *Lady Raebank;* Felix Aylmer, *Mr. Boon;* Joyce Bland, *Nurse Sharp;* Percy Parsons, *Mr. Stillman;* Dilys Davis, *Mrs. Page;* Basil Gill, *Dr. Page;* Joss Ambler, *Dr. A. H. Llewellyn.*

MGM, the first U.S. company to establish a British production unit, kicked off an ambitious program of hands-across-the-sea filming with *A Yank at Oxford* (1938), an entertaining box-office hit with Robert Taylor, Maureen O'Sullivan, and Lionel Barrymore blending into an otherwise English cast. As a follow-up, Metro prepared an adaptation of A. J. Cronin's 1937 novel *The Citadel*, dispatching director King Vidor and this time only *one* American star. Rosalind Russell was well teamed with Robert Donat and splendidly supported by a distinguished array of British stage actors, among them Ralph Richardson, Emlyn Williams, Rex Harrison, Francis L. Sullivan, Mary Clare, and Athene Seyler.

Much of Dr. Cronin's novel ran a close parallel with his own early career as a Scottish doctor in the mining country of South Wales, from which he moved on to fame and fortune in London practice. Ill health eventually forced him to convalesce in Scotland—which led to his successful writing career.

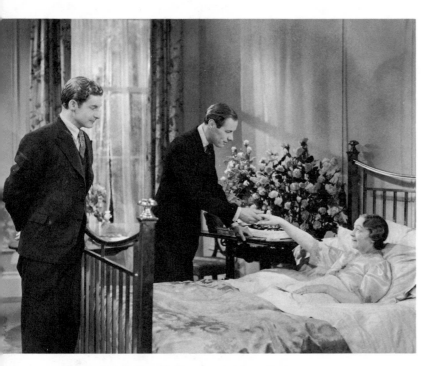

Robert Donat, Rex Harrison, and Athene Seyler

Emlyn Williams, Rosalind Russell, and Robert Donat

The Citadel's Cronin-like Dr. Andrew Manson (Donat) is a Scot who begins doctoring the tubercular miners of the Welsh mining slums, then compromises his youthful ideals when he enters into the treatment of a rich and neurotic London clientele. Against the advice of his ex-schoolteacher wife (Russell), Manson now puts profit over idealism—until the death of a dear friend (Richardson) makes him reevaluate his life and return to serious, small-town medicine.

This was an even more popular motion picture than *A Yank at Oxford*, reaping widespread critical acclaim. In *The New York Times*, Frank S. Nugent praised the movie for combining "the pace of a Hollywood production" with "the honest characterization typical of England's best films."

Of *The Citadel*'s many citations, the most prestigious was its designation as Best Motion Picture of 1938 by the New York Film Critics. In the Oscar sweepstakes, however, it was only a Best Picture runner-up to *You Can't Take It With You*. And, while Donat's brilliant performance lost out to Spencer Tracy for *Boys Town*, a year later *he* would be the victor for *Goodbye, Mr. Chips*, the film with which World War II brought an untimely halt to the MGM/British production division.

Rosalind Russell, Ralph Richardson, and Robert Donat

THE ROAD TO RENO

1938

CREDITS

A Universal Picture. Directed by S. Sylvan Simon. *Produced by* Edmund Grainger. *Screenplay by* Roy Chanslor, Adele Comandini, *and* Brian Marlowe. *Based on an adaptation by* Charles Kenyon *and* F. Hugh Herbert *of the novel Puritan at Large by* I.A.R. Wylie. *Photographed by* George Robinson. *Edited by* Maurice Wright *and* Paul Landres. *Art direction by* Jack Otterson *and* Charles H. Clarke. *Gowns by* Vera West. *Musical direction by* Charles Previn. *Songs:* "Ridin' Home," "I Gave My Heart Away," *and* "Tonight Is the Night" *by* Jimmy McHugh *and* Harold Adamson; *Quando me'n vo'soletta" from* Puccini's *opera* La Bohème. *Running time: 72 minutes.*

CAST

Randolph Scott, *Steve Fortness;* Hope Hampton, *Linda Halliday;* Glenda Farrell, *Sylvia Shane;* Helen Broderick, *Aunt Minerva;* Alan Marshal, *Walter Crawford;* David Oliver, *Salty;* Ted Osborne, *Linda's attorney;* Samuel S. Hinds, *Sylvia's attorney;* Charles Murphy, *Mike;* Spencer Charters, *The judge;* Dorothy Farley, *Mrs. Brumleigh;* Mira McKinney, *Hannah;* Renie Riano, *Woman bailiff.*

The Thirties were loaded with pleasantly innocuous little comedies like *The Road to Reno*, manufactured by all of the Hollywood studios to meet the weekly demands of constantly changing double-bill programs. *The Road to Reno* typifies this kind of movie in that it is neither very good nor very bad, its mediocrity offset by the foolishly diverting story: a blonde opera singer (Hope Hampton) heads for Reno to divorce her handsome rancher-husband (Randolph Scott) so that she can marry an equally attractive Easterner

Hope Hampton as Musetta in the "La Boheme" opera sequence

(Alan Marshal). Not to wonder why such a diva and a strong, silent Westerner ever got together in the first place! But, in the course of this cross-country romantic trifle, the cowboy (who, incidentally, still loves that soprano) has to contend with his Eastern rival, who manages to belie his "dude" status by riding a wild, bucking bronco deliberately chosen to embarrass him in the eyes of his lady. But by the story's end, our prima donna finds she still loves her cowboy, after all, thus obviating any genuine need for this film in the first place!

Randolph Scott was, at thirty-five, equally at home on the range or in the drawing room at this stage of his long career. His leading lady was something else; millionairess Hope Hampton, later to be celebrated as "the Duchess of Park Avenue," was somewhere in her late thirties and attempting a movie comeback. From 1920 to 1926, she had graced such silent epics as *A Modern Salome* and *Love's Penalty*. Married to a financier thirty-three years her senior, Hope had turned from a limping movie career to the operatic stage, before moving on to operetta and then nightclubs.

The Road to Reno, Hope Hampton's talkie debut and her *only* Thirties film, allows her to indulge in her admittedly pleasant singing talents via three pop tunes, as well as Musetta's Waltz Song from Puccini's *La Bohème*, performed in period costume but in a strangely modernistic setting. In the opera house, this aria occurs in the second act. But in *The Road to Reno*, her aria closes both the act and the *opera;* she takes her bows, receives a floral tribute, and leaves the theater!

Apparently, Hope Hampton enjoyed this solitary fling at talking-picture stardom, for she skips through the picture with great glee and a winning Pepsodent smile. She appears so eager to please that it would seem churlish not to wish her a safe return to Park Avenue.

Helen Broderick, Randolph Scott, and Hope Hampton

Miliza Korjus and Luise Rainer

Minna Gombell, Fernand Gravet, Hugh Herbert, and Luise Rainer

THE GREAT WALTZ

1938

CREDITS

A Metro-Goldwyn-Mayer Picture. Directed by Julien Duvivier *and (uncredited)* Josef von Sternberg. *Produced by* Bernard Hyman. *Screenplay by* Samuel Hoffenstein *and* Walter Reisch. *Based on an original story by* Gottfried Reinhardt. *Photographed by* Joseph Ruttenberg. *Edited by* Tom Held. *Music of Johann Strauss II adapted and arranged by* Dimitri Tiomkin. *Lyrics by* Oscar Hammerstein II. *Musical direction by* Arthur Gutman. *Dances staged by* Albertina Rasch. *Art direction by* Cedric Gibbons. *Running time: 102 minutes.*

CAST

Luise Rainer, *Poldi Vogelhuber;* Fernand Gravet, *Johann Strauss;* Miliza Korjus, *Carla Donner;* Hugh Herbert, *Hofbauer;* Lionel Atwill, *Count Hohenfried;* Curt Bois, *Kienzl;* Leonid Kinsky, *Dudelman;* Al Shean, *Cellist;* Minna Gombell, *Mrs. Hofbauer;* George Houston, *Schiller;* Bert Roach, *Vogelhuber;* Greta Meyer, *Mrs. Vogelhuber;* Herman Bing, *Dommayer;* Alma Kruger, *Mrs. Strauss;* Henry Hull, *Franz Joseph;* Sig Rumann, *Wertheimer;* Christian Rub, *Coachman.*

Prior to the wide-screen era of stereophonic sound, the glorious waltz tunes of Johann Strauss II (1825–1899) had never been so well served in a Hollywood motion picture as in MGM's lavish 1938 screen operetta, *The Great Waltz.* The film was a pet project of Metro chief Louis B. Mayer, whose partiality for Strauss's music and love of pure-hearted, escapist entertainment led him to champion this fictional biofilm of the popular nineteenth-century composer. Filmed with a virtual melting pot of European-born talent, both behind and before the cameras, *The Great Waltz* (directed by French-born Julien Duvivier) featured a cast topped by MGM's double-Oscar winner, Viennese Luise Rainer, as Strauss's demure, long-suffering wife. Portraying Strauss was Belgian actor Fernand Gravet (originally spelled "Gravey" in Europe, but Hollywood producers worried about their import being confused with meat sauce), and for the inevitable extramarital flirtation (albeit

Miliza Korjus, Fernand Gravet, Leonid Kinsky, Curt Bois, and bit players

quite innocent in 1938 Hollywood), Mayer imported Warsaw-born coloratura soprano Miliza Korjus ("rhymes with gorgeous!" proclaimed MGM's advertising for the film).

A robust, large-boned woman, Korjus, at Mayer's insistence, received the full MGM treatment. She was slimmed down and glamorized and given special accord by the Metro sound department. As a result, her rather phenomenal singing voice soared with ravishing abandon through such melodies as "I'm in Love with Vienna," "One Day When We Were Young," and the lilting arias from *Die Fledermaus*. Critics (perhaps unfairly) likened the Korjus screen image to Mae West, but most were impressed with the enthusiasm of her performance—and especially that glorious voice. But the lady never made another Hollywood film, and rumor has it that MGM's then reigning soprano, Jeanette

MacDonald, let Mayer know, in no uncertain terms, that there wasn't room for both herself *and* Korjus on that studio lot.

The Great Waltz is little more than a rich cream puff of visual and sonic splendor. But this Viennese pastry provided welcome entertainment in a year notable for its dearth of great movies, and it took home an Academy Award for the swirling, handsomely lit camerawork of Joseph Ruttenberg. Nominations went to Korjus as supporting actress and Tom Held's editing, but, inexplicably, there were no Oscar nods toward those who perhaps made the greatest contributions to *The Great Waltz*—music director Arthur Gutman and arranger Dimitri Tiomkin, who so cleverly adapted Strauss's durable themes to the soundtrack.

GUNGA DIN

1939

CREDITS

A RKO Picture. Produced and directed by George Stevens. *Executive producer:* Pandro S. Berman. *Screenplay by* Joel Sayre *and* Fred Guiol. *Story by* Ben Hecht, Charles MacArthur, *and (uncredited)* William Faulkner. *Suggested by the* Rudyard Kipling *poem. Photographed by* Joseph H. August. *Edited by* Henry Berman *and* John Lockert. *Art direction by* Van Nest Polglase *and* Perry Ferguson. *Set decoration by* Darrell Silvera. *Gowns by* Edward Stevenson. *Technical advisers:* Capt. Clive Morgan, Sgt.-Maj. William Briers, *and* Sir Robert Erskine Holland. *Special effects by* Vernon L. Walker. *Music by* Alfred Newman. *Running time: 117 minutes.*

CAST

Cary Grant, *Cutter;* Victor McLaglen, *MacChesney;* Douglas Fairbanks, Jr., *Ballantine;* Sam Jaffe, *Gunga Din;* Eduardo Ciannelli, *Guru;* Joan Fontaine, *Emmy Stebbins;* Montagu Love, *Colonel Weed;* Robert Coote, *Higginbotham;* Abner Biberman, *Chota;* Lumsden Hare, *Maj. Mitchell;* Cecil Kellaway, *Mr. Stebbins;* Reginald Sheffield, *Journalist;* Ann Evers, Audrey Manners and Fay McKenzie, *Girls at party;* Roland Varno, *Lt. Markham.*

This rousing, Kiplingesque adventure spectacle of imperialist British derring-do on India's mountainous Northwest Frontier was merely "inspired" by that celebrated novelist's poem of the same title. Its bravura entertainment value as a motion picture is fully attributable to the enthusiastic inspiration of screenwriters Joel Sayre and Fred Guiol (and the uncredited contribution of William Faulkner), working from a story treatment by the team of Ben Hecht and Charles MacArthur (also responsible for *The Front Page*). But director George Stevens (here doubling for the first time as his own producer) is the individual most responsible for *Gunga Din*'s expansive flair, epic fun, and almost nonstop movement. Obviously, his cast, topped by clowning Cary Grant, bullish Victor McLaglen, and dashing Douglas Fairbanks, Jr., entered into this project with energy and enthusiasm. And character actor Sam Jaffe is as oddly appealing in the title role of that humble Indian

Eduardo Ciannelli, Victor McLaglen, Douglas Fairbanks, Jr., Cary Grant, and bit players

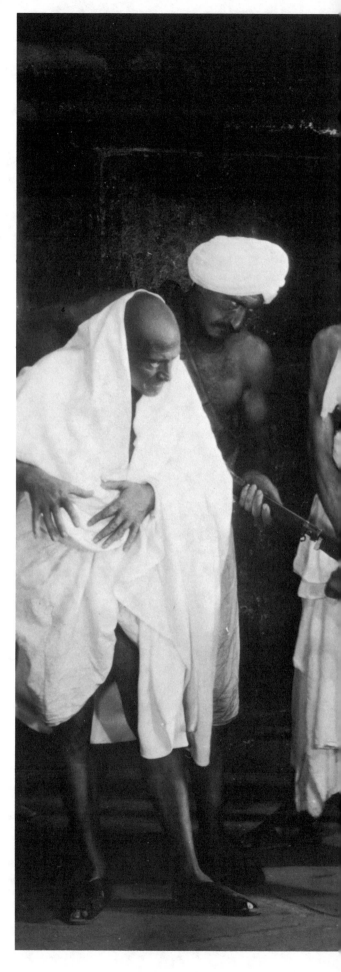

Cary Grant, Victor McLaglen, Joan Fontaine, and Douglas Fairbanks, Jr.

waterboy as bald-pated Eduardo Ciannelli is chilling as the fanatically villainous Guru. Demurely pretty Joan Fontaine pleasantly fulfills the minor-league requirements of femininity in this he-man's yarn.

Gunga Din may be a highly unlikely adventure story, but it certainly isn't heavy, despite its nearly two-hour running time (the version generally shown on TV is considerably shorter). And the smoothness of its telling belies Stevens's report that its production was undertaken with an incomplete screenplay and that some parts (including the bugle scene between Grant and Jaffe) were completely improvised during filming.

The thirty-five-year-old Stevens's previous, recent forays into small-town drama *(Alice Adams),* musicals *(Swing Time),* and comedy *(Vivacious Lady)* hardly suggested the ease with which he would handle the spectacular heroics, humor, and tongue-in-cheek melodrama of *Gunga Din.* Although he wasn't accustomed to directing thousands of extras in spectacular outdoor settings (location scenes were shot near California's Mt. Whitney, at Lone Pine), Stevens handles his red-blooded adventure tale with apparent ease —and the indispensable panoramic skills of cameraman Joseph H. August.

Today, this black-and-white 1939 classic remains far more colorful entertainment than such rainbow-hued derivatives as its 1962 Frank Sinatra–Dean Martin–Peter Lawford remake, *Sergeants 3.*

WUTHERING HEIGHTS

1939

Laurence Olivier and Merle Oberon

Geraldine Fitzgerald, Laurence Olivier, Leo G. Carroll

CREDITS

A United Artists release of a Samuel Goldwyn Production. Directed by William Wyler. *Screenplay by* Ben Hecht *and* Charles MacArthur. *Based on the novel by* Emily Brontë. *Photographed by* Gregg Toland. *Edited by* Daniel Mandell. *Art direction by* James Basevi. *Set decoration by* Julia Heron. *Music by* Alfred Newman. *Costumes by* Omar Kiam. *Running time: 104 minutes.*

CAST

Merle Oberon, *Catherine Earnshaw;* Laurence Olivier, *Heathcliff;* David Niven, *Edgar Linton;* Flora Robson, *Ellen Dean;* Donald Crisp, *Dr. Kenneth;* Hugh Williams, *Hindley Earnshaw;* Geraldine Fitzgerald, *Isabella Linton;* Leo G. Carroll, *Joseph;* Cecil Humphreys, *Judge Linton;* Miles Mander, *Mr. Lockwood;* Sarita Wooton, *Cathy as a child;* Rex Downing, *Heathcliff as a child;* Douglas Scott, *Hindley as a child;* Romaine Callender, *Robert;* Cecil Kellaway, *Mr. Earnshaw.*

Emily Brontë's classic melodrama of tragic love and

revenge was published in 1847 under the pseudonym of Ellis Bell to disguise the fact that its author was a woman. It was her only novel, this wildly imaginative tale of conflicting passions amid the "wuthering" (or stormy) moors of her native Yorkshire. Central to the story is the half-wild gypsy youth Heathcliff who, through his disappointed love for the willfully selfish Cathy, is driven to extreme measures of vindictiveness, culminating in either death or tragedy for all involved. Its well-wrought blend of romance and lurid violence helped make *Wuthering Heights* a perennial nineteenth-century best-seller and a lucrative subject for twentieth-century filmmaking. Research reveals at least four movie versions to date, including a 1920 British adaptation starring Milton Rosmer and Colette Brettel; Luis Buñuel's 1953 Mexican translation, *Abismos de Pasin*, with Jorge Mistral and Irasema Dilian; and a 1970 British remake with Timothy Dalton and Anna Calder-Marshall.

But for many, there's only one *Wuthering Heights,* and that's the haunting, black-and-white Samuel Goldwyn production with Laurence Olivier and Merle Oberon, sensitively directed by William Wyler. Scenarists Ben Hecht and Charles MacArthur altered and simplified the Brontë plot, confining their screenplay to the novel's first seventeen chapters. But the resulting film was immensely popular with both moviegoers and the press, even beating out *Gone With*

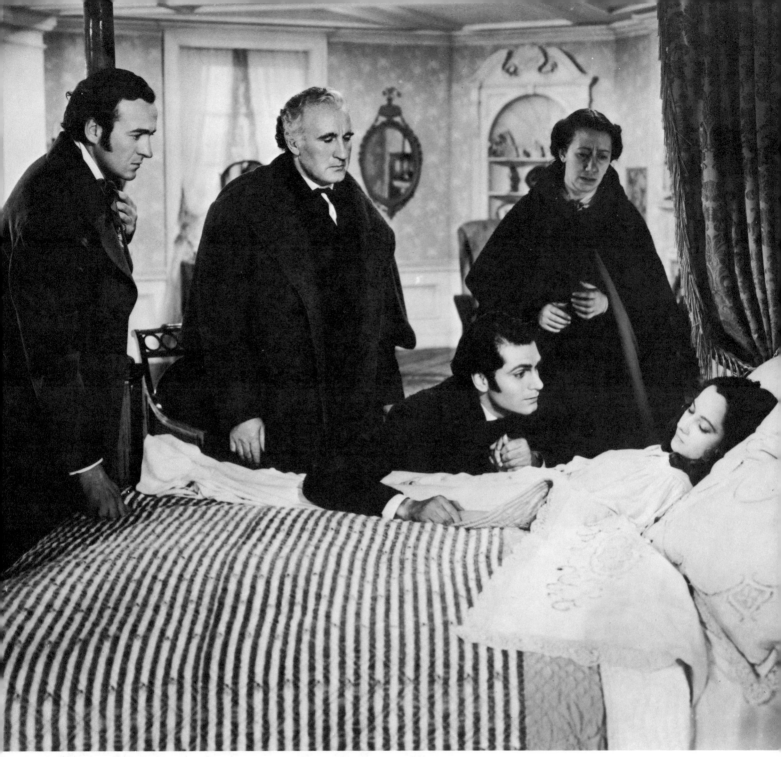

David Niven, Donald Crisp, Laurence Olivier, Flora Robson, and Merle Oberon

the Wind as the New York Film Critic's choice for 1939's Best Picture. Hollywood's Academy granted it *nominations* for Best Picture, Screenplay, Director Wyler, Actor Olivier, Supporting Actress Geraldine Fitzgerald, and Alfred Newman's Score. But, the only contributor to take home an Oscar was cinematographer Gregg Toland, whose moody expressionism was carefully worked out between himself and Wyler to maintain a certain distance from reality.

For Olivier, *Wuthering Heights* marked a major turning point, and he credits Wyler's tough guidance and advice with making him take seriously, for the first time, the art of screen acting. The exotic Merle Oberon, an actress never celebrated for either warmth or great acting talent, nevertheless appears to her best advantage under Wyler's direction (as she did in his *These Three*). Geraldine Fitzgerald also stands out with her spirited interpretation of the fiercely determined Isabella (a role that Vivien Leigh had refused because of its supporting nature.

The fact that this *Wuthering Heights* has withstood the test of time can be credited to the Goldwyn touch, that canny mixture of taste and showmanship that so often inspired the talents in his employ to seek perfection.

DARK VICTORY

1939

Bette Davis and George Brent

CREDITS

A Warner Bros. Picture. Directed by Edmund Goulding. *Produced by* Hal B. Wallis. *Associate producer:* David Lewis. *Screenplay by* Casey Robinson. *Based on the play by* George Emerson Brewer, Jr., *and* Bertram Bloch. *Photographed by* Ernest Haller. *Edited by* William Holmes. *Art direction by* Robert Haas. *Costumes by* Orry-Kelly. *Music by* Max Steiner. *Song:* "Oh, Give Me Time for Tenderness" *by* Elsie Janis *and* Edmund Goulding. *Technical adviser:* Dr. Leo Schulman. *Running time: 106 minutes.*

CAST

Bette Davis, *Judith Traherne;* George Brent, *Dr. Frederick Steele;* Humphrey Bogart, *Michael O'Leary;* Geraldine Fitzgerald, *Ann King;* Ronald Reagan, *Alec Hamm;* Henry Travers, *Dr. Parsons;* Cora Witherspoon, *Carrie Spottswood;* Virginia Brissac, *Martha;* Dorothy Peterson, *Miss Wainwright;* Charles Richman, *Colonel Mantle;* Herbert Rawlinson, *Dr. Carter;* Leonard Mudie, *Dr. Driscoll;* Fay Helm, *Miss Dodd;* Lottie Williams, *Lucy;* Diane Bernard, *Agatha;* Jack Mower, *Veterinarian;* Ila Rhodes, *Secretary.*

Bette Davis copped Academy Awards for *Dangerous* in 1935 and *Jezebel* in 1938. The role for which she deserved one even more was *Dark Victory.* But 1939 was a highly competitive, banner year for Hollywood movies, and *Dark Victory* won only nominations—for Best Picture, Best Actress, and Best Score (Max Steiner), categories in which they lost, respectively, to *Gone With the Wind*, Vivien Leigh, and *The Wizard of Oz.*

In *Dark Victory*'s Judith Traherne, Davis had one of her favorite roles; her costar George Brent thought she gave "the greatest performance of her life" in this movie. Davis fought hard to get this part, urging Warners to acquire the property for her, despite its failure as a 1934 stage vehicle for Tallulah Bankhead. But, with a sensible reworking of the play by screenwriter Casey Robinson, *Dark Victory*'s originally misjudged dramatic values realize their full potential in this adaptation. Under the guidance of Edmund Goulding—like George Cukor, an expert at directing women—*Dark Victory* emerged as a first-rate tear-jerker about a willful heiress who learns that she has a brain tumor. After a successful operation, she falls in love with the

Humphrey Bogart and Bette Davis

Geraldine Fitzgerald and Bette Davis

doctor (Brent) who performed the surgery, but accidentally discovers that his success was only temporary and that she will die within a year. Rejecting her fiancé's affection as mere pity, she sets out to bury her confused feelings in fast living with the horse-and-cocktail set. But the down-to-earth advice of her admiring stableman (Humphrey Bogart) convinces her to seek love and happiness while there's still time, and she weds her doctor. In the movie's poignant final scenes, dwindling eyesight informs her that death is imminent, and she sends her husband off to a medical conference while she and her best friend (Geraldine Fitzgerald) plant a flower bed. Finally, Judith goes indoors to face the end alone.

Bette Davis runs a nearly flawless emotional gamut in *Dark Victory*, and her handling of that difficult final sequence is dulled only slightly by the heavenly choir with which composer Steiner chose to conclude an otherwise laudable score.

Dark Victory is soap opera of the highest caliber, and its star's dedicated artistry prevents its ever becoming maudlin. More than any other, it was this movie that made Davis queen of the Warner Bros. lot and, throughout much of the Forties, Hollywood's first lady of drama.

1939

Jack Haley, Bert Lahr, Judy Garland, Frank Morgan, and Ray Bolger

Margaret Hamilton and Judy Garland

CREDITS

A Metro-Goldwyn-Mayer Picture. Directed by Victor Fleming, *(and, uncredited)* Richard Thorpe *and* King Vidor. *Produced by* Mervyn LeRoy. *Associate producer:* Arthur Freed. *Screenplay by* Noel Langley, Florence Ryerson, *and* Edgar Allan Woolf. *Based on the book by* L. Frank Baum. *Photographed in Technicolor by* Harold Rosson *(opening and closing scenes in sepia). Edited by* Blanche Sewell. *Art direction by* Cedric Gibbons *and* William A. Horning. *Set decoration by* Edwin B. Willis. *Special effects by* Arnold Gillespie. *Costumes by* Adrian. *Music by* Harold Arlen. *Lyrics by* E. Y. Harburg. *Musical adaptation by* Herbert Stothart. *Songs: "Over the Rainbow," "Munchkinland," "Follow the Yellow Brick Road," "If I Only Had a Brain," "We're Off to See the Wizard," "Merry Old Land of Oz," "Laugh a Day Away," "If I Were King," "Courage," "Ding, Dong, the Witch is Dead," "If I Only Had a Heart," "Optimistic Voices,"* and *"The Jitterbug" (cut from the film following its first public preview). Musical numbers staged by* Bobby Connolly. *Character makeups created by* Jack Dawn. *Running time: 100 minutes.*

CAST

Judy Garland, *Dorothy;* Frank Morgan, *Professor Marvel/The Wizard;* Ray Bolger, *Hunk/Scarecrow;* Bert Lahr, *Zeke/Cowardly Lion;* Jack Haley, *Hickory/Tin Woodman;* Billie Burke, *Glinda;* Margaret Hamilton, *Miss Gulch/Wicked Witch;* Charley Grapewin, *Uncle Henry;* Clara Blandick, *Auntie Em;* Pat Walshe, *Nikko.*

This inspired musical fantasy has so sustained its popularity over the years that it has, as this book is written, enjoyed a record twenty-three airings on prime-time network television. The movie remains in a class by itself, for fantasy of this sort has seldom proven successful on the screen. But MGM, inspired by the popularity of Walt Disney's animated *Snow White and the Seven Dwarfs* (1937), struck a goldmine with this delightful musical adaptation of a classic children's story that began and ended in sepia-toned Kansas, in-between which MGM's art and special-effects departments had a field day creating all the magical, Technicolor wonders of Oz.

Sixteen-year-old Judy Garland, in the role for which she's best remembered, had just the right quality of vulnerable sincerity for Dorothy, the Kansas teen-ager who's transported to Oz by a cyclone. There, she's introduced to all manner of friendly and frightening creatures before returning, unharmed, to friends and family. It's interesting to note that Garland's lifetime musical trademark, "Over the Rainbow," which was added to the movie almost as an afterthought, was executive-ordered to be cut out, after the first public preview. Fortunately, saner heads prevailed. The number was restored and went on to win 1939's Best Song Oscar.

Of *The Wizard of Oz's* wonderful cast, few ever had roles more memorable than they portrayed here. Bert Lahr, Jack Haley, and Margaret Hamilton have never been more celebrated than as the Cowardly Lion, Tin Woodman, and Wicked Witch of this beloved film. And Ray Bolger's Scarecrow rivals only his stage-and-screen *Where's Charley?* Victor Fleming, who replaced Richard Thorpe two weeks into filming, received sole director credit for the film, although the last weeks of shooting were handled by King Vidor, after Fleming, in turn, left to replace George Cukor as director of *Gone With the Wind.*

The Wizard of Oz was nominated for a Best Picture Academy Award but lost to *Gone With the Wind.* It did win an Oscar for Herbert Stothart's scoring, in addition to the aforementioned "Over the Rainbow." And Judy Garland was awarded a miniature statuette for her outstanding juvenile work that year.

Jack Haley, Ray Bolger, Judy Garland, and Bert Lahr

DRUMS ALONG THE MOHAWK

1939

CREDITS

A 20th Century-Fox Picture. Directed by John Ford. *Produced by* Darryl F. Zanuck. *Associate producer:* Raymond Griffith. *Screenplay by* Lamar Trotti *and* Sonya Levien. *Based on the novel by* Walter D. Edmonds. *Photographed in Technicolor by* Bert Glennon *and* Ray Rennahan. *Edited by* Robert Simpson. *Music by* Alfred Newman. *Art direction by* Richard Day *and* Mark Lee Kirk. *Set decoration by* Thomas Little. *Costumes by* Gwen Wakeling. *Running time: 103 minutes.*

CAST

Claudette Colbert, *Magdelana "Lana" Martin;* Henry Fonda, *Gilbert Martin;* Edna May Oliver, *Sarah McKlennar;* Eddie Collins, *Christian Reall;* John Carradine, *Caldwell;* Dorris Bowdon, *Mary Reall;* Jessie Ralph, *Mrs. Weaver;* Arthur Shields, *Father Rosenkranz;* Robert Lowery, *John Weaver;* Roger Imhof, *Gen. Nicholas Herkimer;* Francis Ford, *Joe Boleo;* Ward Bond, *Adam Hartmann;* Kay Linaker, *Mrs. Demooth;* Russell Simpson, *Dr. Petry;* Chief Big Tree, *Blue Back;* Spencer Charters, *Innkeeper;* Arthur Aylesworth, *George;* Si Jenks, *Jacob Small;* J. Ronald "Jack" Pennick, *Amos;* Charles Tannen, *Robert Johnson;* Paul McVey, *Capt. Mark Demooth;* Elizabeth Jones, *Mrs. Reall;* Lionel Pape, *General;* Clarence Wilson, *Paymaster;* Edwin Maxwell, *Pastor;* Clara Blandick, *Mrs. Borst;* Beulah Hall Jones, *Daisy;* Robert Greig, *Mr. Borst;* Tom Tyler, *Morgan;* Noble Johnson, *Indian;* Mae Marsh, *Pioneer woman.*

Walter D. Edmonds's popular 1936 novel vividly depicted events in upstate New York's Mohawk Valley in the years 1775–1783 and how the Revolutionary War affected its farmers and residents. Three years later, producer Darryl F. Zanuck and director John Ford brought this story to the screen with a striking eye to period detail. This was Ford's first experience with the then increasingly popular three-color Technicolor process, and he was fortunate in having the expertise of cinematographers Bert Glennon and Ray Rennahan.

Drums Along the Mohawk sacrificed some of the detail in Edmonds's novel, eliding events into an episodic (but essentially faithful) screenplay, as adapted by Lamar Trotti and Sonya Levien. This is a stirring pioneer saga of considerable interest as it takes the audience from a well-to-do Albany home to the near wilderness of the Deerfield settlement's farms and fortress. Claudette Colbert portrays the

Claudette Colbert, Edna May Oliver, and Dorris Bowdon

cultured young woman who takes her chances with marriage to farmer Henry Fonda, traveling by covered wagon to his upstate home, where she joins him in the hardships of warring Indians, white renegades, death, childbirth, and a fire that destroys their home and possessions.

The movie's beautiful Technicolor scenery may tend to soften the impression of pioneering hardships. And 1939 censorship restrictions prevent our seeing the more horrifying effects of Indian violence, although Ford manages vividly to suggest what he cannot show.

A fine supporting cast helps make *Drums Along the Mohawk* the memorable entertainment it remains today. Gruff, vinegary, and horse-faced Edna May Oliver won the film's only Oscar nomination, but she lost to Hattie McDaniel for *Gone With the Wind*. There haven't been many motion pictures dealing with this period in America's past—which makes *Drums Along the Mohawk*'s excellence all the more worthy of revisiting.

THE WOMEN

1939

*Rosalind Russell, Joan Fontaine, and
Norma Shearer*

Norma Shearer, *Mary Haines;* Joan Crawford, *Crystal Allen;* Rosalind Russell, *Sylvia Fowler;* Mary Boland, *Countess De Lave;* Paulette Goddard, *Miriam Aarons;* Joan Fontaine, *Peggy Day;* Lucile Watson, *Mrs. Morehead;* Phyllis Povah, *Edith Potter;* Florence Nash, *Nancy Blake;* Virginia Weidler, *Little Mary;* Ruth Hussey, *Miss Watts;* Muriel Hutchison, *Jane;* Margaret Dumont, *Mrs. Wagstaff;* Dennie Moore, *Olga;* Mary Cecil, *Maggie;* Marjorie Main, *Lucy;* Esther Dale, *Ingrid;* Hedda Hopper, *Dolly De Peyster;* Priscilla Lawson, *Hairdresser;* Ann Morriss, *Exercise instructor;* Mary Beth Hughes, *Miss Trimmerback;* Virginia Grey, *Pat;* Cora Witherspoon, *Mrs. Van Adams;* Theresa Harris, *Olive;* Vera Vague, *Receptionist;* Judith Allen, *Model;* Aileen Pringle, *Saleslady.*

Joan Crawford and Virginia Grey

A Metro-Goldwyn-Mayer Picture. Directed by George Cukor. *Produced by* Hunt Stromberg. *Screenplay by* Anita Loos, Jane Murfin, *and (uncredited)* Donald Ogden Stewart *and* F. Scott Fitzgerald. *Based on the play by* Clare Boothe. *Photographed by* Oliver T. Marsh *and* Joseph Ruttenberg. *Edited by* Robert J. Kern. *Art direction by* Cedric Gibbons *and* Wade B. Rubottom. *Set decoration by* Edwin B. Willis. *Gowns and Technicolor fashion show by* Adrian. *Music by* Edward Ward. *Running time: 132 minutes.*

Years before she was the politically active wife of *Time* titan Henry Luce, Clare Boothe enjoyed a successful career as editor of *Vanity Fair* magazine, syndicated newspaper columnist, and author of two successful Broadway comedies, *The Women* and *Kiss the Boys Good-Bye.* The former, a long-running 1936 hit, was reportedly inspired by caustic gossip overhead by Boothe in a nightclub ladies' room. Lightweight and episodic, *The Women* employed a large, all-female cast to dissect the superficial lives of several Park Avenue matrons whose days are filled with bridge, beauty-parlor appointments, and bitchery involving one another's marital ups and downs.

In 1939, under George Cukor's enthusiastic direction, MGM brought this hit comedy to the movies, retaining most of Boothe's original bite, although a few of her cleverest lines were eliminated to pacify the censors. But the episodic narrative retained its all-female milieu, and a fine cast played *The Women* to its hilt. Norma Shearer drew audience sympathy as the nice matron who finds she's losing her husband to a ruthless shopgirl (Joan Crawford), with Rosalind Russell hilarious as this smart set's fast-talking, busybody. Surrounding them with varying degrees of wiles, wit, and feminine wisdom are the clever characterizations of Paulette Goddard, Mary Boland, Phyllis Povah, Joan Fontaine, and—in a standout bit—Virginia Grey, as a wised-up colleague of Crawford's.

MGM garnished this brilliant black-and-white film with a Technicolor fashion-show sequence featuring the creations of their star-designer, Adrian. But such gimmickry was unnecessary, for the screen fairly crackles with clever writing, acted to perfection by a cast that could not have been improved on (and certainly *not* bettered in its 1956 remake, *The Opposite Sex.*)

Like many another great motion picture, *The Women* took no Oscars, although it was a top box-office hit of the 1939–1940 season.

*Rosalind Russell and
Joan Crawford*

*Paulette Goddard, Mary
Boland, and Norma
Shearer*

MR. SMITH GOES
TO WASHINGTON

1939

James Stewart and Jean Arthur

Claude Rains, James Stewart

A Columbia Picture. Produced and directed by Frank Capra. *Screenplay by* Sidney Buchman. *Based on* Lewis R. Foster's *story "The Gentleman from Montana." Photographed by* Joseph Walker. *Edited by* Gene Havlick and Al Clark. *Art direction by* Lionel Banks. *Music by* Dimitri Tiomkin. *Gowns by* Kalloch. Montage effects by Slavko Vorkapich. *Technical adviser:* Jim Preston. *Running time: 125 minutes.*

CAST

Jean Arthur, *Clarissa Saunders;* James Stewart, *Jefferson Smith;* Claude Rains, *Sen. Joseph Paine;* Edward Arnold, *Jim Taylor;* Guy Kibbee, *Gov. Hubert Hopper;* Thomas Mitchell, *Diz Moore;* Eugene Pallette, *Chick McGann;* Beulah Bondi, *Ma Smith;* H. B. Warner, *Sen. Agnew;* Harry Carey, *President of the Senate;* Astrid Allwyn, *Susan Paine;* Ruth Donnelly, *Emma Hopper;* Grant Mitchell, *Sen. MacPherson;* Porter Hall, *Sen. Monroe;* Pierre Watkin, *Sen. Barnes;* Charles Lane, *Nosey;* William Demarest, *Bill Griffith;* Dick Elliott, *Carl Cook;* H. V. Kaltenborn, *Broadcaster;* Jack Carson, *Sweeney;* Joe King, *Summers;* Paul Stanton, *Flood;* Russell Simpson, *Allen;* Stanley Andrews, *Sen. Hodges;* Walter Soderling, *Sen. Pickett;* Byron Foulger, *Hopper's secretary;* Dickie Jones, *Page;* Allan Cavan, *Ragner;* Maurice Costello, *Diggs;* Ann Doran and Helen Jerome Eddy, *Paine's secretaries.*

James Stewart, Edward Arnold, Allan Cavan

Director Frank Capra's personal commitment to flag-waving commentary on American idealism and political chicanery centers particularly on a trio of movies: *Mr. Deeds Goes to Town* (1936), *Mr. Smith Goes to Washington* (1939), and *Meet John Doe* (1941). Mixing comedy with drama and amusingly naive heroes with corrupt, power-hungry villains, Capra therein weaves three variations on the theme of right overcoming might. *Mr. Smith Goes to Washington* is the best of the lot, a triumphant blend of script, direction, and inspired performances.

The nation's capital, of course, provides the setting for Sidney Buchman's well-wrought screenplay about a green-from-Wisconsin freshman senator (James Stewart) who learns the hard way about Washington graft and corruption, which he idealistically discloses in a climactic speech before the Senate. This sequence, with its memorable filibuster, reveals Jimmy Stewart at the peak of his power as a populist actor. In the progress of this well-thought-out characterization, Stewart's subtle range of facets stamps his Jefferson Smith as the single most powerful performance of

a long and distinguished career. In a year of extraordinarily fine acting, the Oscar Stewart should have won went to Robert Donat for *Goodbye, Mr. Chips.* But the New York Film Critics, in turn, bypassed Donat in favor of Stewart for their Best Actor of 1939 award. *Mr. Smith Goes to Washington* did manage to collect an impressive eleven nominations, including ones for Best Picture and Director Capra. But the only winner was Lewis R. Foster, for his Best Original Story.

The movie isn't entirely Jimmy Stewart's, however, so far as acting goes. Claude Rains, in particular, offers a masterful display of corruption battling conscience. And the uniquely child-voiced Jean Arthur alternates endearingly between warm support and tart cynicism as the all-wise Girl Friday who's instrumental in helping Smith beat those governmental odds. And equally worthy of note are the well-mannered ruthlessness of Edward Arnold and the wryly amusing Harry Carey in a near pantomimic cameo as President of the Senate. Very much the entertaining sum of its brilliant parts, *Mr. Smith Goes to Washington* is popular Thirties moviemaking at its best.

THE ROARING TWENTIES

1939

Humphrey Bogart and James Cagney

A Warner Bros. Picture. Directed by Raoul Walsh *and (uncredited)* Anatole Litvak. *Executive producer:* Hal B. Wallis. *Associate producer:* Samuel Bischoff. *Screenplay by* Jerry Wald, Richard Macauley, *and* Robert Rossen. *Story by* Mark Hellinger. *Photographed by* Ernest Haller. *Edited by* Jack Killifer. *Art direction by* Max Parker. *Music by* Heinz Roemheld *and* Ray Heindorf. *Songs:* "My Melancholy Baby" *by* Ernie Burnett *and* George A. Norton; "I'm Just Wild About Harry" *by* Eubie Blake *and* Noble Sissle; "It Had to Be You" *by* Isham Jones *and* Gus Kahn; "In a Shanty in Old Shanty Town" *by* Jack Little, Joseph Young, *and* John Siras. *Costumes by* Milo Anderson. *Special effects by* Byron Haskin *and* Edwin DuPar. *Running time: 104 minutes.*

CAST

James Cagney, *Eddie Bartlett;* Priscilla Lane, *Jean Sherman;* Humphrey Bogart, *George Hally;* Jeffrey Lynn, *Lloyd Hart;* Gladys George, *Panama Smith;* Frank McHugh, *Danny Green;* Paul Kelly, *Nick Brown;* Elisabeth Risdon, *Mrs. Sherman;* Ed Keane, *Pete Henderson;* Joseph Sawyer, *Sgt. Pete Jones;* Abner Biberman, *Lefty;* George Humbert, *Luigi the proprietor;* Clay Clement, *Bramfield the broker;* Don Thaddeus Kerr, *Bobby Hart;* Ray Cooke, *Orderly;* Robert Dobson, *Lieutenant;* John Harron, *Soldier;* Vera Lewis, *Mrs. Gray;* Murray Alper and Dick Wessel, *Mechanics;* Joseph Crehan, *Fletcher the foreman;* Norman Willis, *Bootlegger;* Eddie Acuff, Milton Kibbee, and John Ridgely, *Cab drivers;* Ann Codee, *Saleswoman;* Jack Norton, *Drunk;* Nat Carr, *Policeman.*

The strength of James Cagney's energetic acting talent saved not a few of the routine program pictures he made for Warner Bros. in the Thirties. And the actor's tough, dynamic style made him, along with Edward G. Robinson, the ideal movie gangster, especially in good scripts like *The Public Enemy, Angels With Dirty Faces,* and—capping the decade—*The Roaring Twenties.* This one was directed for the most part by Raoul Walsh, who took over from Anatole Litvak. Cagney worked well with Walsh, and although the actor was now tired of the genre, ten years later he would return to Warners for one last salute to gangsterdom, the Walsh-directed classic *White Heat.*

The Roaring Twenties sprawls over the years between World War I and the mid-Thirties to tell, in semi-documentary fashion, the story of three veterans. Jeffrey Lynn becomes a lawyer, Humphrey Bogart turns to bootlegging, and Cagney drives a taxi, later drifting into the bootleg-liquor business himself, in league with nightclub gal

Jeffrey Lynn, James Cagney, and Priscilla Lane

James Cagney, Gladys George, and Ben Welden

James Cagney, Gladys George, and Nat Carr

Gladys George. While she carries a torch for Cagney, he's interested only in sweet young singer Priscilla Lane, who's in love with—and marries—crusading attorney Jeffrey Lynn.

The stock-market crash wipes out Cagney's underworld racket, but an old gangland rivalry with Bogart continues, resulting in the latter's murder by Cagney. In the film's memorable finale, Cagney is gunned down in front of a church by Bogart's henchmen as Gladys George and a policeman look on. When the cop asks, "What was his business?" she has the classic line: "He used to be a big shot."

The Roaring Twenties is an underworld movie in the best Warner Bros. action-melodrama tradition. But the golden era of the Thirties gangster film ended with a dying Cagney staggering across the steps of that church.

THE CAT AND THE CANARY

1939

Paulette Goddard and the disguised killer

Bob Hope and Paulette Goddard

CREDITS

A Paramount Picture. Directed by Elliott Nugent. *Produced by* Arthur Hornblow, Jr. *Screenplay by* Walter De Leon *and* Lynn Starling. *Based on the stage play by* John Willard. *Photographed by* Charles Lang. *Edited by* Archie Marshek. *Art direction by* Hans Dreier *and* Robert Usher. *Music by* Dr. Ernst Toch. *Running time: 74 minutes.*

CAST

Bob Hope, *Wally Hampton;* Paulette Goddard, *Joyce Norman;* John Beal, *Fred Blythe;* Douglass Montgomery; *Charlie Wilder;* Gale Sondergaard, *Miss Lu;* Nydia Westman, *Cicily;* Elizabeth Patterson, *Aunt Susan;* George Zucco, *Lawyer Crosby;* Willard Robertson, *Hendricks;* George Regas, Nick Thompson, and Chief Thundercloud, *Indian guides;* Milton Kibbee, *Photographer;* Charles Lane and Frank Melton, *Reporters;* William Abby, *The Cat.*

In turning that hoary old stage melodrama *The Cat and the Canary* into a comedy vehicle for the talents of stage-trained contractee Bob Hope, Paramount provided him with a step up to stardom after playing in the shadow of comedienne Martha Raye in films like *College Swing* and *Give Me a Sailor. The Cat and the Canary* also provided his leading lady, Paulette Goddard, with her first starring part. The movie's great success fostered an equally popular Hope-Goddard blend of chills and laughter entitled *The Ghost Breakers* (1940).

They made a good film team. Hope's amusing blend of chicken-hearted bravado and smart-alecky audacity crumpled easily when faced with danger, generating infectious audience amusement. And, for a comedian, he was unusually personable. Audiences could *believe* Bob might get the girl when the movie ended, even one as striking as Paulette, whose glamorous vivacity made a perfect foil for his never-ending gags.

The Cat and the Canary had originally been filmed as a Universal silent in 1927 and was remade with sound in 1930 as *The Cat Creeps.* Both of these versions were straight thrillers. Gearing it up for laughs and Bob Hope in 1939 was an inspired decision, and the Walter De Leon—Lynn Starling rewrite of John Willard's old play afforded Hope enough jokes to properly balance the chills. But there's still plenty of suspense, mystery, and mayhem in a sinister, swamp-located family manse in which the cleverly disguised killer is methodically eliminating those standing between himself and a sizable inheritance. With the plot hinging on heiress Goddard's remaining sane and sound within the walls of this sinister abode, it not surprisingly develops that her life is very much in jeopardy as panels slide, bookcases swing out, and clawed hands clutch at her, while the bumbling Hope appears unlikely to save her from a dire fate—which, of course, is as misleading as the many red herrings of the plot.

Arthur Hornblow, Jr.'s handsome production offers appropriately atmospheric sets, moody photography, and an execellent supporting cast, dominated by sinister Gale Sondergaard as the obligatory black-garbed housekeeper—with matching cat. And Elliott Nugent, who had directed Hope in *Give Me a Sailor* and *Never Say Die,* mixes all of these elements smartly, maintaining a happy balance between screams of laughter and screams of fright. For Hope and Goddard, *The Cat and the Canary* anticipated their vintage Forties years at Paramount.

George Zucco, Gale Sondergaard, Douglass Montgomery, Bob Hope, John Beal, Paulette Goddard, Elizabeth Patterson, and Nydia Westman

Gale Sondergaard, Paulette Goddard, Bob Hope, and George Zucco

DESTRY RIDES AGAIN

1939

Charles Winninger, Una Merkel, James Stewart, Irene Hervey, and Jack Carson

CREDITS

A Universal Picture. Directed by George Marshall. *Produced by* Joe Pasternak. *Screenplay by* Felix Jackson, Gertrude Purcell, *and* Henry Meyers. *Based on the novel by* Max Brand. *Photographed by* Hal Mohr. *Edited by* Milton Carruth. *Art direction by* Jack Otterson. *Music by* Frank Skinner. *Songs: "Little Joe," "You've Got That Look," and "The Boys in the Back Room" by* Frederick Hollander *and* Frank Loesser. *Costumes by* Vera West. *Running time: 94 minutes.*

CAST

Marlene Dietrich, *Frenchy;* James Stewart, *Tom Destry, Jr.,* Mischa Auer, *Boris Callahan;* Charles Winninger, *Washington Dimsdale;* Brian Donlevy, *Kent;* Allen Jenkins, *Gyp Watson;* Warren Hymer, *Bugs Watson;* Irene Hervey, *Janice Tyndall;* Una Merkel, *Lily Belle Callahan;* Billy Gilbert, *Loupgerou;* Samuel S. Hinds, *Judge Slade;* Jack Carson, *Jack Tyndall;* Tom Fadden, *Lem Claggett;* Virginia Brissac, *Sophie Claggett;* Edmund MacDonald, *Rockwell;* Lillian Yarbo, *Clara;* Joe King, *Sheriff Keogh;* Dickie Jones, *Claggett boy;* Ann Todd, *Claggett girl;* Harry Cording, *Rowdy;* Minerva Urecal, *Mrs. DeWitt.*

After splitting professionally in 1935 from her mentor Josef von Sternberg, Marlene Dietrich had difficulty finding roles suitable to the exotic screen image with which that director had so closely identified her in the public's eye in their seven pictures together. And by 1939 her career and magnetism had sharply declined with such unpopular entertainments as the British-made *Knight Without Armour* (1936) and Ernst Lubitsch's stultifying *Angel* (1937). Thus it took a great deal of faith in Dietrich for producer Joe Pasternak to persuade Universal that she should play the tough but tender dance-hall singer Frenchy in *Destry Rides Again.*

In 1932, Max Brand's novel had become a standard Tom Mix Western. But Pasternak's 1939 remake was much altered to accommodate the mild-mannered personality of Jimmy Stewart, with the Frenchy role built up especially for Dietrich. Felix Jackson, Gertrude Purcell, and Henry Meyers reworked the Brand story into a rousing seriocomic Western about a lawless town brought around to law and order by a gunless deputy sheriff, and George Marshall's fast-paced direction created a minor miracle—and one of 1939's surprise box-office hits.

Marlene Dietrich sings "You've Got That Look."

James Stewart, Marlene Dietrich, and Brian Donlevy

Marlene Dietrich, Una Merkel

Stewart proved himself as adept at Westerns as at drawing-room comedy, and Charles Winninger, Una Merkel, Brian Donlevy, and Mischa Auer alternately helped generate laughter and tension in top-notch supporting roles. But it was Marlene Dietrich—with her insinuating bass-baritone singing of "Little Joe," "You've Got That Look" and, especially, "The Boys in the Backroom"—who quite stole the show in her deglamorized makeup and gold-gilt curls as the plucky, flashy barroom song-slinger whose tough, scrappy façade masks a gold-hearted sentimentalist. *Destry Rides Again* revealed a more human and humorous Dietrich than her public had previously known, and they loved her. The film rejuvenated her waning career and led to such action-oriented Universal entertainments as *Seven Sinners, The Spoilers,* and *Pittsburgh,* opposite John Wayne and Randolph Scott.

Marlene Dietrich and James Stewart

GONE WITH THE WIND

1939

Vivien Leigh and Clark Gable

Vivien Leigh as Scarlett O'Hara

CREDITS

A Metro-Goldwyn-Mayer release of a Selznick International Picture. Directed by Victor Fleming *and (uncredited)* William Cameron Menzies, George Cukor, *and* Sam Wood. *Produced by* David O. Selznick. *Second-unit direction by* Reeves Eason. *Screenplay by* Sidney Howard *and (uncredited)* Ben Hecht, F. Scott Fitzgerald, John van Druten, Oliver H. P. Garrett, *and* Jo Swerling. *Based on the novel by* Margaret Mitchell. *Photographed in Technicolor by* Ernest Haller *and* Ray Rennahan. *Edited by* Hal C. Kern *and* James E. Newcom. *Production design by* William Cameron Menzies. *Interiors by* Joseph B. Platt. *Art direction by* Lyle Wheeler. *Interior decoration by* Edward G. Boyle. *Costumes by* Walter Plunkett. *Music by* Max Steiner. *Special effects by* Jack Cosgrove *and* Lee Zavitz. *Technical advisers:* Susan Myrick *and* Will Price. *Running time: 222 minutes.*

The Burning of Atlanta

CAST

Clark Gable, *Rhett Butler;* Vivien Leigh, *Scarlett O'Hara;*
Leslie Howard, *Ashley Wilkes;* Olivia de Havilland, *Melanie
Hamilton;* Hattie McDaniel, *Mammy;* Thomas Mitchell,
Gerald O'Hara; Barbara O'Neil, *Ellen O'Hara;* Carroll Nye,
Frank Kennedy; Laura Hope Crews, *Aunt Pittypat
Hamilton;* Harry Davenport, *Dr. Meade;* Rand Brooks,
Charles Hamilton; Ona Munson, *Belle Watling;* Ann
Rutherford, *Careen O'Hara;* Oscar Polk, *Pork;* Butterfly
McQueen, *Prissy;* Evelyn Keyes, *Suellen O'Hara;* Victor
Jory, *Jonas Wilkerson;* Isabel Jewell, *Emmy Slattery;* Cam-
mie King, *Bonnie Blue Butler;* Jane Darwell, *Dolly Merri-
wether;* Ward Bond, *Tom, a Yankee captain;* George
Reeves, *Brent Tarleton;* Fred Crane, *Stuart Tarleton;* Paul
Hurst, *Yankee deserter;* Mickey Kuhn, *Beau Wilkes.*

Vivien Leigh and Butterfly McQueen

Vivien Leigh, Leslie Howard, Mickey Kuhn, and Clark Gable

Hattie McDaniel, Olivia de Havilland, and Vivien Leigh

Hollywood's best-remembered and most-publicized motion picture has long since been surpassed as a moneymaker by box-office blockbusters like *The Sound of Music* and *The Godfather*, due to the rapid inflation of ticket prices since 1939. But its legendary reputation and continuing appeal have made David O. Selznick's Civil War masterpiece a film whose revival value seems never-ending.

So much has been written about *Gone With the Wind* that it is quite impossible to add anything new within these pages. But it is interesting to note that Margaret Mitchell's 1,037-page 1936 best-seller was produced at a cost of $3.7 million in 1939 (a mere twenty years later, the same movie would have cost an estimated $40 million!). In 1978, CBS paid $35 million for twenty-year television rights to the epic film.

Gone With the Wind centers on Scarlett O'Hara, a fiery, plantation-bred daughter of the Confederacy, detailing her shameless pursuit of aristocratic Ashley Wilkes and her impassioned love-hate relationship with a man she eventually marries, roguish Rhett Butler. After much controversy over the film's casting, these roles were assigned to Vivien Leigh (a virtually unknown actress from England), Leslie Howard, and Clark Gable, none of whom enjoyed the movie's long, harrowing production schedule with its various changes in script and direction (Victor Fleming alone received on-screen credit).

This landmark motion picture earned a then record ten Oscars, including those for Best Picture, Best Actress Leigh, Supporting Actress Hattie McDaniel—a "first" for a black performer—Director Fleming, Screenplay, Cinematography, Art Direction, Editing, Special Effects, and a Special Award, for his achievements in design and color, to William Cameron Menzies. Fittingly, David O. Selznick was given 1939's Irving G. Thalberg Memorial Award "for the most consistent high level of production achievement by an individual producer."